I Dreamed I Saw
Joe Hill Last Night

JOE HILL
GÄVLE, SVERIGE
7. OKTOBER 1879
SALT LAKE CITY, USA
19 NOVEMBER 1915
UNION ORGANIZER
LABOR AGITATOR
CARTOONIST. POET
MUSICIAN. COMPOSER
ITINERANT WORKER
ARBETARSÅNGAREN
MURDERED BY THE JUDICIARY IN COLLUSION WITH THE MINE OWNERS WHO WISHED TO SILENCE HIS SONGS BUT THE SONGS ARE STILL BEING SUNG!
INDUSTRIAL WORKERS OF THE WORLD
3435 N. SHEFFIELD AVENUE Suite 202
CHICAGO ILLINOIS, 60657 USA
IF WE WORKERS TAKE A NOTION
WE CAN STOP ALL SPEEDING TRAINS
EVERY SHIP UPON THE OCEAN
WE CAN TIE WITH MIGHTY CHAINS
EVERY WHEEL IN THE CREATION
EVERY MINE AND EVERY MILL
FLEETS AND ARMIES
OF ALL NATIONS
WILL AT OUR COMMAND
STAND STILL
SÖRJ EJ, ORGANISERA

I Dreamed I Saw Joe Hill Last Night

The History of a Classic American Labor Song

CRAIG SMITH

McFarland & Company, Inc., Publishers

Jefferson, North Carolina

Frontispiece: Carlos Cortéz (Milwaukee-Chicago, 1923-2005), Joe Hill, linocut, 33" × 23⅛" (paper size) (image courtesy of the National Museum of Mexican Art Permanent Collection, 1990.27, Gift of the artist, photo: Kathleen Culbert-Aguilar).

LIBRARY OF CONGRESS CATALOGING-IN-PUBLICATION DATA

Names: Smith, Craig, 1947– author.
Title: I dreamed I saw Joe Hill last night : the history of a classic American labor song / Craig Smith.
Description: Jefferson, North Carolina : McFarland & Company, Inc., Publishers, 2024. | Includes bibliographical references and index.
Identifiers: LCCN 2024044351 | ISBN 9781476696515 (paperback : acid free paper) ∞
ISBN 9781476654256 (ebook)
Subjects: LCSH: Joe Hill (Song) | Work songs—United States—History and criticism. | Protest songs—United States—History and criticism. | Working class—United States—Songs and music—History and criticism. | Working class—United States—History. | Hill, Joe, 1879-1915.
Classification: LCC ML3780 .S64 2024 | DDC 781.5/920973—dc23/eng/20240924
LC record available at https://lccn.loc.gov/2024044351

BRITISH LIBRARY CATALOGUING DATA ARE AVAILABLE

ISBN (print) 978-1-4766-9651-5
ISBN (ebook) 978-1-4766-5425-6

Front cover image: Joe Hill (Utah Division of Archives and Records Service)

Printed in the United States of America

McFarland & Company, Inc., Publishers
 Box 611, Jefferson, North Carolina 28640
  www.mcfarlandpub.com

For Lynda,
my life companion on the journey

"This was the song of Joe Hill, an ordinary worker
who was killed on trumped-up charges.
Its words summoned the unfortunate people
to organized struggle. Joe Hill is immortal,
as a just cause is immortal."
—*Paul Robeson*

"History isn't just something we read;
it's also something we *hear*."
—*Jon Meacham & Tim McGraw*

Table of Contents

Table of Contents

"Joe Hill"

I dreamed I saw Joe Hill last night,
Alive as you and me.
Says I, "But Joe, you're ten years dead."
"I never died," says he.
"I never died," says he.

"In Salt Lake, Joe," says I to him,
Him standing by my bed,
"They framed you on a murder charge."
Says Joe, "But I ain't dead."
Says Joe, "But I ain't dead."

"The copper bosses killed you, Joe.
They shot you, Joe," says I.
"Takes more than guns to kill a man,"
Says Joe, "I didn't die."
Says Joe, "I didn't die."

And standing there as big as life
And smiling with his eyes,
Joe says, "What they forgot to kill
Went on to organize,
Went on to organize."

"Joe Hill ain't dead," he says to me,
"Joe Hill ain't never died."
Where working men are out on strike
Joe Hill is at their side,
Joe Hill is at their side.

"From San Diego up to Maine
In every mine and mill,
Where workers strike and organize,"
Says he, "You'll find Joe Hill."
Says he, "You'll find Joe Hill."

"Joe Hill"

I dreamed I saw Joe Hill last night,
Alive as you or me
Says I, "But Joe, you're ten years dead."
"I never died," says he.
"I never died," says he.

Preface

IN THE BEGINNING were the words, a seventy-word, three-stanza poem that should never have needed to be written. But the man whom the poem commemorates did exist. He was not a myth, though his life would become the stuff of legend, and his legacy one of enormous proportions. He was a real man, a man who was executed for a crime I believe he did not commit. The man whom the poem spoke of was an individual who had joined an organization that sought to unite workingmen and women, a labor union that was hailed by those who joined it but hated by those who considered it dangerous. This man became a prominent spokesman for his union—and a thorn in the sides of its opponents. By falsely accusing him of being a criminal and a symbol of a radical organization, and by executing this one individual, the anti-union establishment and authorities intended to send a warning message to that organization. The man's death, then, was born out of not justice but vengeance.

So the poem did need to be written. It needed to be written to send its own message to workers everywhere, as well as to the bosses that subjugate workers: you may kill one of us, but we will live on as long as there are people who stand up for their rights.

I hold a special reverence for songs that defy being pigeonholed, songs that have the capacity to lift us out of the abyss of hopelessness, songs that inspire us to do what is just for all peoples, songs that speak to us as brothers and sisters in a single human race. "Joe Hill" is one of those songs.

I Dreamed I Saw Joe Hill Last Night is an account of that song. What follows is not a scholarly treatise on a literary piece of work. I do not have the objectivity or academic tools for such an approach. What follows is a subjective interpretation of the story of the song "Joe Hill," from its origin through its long trajectory up to the present day. This book is, in effect, an idiosyncratic essay based on what I have read on the

1

subject and what I have gained from people I have interviewed in this regard.

It is also a celebration of the power of song, how a song can galvanize a single moment or an international movement. One thing I learned from the research I have conducted, and from people who know the song and people who sing the song, is this: "Joe Hill" says a lot about America. It personifies what America is supposed to be all about—written by an English-born immigrant and set to music by an American-born composer, it chronicles another immigrant, one from Sweden.

What its composer Earl Robinson once said of it remains relevant: Go to the memorial service of almost any leftwing old-timer and you'll hear "Joe Hill" as the anthem everybody knows.[1] Al Hayes's words will bring tears to their eyes as they recall the movements of their youth when the spirit of Joe Hill inspired them to acts of solidarity.

The lyrics are memorable, and the melody, once heard, is unforgettable. There is no mixed message in "Joe Hill." It is as direct as a song can be, a work that eulogizes a long-dead labor icon and spreads the call for workers to organize, and for all peoples to stand tall for justice and freedom.

The song likewise says a lot about the world, for it is immediately recognized in countries whose people do not speak or understand the language in which the song was written. It speaks of and to workingmen and women everywhere who are subjected to any form of oppression that is meant to keep them down. It speaks of and to women and men everywhere who continue to rise up for justice, who continue to fight for their rights, and who continue to occupy the front lines for freedom. In that sense, "Joe Hill" speaks to all of us.

I hope that the present book brings you back to the song as well as to an understanding of how significant a song such as "Joe Hill" can be to the ongoing struggle for human rights everywhere. Over the years "Joe Hill" has emerged from the throats of thousands, perhaps millions, of people. It is everyone's song now. As such we have the right—and the responsibility—not only to preserve it but also to project it forward.

Prologue:
Campfires

"Human beings have always been fascinated by camp-fires. The campfire is a magnet; it's the center of human activity."—Doug Wood

CAMPFIRES, and the stories told around them and the songs sung around them, have long occupied a familiar place in American lore as well as in cultures around the world. Images of campfires have come to us from every medium of the arts—movies, literature, dance, music—and from oral traditions handed down through generations. They are where we interact with nature, where we cook food, gain warmth, and feel protected, what writer Joan Didion described as keeping the human voice "raised against the night, the wind, the rustlings in the brush."[1] They are where we sing and dance and stage gatherings and revivals, both religious and secular.

Regardless of how we construct campfires—pyramid style, log cabin style, or however our parents, grandparents, or group leaders did—what is important about them is not how they are built but how they bring us together, how they foster a sense of community.

In 2014 a freelance writer named Rachel Nuwer published an essay that underscores the significance of campfires. She suggests that our ancient ancestors weren't so different from us today, how we often gather at nighttime to eat and drink and swap stories. Nuwer writes that ending the day around a campfire, complete with stories and songs and developing relationships, ultimately shaped cultures and may have helped develop our ability to understand one another, cooperate, and internalize culture.[2]

In her piece Nuwer refers to research published in *Proceedings of the National Academy of Science* by anthropologist Polly Wiessner, who once lived with the Bushmen of Botswana and Namibia. Wiessner concluded that while three-quarters of daytime conversations centered on work-related talk, at night a greater percentage of conversations centered on stories, dancing, spirituality, or singing.

This story begins with singing around a campfire.

= 1 =

In the Beginning: Alfred and Earl

"Singing is inspirational, more inspirational than talk.
It arouses people more, makes them feel part of things."
—John Handcox

TWILIGHT: A FRIDAY in late June. Preparations were underway for a group sing-along. Soon, counselors would ignite the firewood that had been collected and laid in place and campers would gather around to participate in a program of songs associated with a legendary labor union, the Industrial Workers of the World (IWW). Among the songs scheduled for that evening's tribute to the Wobblies, as IWW members were known, were several written by the union's best-known songwriter, the martyr Joe Hill.

The setting was idyllic. The year was 1936. This was Camp Unity, outside of the village of Wingdale, east of Poughkepsie in New York's Dutchess County. Unity was situated at the shores of Lake Ellis (now Ellis Pond) at the westernmost foothills of the Berkshire Mountains along the New York and Connecticut state line. Founded in 1927, Unity was one of many workers retreats that had been established outside of large East Coast cities in the decade following World War I by politically left-leaning groups, among them the Communist Party USA (CPUSA) and related socialist organizations. Camp Unity, like the IWW before it, welcomed people of all races, creeds, religions, and political persuasions—what the FBI once referred to as a most unusual clientele—but had no room for Fascists, bigots, racists, or anti–Semites. Unity was pro-labor, and as such provided a place where like-minded people could come together to escape the cities for recreation and discussion as well as for some peace and quiet. Unity referred to itself as the first proletarian summer colony and the first interracial adult camp in America. "You will sleep like a Rip Van Winkle in the comfortable bunks at Unity," declared an advertisement in *The Crisis*, the official magazine of the National Association for the Advancement of Colored People (NAACP).

While the politics of the camp were never far from the surface, Unity was no indoctrination facility, unlike Camp Siegfried in Yaphank, Long Island. Siegfried was one of many camps across the nation owned by the pro–Nazi *Amerikadeutscher Volksbund* or German American Bund (GAB), which had been formed that year, calling itself an organization for patriotic Americans of German stock to come together and promote Nazi Party values. Charged with raising future leaders of America who were steeped in Nazi ideals, the Bund grew to a membership in the tens of thousands nationwide before it collapsed after the onset of World War II. Camp Siegfried even had its own train on the Long Island Railroad, the Siegfried Special.

If the campers at Unity were decidedly progressive, they also displayed an open and positive approach to America. They were proud of the country's revolutionary past and optimistic about its democratic future. When members of the Fish Committee, named for New York's ardent anti-communist Representative Hamilton Fish, visited Unity in 1930 for what it termed an inspection of suspected subversive activities, they were met with ridicule as campers laughingly escorted them off the premises.

MANY OF THOSE in attendance at the June campfire sing-along led lives characterized by long hours in factories and sweatshops and lived in cramped apartments and tenements surrounded by the noise of urban life. The bucolic setting of Unity provided a refuge from their daily labor. There they could revel in music and theater and other camp entertainments. There they could walk in silence in the woods, breathe in the air that wafted over the lake, and forget about the stench of where they worked or the foul air where they lived. Camp Unity provided a metaphorical and literal breath of fresh air and, just as importantly, it gave people a sense of belonging to a community. Away from city crowds and their normal routines they could look forward to the respite that outdoor activities can offer, a buffer against the tensions of the modern day industrial existence.

As the campers gathered around the fire that June evening in 1936, they could share a sigh of relief. It was hot enough where they were, but at least they were not seventy miles south on the asphalt of New York. That summer the city was suffering through a debilitating heat wave:

HEAT RECORDS SHATTERED
WITH 102.3 DEGREES HERE;
NATION'S DEATH TOLL 245

read one headline in *The New York Times*. Chefs were frying eggs in pans on sidewalks, and shoes were sticking to buckling streets. Workers in factories were fainting. The city would eventually record a single day record high temperature of 106 degrees on July 9.

The severe heat wasn't limited to the East. In June eight states experienced temperatures of 110 degrees or higher. In the Midwest, drought continued to plague farmers. Crops were failing. Deaths were mounting up. By the time the heat gradually subsided, in September, some 5,000 fatalities attributed to it would be recorded in the United States.

Depression

IN THE SUMMER of 1936 the country was approaching the seventh anniversary of the October 1929 stock market crash. The decade of the 1920s, dubbed in America the Roaring Twenties, were years when many investors engaged in sprees of wildly speculative stock buying, often using borrowed money that left them vulnerable to market fluctuations. They were also years of great economic disparities between haves and have-nots. The late 1920s contained warning signs of impending financial disaster, but the signs were largely ignored. The bubble finally burst on October 29. That day, Black Tuesday, would forever be labeled the poster date for America's descent into the most calamitous economic crisis in the country's history, the Great Depression.

In a matter of days financial markets registered a loss of $30 billion, the equivalent of some $400 billion in today's dollars. Nearly a quarter of the labor force was thrown out of work. Tens of thousands of banks and businesses failed.

The numbers were, and still are, staggering. The statistics don't lie. But this many decades removed from that cataclysm, and with few remaining survivors of that time to personally recall it, what is in danger of being glossed over is the sheer depth of individual suffering during the Depression—something more fully realized when examining the photographic images from that time: the face of the mother with her family and their possessions evicted onto the street; the hollow look of the self-made men, now forgotten men, standing in lines for jobs or bread or selling apples on street corners; the unwashed children sifting through garbage dumps for anything of sustenance; people huddled in

"Hooverville" shacks, disparagingly named for the president many felt had abandoned them.

And beyond the grim statistics and pictures lay another casualty of the calamity—the loss of confidence by Americans in their own country. The nation appeared to be coming apart, its very fabric unraveling.

Americans were no strangers to economic turbulence or catastrophic events, having endured a recession ten years earlier as well as the influenza epidemic that cost more than 600,000 American lives and millions more around the world. But the sheer scale of the Great Depression was unprecedented. "In all our history," writes historian Carl Degler, "no other economic collapse brought so many Americans to near starvation, endured so long, or came so close to overturning the basic institutions of American life."[1]

Buck Up!

NO ONE was more aware of that than the incoming president. At his inauguration on March 4, 1933, Franklin D. Roosevelt delivered his famous "nothing to fear but fear itself" speech, but his remarks contained a statement of equal significance: "This nation asks for action, and action now!" In the first one hundred days of his administration he answered that call with the plethora of legislation known as the New Deal. Humorist Will Rogers responded that America hasn't been this happy in three years. Let this country get hungry and they are going to eat, he said, no matter what happens to budgets, income taxes or Wall Street. Washington mustn't forget who rules when it comes to a showdown.[2]

The ideas contained in the New Deal were not entirely new. Some were extensions of efforts by Roosevelt's predecessor, Herbert Hoover; others were experimental. Some worked and some didn't. Proponents of the New Deal extolled its visionary aspects and applauded the expanded role of the federal government. Opponents of the New Deal labeled it as socialist policy that went against the grain of American individualism, claiming that it would frighten business away and make Americans lazy by growing accustomed to entitlements.

Franklin Roosevelt was fifty-one years old when he assumed office. Despite his previous service in the New York State Senate, as assistant secretary of the Navy, and governor of New York, many in the political arena dismissed this Harvard-educated son of wealth as a lightweight. He had no end of detractors, among them the blustery Senator Huey Long of Louisiana and the equally blustery Father Charles Coughlin, whose popular radio broadcasts reached millions of listeners with its anti–Semitic and pro–Nazi message. But FDR would show himself to be a consummate politician—"and he did it so well that he saved the nation."[3] He possessed two critical qualities that proved indispensable to the turbulent times—an unbridled optimism and a can-do attitude. For FDR, pessimism was not an option.

In the closing scene of his 1936 film *Modern Times*, about people facing declining prospects in an increasingly mechanized world, Charlie Chaplin, in his valedictory appearance as The Little Tramp, cheers up his companion after she mutters, "What's the use in trying?" "Buck up," the Tramp responds (on the silent screen). "Never say die. We'll find a way!"

Franklin Roosevelt was trying to find a way. His *modus operandi* was to try something, and if it didn't work to try something else. In a word, he brought to the country what may be his greatest legacy—hope.

Dust

> "To have lost, wantonly the ancient forests, the vast grasslands is our madness."—Wendell Berry

AT THE TIME of the Camp Unity sing-a-along, the nation was beginning to recover from its low point in 1932, but was still in a slump. If the worst economic crisis in American history wasn't enough to deal with, much of the middle part of the country was reeling from the effects of the greatest natural disaster the nation had ever confronted—the Dust Bowl. Just as years of speculative buying and selling had contributed to the stock market crash, years of stripping the natural grasslands of the Great Plains, in an effort to introduce more profitable crops, had led to a decimation of the very root system that held the soil in place. The region became a disaster waiting to happen, and when drought struck, in the early 1930s, an area touching six states—stretching from Red Cloud, Nebraska, down across Kansas and the Oklahoma and Texas panhandles as far south as Lubbock and west past Springfield, Colorado, and Clayton, New Mexico—was becoming a wasteland, at its peak one hundred million acres.

In his book *Notes on the State of Virginia*, first completed in 1781, Thomas Jefferson argued that America should be founded on an agrarian ideology, one that values rural society over urban society and the independent farmer over the paid worker. It was a perfectly logical position at the time: the United States was still twenty years shy of the

Louisiana Purchase, a transaction completed by Jefferson himself, that doubled the size of the nation and opened the era of westward expansion. But in the 1930s, for many Americans the Dust Bowl signaled the end of that ideal. Now, with the double disasters of Depression and Dust, urban workers and rural farmers alike were facing growing uncertainties and unprecedented dire circumstances.

To many observers—among them Dorothea Lange, who would take iconic photographs of the Dust Bowl; Woody Guthrie, who would write unforgettable songs about the calamity; John Steinbeck, who would publish the great American novel about the Dust Bowl; and filmmaker Pare Lorentz, whose documentary *The Plow That Broke the Plains* chronicled the agricultural abuse of the Great Plains—the combined catastrophes seemed to validate a growing sense of apocalypse, a fear that the capitalist system itself was on the brink of collapse.

Dictators

> "After the Great Crash of 1929, the tempo of counter-revolution accelerated, and after 1934 the drift toward World War II became irreversible."—Robert G. Colodny

DEPRESSION AND DUST: At the same time that Americans—the campers at Unity among them—were grappling with these two calamities, they were aware of a third ominous development. This was the rise of authoritarian dictators in other parts of the word. Would America be able to restore its system of democratic capitalism? Or, in the wake of its financial and agricultural crises, would the country go the way of Soviet Communism, German Nazism, or Italian and Spanish Fascism?

After the First World War reparations levied by the victorious Allies through the Treaty of Versailles against the defeated nations contributed to a sense of disillusionment and disorder over much of Europe. The new world order envisioned by that treaty soon lay in shambles. Economist John Maynard Keynes, a member of the British delegation to the Paris peace talks, warned that if the Allies abused their "momentary victorious power to destroy Germany and Austro-Hungary, now prostrate, they invited their own destruction."[4] He further predicted that the standard of life in some industrial nations could deteriorate to the point of starvation for some peoples, leading to depression, desperation, and the dismantling of civilization itself. These circumstances proved ripe for the rise of nationalistic and jingoistic political parties.

In 1922 Benito Mussolini and his followers marched on Rome,

inaugurating the Fascist era in that country. Germany's soaring unemployment and sinking industrial production contributed to the rise of Adolf Hitler's National Socialist Party, the Nazis. Japan invaded Manchuria and China. In June 1936, the very month that Camp Unity was holding its sing-along, Anastasio Somoza, commander of Nicaragua's National Guard, took power in that country, beginning a forty-two year family reign. The following month a military rebellion would break out in Spain. Backed by staunch rightists, monarchists, and the conservative Roman Catholic hierarchy, the uprising, led by General Francisco Franco, launched the three-year Spanish Civil War that would result in four decades of dictatorship.

In the face of these developments much of America remained outwardly isolationist, despite the fact that with its involvements in Mexico, the 1893 overthrow of the Hawaiian monarchy, and its 1898 actions in Cuba and the Philippines during the Spanish-American War, the United States was clearly loosening its position as an isolated nation.

All of these crises—Depression, Dust, and Dictators—fed concern around the country about the future of America's democratic way of life. In his inaugural address Franklin Roosevelt had declared that we do not distrust the future of democracy, but political commentator Walter Lippmann worried that the twentieth century would be a Fascist century.

These crises were familiar to the group that gathered around a campfire on that June evening at Camp Unity. Two of the adult participants in the program were a writer named Alfred Hayes and a musician and composer named Earl Robinson.

Alfred: Shake the Midtown Towers!

DARK, DANTEAN, AND WITTY: That is how one observer[5] characterized Alfred Hayes as a young man of twenty-three, when he was already establishing himself as a poet and a rising star of the working class literary left.

Hayes was born into a Jewish family in the Whitechapel district of London on April 18, 1911. Whitechapel at that time was industrial, dirty, overcrowded, and characterized by crime. The notorious Jack the Ripper murders took place there, and the conditions of abject poverty in that neighborhood would later inspire the founding of the Salvation Army.

Three years after Alfred's birth the Hayeses immigrated to the United States. There they settled on 117th Street among other working families in the Jewish section of New York City's Harlem neighborhood. Harlem was not yet the black mecca it would become in the aftermath of the Harlem Renaissance, a period that roughly began after the end of World War I with the influx of black residents, among them such prominent figures as W.E.B. DuBois, Langston Hughes, and Zora Neale Hurston.

Alfred attended Commerce High School and the City College of New York, now part of the City University of New York. His father, a hairdresser and trained violinist, wanted him to focus on something practical, such as accounting, but early on the younger Hayes was drawn to politics, poetry, and drama, particularly after his schoolboy recitation of Edgar Allan Poe's "The Bells" met with a thunderous reception—a performance he would be called upon numerous times to repeat. This caused tension between him and his parents, a rift that was never fully reconciled. But clearly, Alfred Hayes was already deciding on the trajectory his life would lead. He did follow, however, his father's example in one respect: The elder Hayes liked to gamble and play the horses, and soon enough the son showed similar interests.

Alfred worked as a copyboy at the *New York American*, where one of his first assignments took him to the city morgue, an experience he found understandably gruesome. He later worked as a crime reporter for the *Daily Mirror* as well as a series of odd jobs, including a brief stint with the Federal Writers' Project. At the same time he was reading the Old Testament. Historian Alan Wald suggests that those two experiences—the morgue and his reading of the Bible, from which he seemed to discern the unrelenting presence of evil—intensified in Hayes a morose cast from childhood, a demeanor bordering on manic-depressive.[6] This dark outlook would characterize much of his later literary output.

In 2018 British documentary filmmaker Alex Harvey described the young Hayes as a genuine blue-collar intellectual who was more at home with fellow gamblers than with Greenwich Village literati.[7] Wald paints a similar picture, referring to Hayes as the Byron of the pool halls. He describes Hayes as a young man with a strikingly handsome face who preferred to hang out with cabdrivers in pinball palaces and who had no patience for any form of pretentiousness. He was young, and he carried the determination of the young to define himself and the times in which he lived.

AT SEVENTEEN, Alfred Hayes joined the Young Communist League (YCL) and began publishing in radical magazines. Two of his notable early efforts are the poems "In a Coffee Pot" and "Into the Streets May

First." "In a Coffee Pot" was published in the 1934 debut issue of *Partisan Review*, the New York City–based literary journal that was launched by the John Reed Clubs.

Founded in 1929, the Reed clubs were named in honor of the Harvard-educated journalist and propagandist who had worked for the socialist magazine *The Masses* and was best-known for his books *Insurgent Mexico*, about the 1910 revolution in that country, and *Ten Days That Shook the World*, that chronicled the 1917 Bolshevik Revolution in Russia. Reed also helped stage a massive pro–IWW pageant in New York's Madison Square Garden during a 1914 textile strike in Paterson, New Jersey. Reporting for *Metropolitan Magazine*, then edited by former president Theodore Roosevelt, Reed was arrested and, while in jail, conceived of a grand show that would dramatize the causes of the strike. It proved to be a huge propaganda success.

Reed's career ended prematurely when he died in a typhus epidemic in Russia in 1920 and was buried in the Kremlin Wall. With chapters in cities throughout America, the John Reed Clubs were designed to bring together socially conscious artists and writers. The clubs' slogan was "Art is a weapon in the class struggle."

"Into the Streets May First" appeared that same year in *New Masses,* the Communist Party's national artistic and literary magazine that succeeded *The Masses*. Whereas the "Coffee Pot" poem deals with unemployment during the Great Depression, "Into the Streets May First" sounds the call for May Day demonstrations:

> Into the streets May First,
> Into the roaring Square.
> Shake the midtown towers,
> Shatter the downtown air!

The same year that he published "Into the Streets May First" Alfred Hayes delivered the keynote address at a conference of John Reed Clubs. There he called on members of those clubs and all similar organizations to put aside sectarianism to make room for a broad cultural front that would accommodate all like-minded intellectuals and artists in the struggle against Fascism.

Both the Young Communist League and the John Reed Clubs were affiliated with the Communist Party USA and were part of a larger movement called the Popular Front, which opposed Fascism. Established in 1919, two years after the Russian October Revolution, the CPUSA in the 1920s promoted industrial unionism and the organization of unskilled immigrants, African Americans, and women into the workforce. The party became an influential voice in the struggles for democratic and civil rights through its opposition to racism and racial segregation.

In the early years of the Great Depression the CPUSA remained active within the unemployment movement and extended its influence to liberal, cultural, and students organizations, such as the YCL and Reed Clubs. Party members made strides in building up labor unions, particularly after the 1935 National Labor Relations Act, also known as the Wagner Act after its primary author, Democratic New York Senator Robert F. Wagner, guaranteed the basic right of private sector employees to organize trade unions, engage in collective bargaining for better conditions and terms at work, and take collective action, including strikes. American communists also were among the first to volunteer to fight Fascism in the Spanish Civil War.

The 1917 Russian Revolution gave rise to the first Red Scare in America, causing widespread fear about the threat of communism or other radical leftist movements in the United States. That same year federal agents ransacked the offices of the Industrial Workers of the World. Socialist Party leader Eugene Debs was jailed for sedition. In 1919 U.S. Attorney General A. Mitchell Palmer unleashed the first of two raids that resulted in the arrest of some 4,000 leftists, three-quarters of whom were deported.

While the CPUSA did exert some influence in American life, particularly in the 1920s and 1930s with some 65,000 or more members, its impact would peak during the years of the Great Depression and wane thereafter. Alfred Hayes remained committed to many of the party's progressive policies, but later began to chafe against what he interpreted as restrictions on his literary freedom. Hayes was a versatile writer experimenting with fiction, essays, and criticism as well as poetry, and while many of his fellow leftist writers adhered more closely to political party lines Hayes was influenced by such European writers as Charles Baudelaire and Heinrich Heine as well as techniques of the American "moderns," prominent among them Ezra Pound and T.S. Eliot.

In the September 18, 1934, issue of *New Masses*, Hayes published another poem, a short piece entitled "I Dreamed I Saw Joe Hill Again."

> And standing there as big as life,
> And smiling with his eyes,
> Says Joe, "What they forgot to kill
> Went on to organize."
>
> "Joe Hill ain't dead," he says to me,
> "Joe Hill ain't never died."

Where workingmen are out on strike,
Joe Hill is at their side.

"From San Diego up to Maine,
In every mine and mill,
Where workers fight and organize,"
Says he, "You'll find Joe Hill."

With this brief poem, the saga of the song "Joe Hill" was born.

Earl: In on the Action

"MOMMER MADE MUSICIANS of us,"[8] Earl Robinson wrote in his autobiography many years later, and indeed she did. Hazel Robinson had studied piano, harp, violin, and cello, and was accomplished enough on the latter instrument to play in a local symphony. She insisted that her three children practice music every night while she cleaned up after dinner, which Earl and his siblings were more than happy to do to avoid the drudgery of washing dishes.

Robinson was born on July 2, 1910, in Seattle, Washington, a city that one year earlier had hosted an international fair, the Alaska-Yukon-Pacific Exposition, a fair designed to celebrate the increasing significance of the Pacific Northwest in general and Seattle in particular as a center for trade, shipping, and culture. Earl Robinson came by both his

A young Alfred Hayes, pictured here in the early 1930s, around the time he created "Joe Hill."

musical and political passions early. Growing up he studied piano, violin, and viola. While his future collaborator Alfred Hayes was coming of age in a household wherein his ambitions contributed to a contentious home atmosphere, Robinson suffered no such trouble. With his enthusiastic embrace of the artistic and political atmosphere of his home he enjoyed the warmth of his family unit. On vacations, it was common for the five Robinsons to pack up the car, drive around the state, pitch their tents whenever and wherever the spirit moved, and hold family sing-a-longs around campfires. Earl's father, Morris, was a lifelong liberal Democrat who asserted that it was wrong for ten percent of the country to have all the money and ninety percent to have nothing.

Robinson sang in choirs, continued to study classical piano, and played with a dance band in high school. He attended the University of Washington (the campus of which had been developed from the site of the Pacific Exposition), where he enrolled in all available music courses, including music history, harmony, and composition. He also listened to recordings by Duke Ellington and a singer named Paul Robeson. In 1933 he received a Bachelor of Music degree and a Teaching Certificate. Earl was now qualified to teach and supervise public school music programs, but first he seized on a unique opportunity.

In March 1934 Robinson accepted an offer to be the pianist in an orchestra aboard the cruise ship *President Jackson* that was bound for Asia. During that voyage he bought a guitar from a passenger for two dollars. That simple transaction changed his life. Folk instruments— banjo, recorder, accordion, and others in addition to the guitar—would increasingly find their way into his compositions. The guitar eventually helped him become a folksinger. He began to gather folksongs and to assimilate the music of his own country.

Back in Seattle, Robinson and two friends decided to head east by way of California, New Mexico, Texas, and the Southern states. Along the way he taught himself to play his newly acquired guitar and occasionally sang for his supper. He also witnessed incidents of racial prejudice that left lifelong impressions upon him.

Union Square

IN NEW YORK in the 1930s Union Square, at the convergence of several New York City streets—its name originated from its location at the intersection of Bloomingdale Road (now Broadway) and Bowery Road (now Fourth Avenue)—was alive with political activity and speakers expounding on the virtues of various political persuasions. While he studied with famed composers Hanns Eisler and Aaron Copland, Earl Robinson gravitated to the square.

In 1933 novelist and playwright Albert Halper had published *Union Square*, a novel that traces the lives of Depression-era New Yorkers living in that neighborhood. He was one of a number of writers, among them Nathanael West and John Dos Passos, who were publishing proletarian novels that questioned the causes and effects of capitalist exploitation. Earl Robinson read Halper's book, and now he wanted a taste of that life. He was drawn into what he called the seething conflict, where he witnessed clashing ideologies as well as police violence against both workers and the unemployed. He felt a tension in the air that was ready to snap at any moment, and he wanted in on the action.

Of the range of soapbox orators he heard in Union Square, Robinson considered the communists the most disciplined and effective, with a program that promoted union organization and employee rights. They also published what he considered readable papers such as the *New Masses*.

In June 1934, like Alfred Hayes before him, Earl Robinson joined the Young Communist League. He also became involved in the Workers Laboratory Theatre, which later became the Theatre of Action (TAC). Instead of competing with other leftwing factions, the TAC promoted alliances with other like-minded groups, precisely what Alfred Hayes had encouraged in his address to a convention of the John Reed Clubs. The TAC stood apart from what it termed bourgeois Broadway, and embraced the slogan, "Theatre is a weapon in the class struggle," echoing the motto of the Reed Clubs.

Among the writers and artists Robinson met at the Theatre of Action was a man named Robert Steck. A staff member of *New Theater* magazine, Steck worked during the summer at an upstate camp called Unity.

Camp Unity 1936

MIT A U, *Mit an N, mit an I_T_Y: Unity, Unity, Ay Yi-Yi!* So sounded some enthusiastic cheerleading from Unity campers. In 1936 Robert Steck invited Earl Robinson to come to the camp that summer as its musical director. Steck wanted Robinson not only to be in charge of the camp's musical program but also to have the freedom to compose and bring American music into the movement. As Robinson had already begun to collect American songs with working-class content, he happily took on the job, attracted by the musical opportunities it offered as well as by Camp Unity's progressive politics and its acceptance of all races, creeds, and religions. It was an easy decision, given the idealism he had developed in the wake of his Union Square observations, his reading of communist publications, the influence of his father's contempt for politicians, and his own travels through the South.

Robinson had been promoting the book *Negro Songs of Protest*, a compilation featuring the music and lyrics of twenty-four songs published by music collector Lawrence Gellert in 1936 with an introduction by Harlem Renaissance poet Langston Hughes, who termed it a work of inestimable value. Now Robinson also embraced the songs of the Industrial Workers of the World, including many by Joe Hill. He planned a program of IWW songs for a Friday evening in June. That afternoon the camp's drama director, a man named Alfred Hayes, handed him a poem to see if it might be made into a song.

IN THE INTERIM between its original composition and the day of the Camp Unity sing-along, Hayes's "I Dreamed I Saw Joe Hill Again" had grown from the three stanzas published two years earlier to six stanzas, with its title changed to "I Dreamed I Saw Joe Hill Last Night" or, simply, "Joe Hill."

When exactly Hayes wrote the original poem and when he expanded it remain uncertain. Several commentators, including historian Patrick Renshaw and Joe Hill biographer Gibbs Smith, have taken the third line of the poem literally—"Says I but Joe you're ten years dead"—to place the date of its writing (Hill died in 1915). Labor historian Archie Green, however, argues that this would mean that the poem was first written in 1925, when Alfred Hayes was only fourteen years old and as yet politically unformed.

Different songwriters and composers require different lengths of time to do their work, but the precise date of the poem's original writing meant little to Earl Robinson. That day at Camp Unity he was in a hurry. He took the poem and his guitar into a tent and forty-five minutes later emerged with a finished song. I wanted it that night, he later said.

The structure of Hayes's poem, written in rhyme, not free verse, made it a prime candidate for conversion into a song. In addition to composing the music, Robinson contributed two elements that lifted Hayes's lyric to another level: he repeated the last line of each stanza, for emphasis, and closed the song by repeating the entire first stanza. The first and last stanzas now stood as:

I dreamed I saw Joe Hill last night
alive as you and me.
Says I, "But Joe, you're ten years dead."
"I never died," says he.
"I never died," says he.

That night at Camp Unity the newly created "Joe Hill" joined such established labor union songs as "Hallelujah I'm a Bum" by Harry "Haywire Mac" McClintock and "Solidarity Forever" by Ralph Chaplin, as well as several Joe Hill originals, among them "There is Power in a Union," "The Rebel Girl," and "The Preacher and the Slave," also known as "Pie in the Sky."

Robinson was drawn to Hill not as a composer—Hill, like Woody Guthrie after him, often simply lifted tunes from existing songs to accommodate his new lyrics—but for the power of his lyrics. (Steal all you want, Robinson would later write in his autobiography, but only from the best places.) He sensed the same power in Hayes's lyrics. "Al's words could certainly stand on their own as a poem in strict iambic meter," Robinson wrote, "but for my purpose it seemed right to repeat the last line—better for joining in on, and the key to shaping a more finished tune."[9]

The newly crafted Hayes-Robinson ballad would later appear in the Wobbly publication *IWW Songs*, better known as the *Little Red Songbook*. Launched in 1909, the songbook would go through thirty-six editions until 1995. It was a compilation of tunes, songs, even hymns designed to boost morale among workers, and its subtitle says it all: "To Fan the Flames of Discontent."

As Robinson later remembered, the new song "Joe Hill" didn't draw prolonged applause that night when he debuted it around Unity's campfire. Nevertheless, on that Friday night in June the song began its storied journey around the world, one that continues to this day.

But who was Joe Hill?

≈ 2 ≈

The Poet Laureate of Labor

"Pin his ear to the wisdom post,
And make his words sledge hammers of truth"
—James Weldon Johnson

As ONE OF SWEDEN's prominent seaports, Gävle has a long history as an active shipping center and railroad hub. The city—its name is believed to derive from the Old Swedish *gavel*, meaning river banks—straddles the Gävle River where it flows into the Gulf of Bothnia, the northernmost arm of the Baltic Sea, nearly 100 miles north of the capital of Stockholm. In the late nineteenth century, in the working class neighborhood on the south bank of the river known as Gamla Gefle—Old Gävle—lived the family of Olof and Margareta Catharina Hägglund. On October 7, 1879, a child was born to the Hägglunds, a son they christened Joel Emanuel. He was the fourth of nine Hägglund children, six of whom would survive into adulthood.

Olof was a conductor on the Gävle-Dala Railway, the train line that since its completion in 1859 had run between Gävle and the mines of northern Sweden. The Hägglunds were a religious and musical family, and Olof and his wife, known as Catharina, who was a fine singer, often led the family in song. They also taught each of their children to play the family organ, which Olof, himself a talented player, had built.

Joel Emanuel displayed a precocious talent for music—learning to play the violin, guitar, piano, and accordion—and for creating songs. It would be years before he combined his instrumental and writing talents into the songs that he wrote for the Industrial Workers of the World in the United States, songs that would earn him admiration and accolades from his union brothers and sisters and anger and animosity from his enemies. But as a boy in the surroundings of his home and family he was already creating little comic tunes. He often borrowed melodies from the hymnbook of the Salvation Army, an irony that would not be lost on him later in America, where that organization—which he would mock as the "Starvation" Army—became a favorite target for his satirical songs.

In 1886 Olof Hägglund was injured on the job. Perhaps because he considered the accident his own fault or because there was no health insurance or workers' compensation in Sweden at that time, he did not seek medical attention. One year later, in surgery for treatment of an illness that may or may not have been related to his earlier injury, Olof died on the operating table. He was forty-one. His death spelled economic disaster for the Hägglunds. Catharina, herself only forty-three, was left with six children aged twelve and under. The fatherless family struggled to make ends meet but often could not, and at times went hungry. At the age of thirteen Joel Hägglund went to work in a factory.

There had been some efforts to unionize in Gävle's factories, but factory owners, civil and military authorities, as well as the archconservative Church of Sweden opposed such activity. So young Joel went to work in a non-union rope factory and there fell ill with skin and glandular tuberculosis. While the disease can be hereditary, by the late nineteenth-century European epidemiologists were suggesting that it could be linked to certain industrial conditions. For instance, fine dust particles prevalent in flax, the raw organic material for rope, could cause lung damage, making workers more vulnerable to tuberculosis. Having grown up in a house where potentially dangerous working conditions had taken his father from him, Joel now faced his own first exposure to the hazards often endured by industrial workers. It was an experience he would never forget. He underwent treatment in Stockholm and, seemingly against the odds, recovered and returned to Gävle, where he went to work at the port.

For fifteen years following her husband's death Margareta Catharina did her best to keep the family together, but she herself suffered from excruciating back pain and had undergone several operations. In January 1902 Catharina died. She was fifty-seven. After her death the Hägglund siblings sold the family home and went their separate ways.

Joel was twenty-three years old. He had grown up in a devout household, though formal religion held little grip on him. He had learned to play several musical instruments. He had witnessed the deaths of his father and his mother, and had escaped his own first serious health scare. He saw no future for himself in his native country, and he was not alone.

In the decades around the turn of the century some one million Swedes immigrated to the United States, convinced by true or trumped up reports circulating at the time that painted a picture of America as the land of opportunity, a place where even an unskilled worker was only as limited as his imagination and grit. So Joel and his brother Paul traveled to Liverpool, England, where on October 18, 1902, they embarked on the Cunard Line ship *Saxonia*, bound for the United States.

Ten days later they arrived in New York Harbor, two new arrivals among hundreds, if not thousands, of new immigrants (the *Saxonia* itself could accommodate nearly two thousand). They were in the New World and knew no one. Soon enough they adapted to their new language, perhaps having studied it in Sweden, and assumed new names. Paul changed his name to Hedlund, later married an American girl—he had left behind a wife in Sweden—and settled in Pennsylvania, where he followed his father's footsteps by going to work for a railroad.

Joel, now calling himself Joseph Hillstrom, became an itinerant laborer. For the next few years his steps are hard to verify. Did he sweep the floors in a Bowery saloon? Did he somehow meet John Reed in Philadelphia? Did he work in a Chicago machine shop, only to be fired for trying to unionize the employees? Did he stack wheat in the Dakotas and labor in Colorado mines? Perhaps. What is certain is that he was following a classic American pattern of moving west in search of better opportunity. By 1906 he was in San Francisco, where he witnessed the earthquake that rocked that city, and he sent a report about it to his hometown newspaper in Gävle. Now on the West Coast of the United States and with a new name, the former Joel Hägglund discovered the Industrial Workers of the World and there recognized his calling. Now he had not just moved to another country. He had moved from his past to his future.

The Wobblies

> Let us new lessons learn,
> All workers,
> New Life-ways make.
> One union form.
> —Langston Hughes

IN 1893, NINE YEARS before the Hägglund brothers arrived in America, a historian named Frederick Jackson Turner delivered a paper at the World's Columbian Exposition in Chicago entitled "The Significance of the Frontier in American History." An avid outdoorsman himself, Turner argued that the American was a new individual, different from his European predecessors, and that this new individual had been formed by the frontier experience of, among other factors, the restless move westward drawn by an abundance of free land. With the 1890 census declaring the American frontier closed, Turner argued that the energy of the new American character—with its distinctive traits of self-reliance, mobility, and optimism molded by that westward movement—would find a new frontier in a new morality, a new social conscience.

Turner's thesis became popular, particularly its underscoring of the notion of rugged individualism that has so frequently marked American culture and attitudes since. But Joseph Hillstrom and thousands of other immigrants to the American West were coming face-to-face with less commendable aspects of America and the American character. Workers in a number of industries were laboring and living in appalling conditions under the thumbs of oppressive bosses who displayed no sense of Turner's new social conscience.

In Colorado, confrontations between miners and mine operators were turning violent. The Western Federation of Miners—founded in 1893, it would change its name in 1916 to the International Union of Mine, Mill, and Smelter Workers—was on strike, and there were clashes between the union and state militias and hired company thugs over the basic right to organize. The exploitation of workers is a recurring theme in American history, and a former miner named Haywood decided to do something about it.

William Dudley "Big Bill" Haywood, massive, stoop-shouldered, and blind in one eye from a childhood accident—John Reed described his face as a scarred battlefield—had been a cowboy and homesteader and a miner before going to work for the Western Federation of Miners. Haywood and his fellow organizers envisioned One Big Union, the OBU, an amalgamation of smaller organizations that, when united, could wield greater economic power than could lesser, divided unions.

On June 27, 1905, Haywood stepped to the front of Brand's Hall in Chicago, slammed a loose board on a table to get the attention of those assembled, and declared, "Fellow workers, this is the Continental Congress of the Working Class. We are here to confederate the workers of this country into a working-class movement in possession of the economic powers, the means of life, in control of the machinery of production and distribution without regard to capitalist masters."[1]

On stage with Haywood were Eugene V. Debs of the Socialist Party, Daniel De Leon, leader of the Socialist Labor Party, activist Mary Harris "Mother" Jones, and Lucy Parsons. Born in Ireland, Jones was a legendary union organizer who had come to America as a child and worked on railways. After she lost her husband and four children in the 1867 yellow fever epidemic in Tennessee and her dress shop in the great Chicago Fire of 1871, she devoted herself to the struggles of miners. President Theodore Roosevelt once called her the most dangerous woman in America, and she is forever remembered for her marching words, "Pray for the dead and fight like hell for the living."

Lucy Parsons was the widow of Albert Parsons, one of several labor martyrs executed in the wake of the Haymarket riot in Chicago, one of the events that ultimately contributed to the convention in June 1905. The incident occurred on May 4, 1886, when a peaceful demonstration by workers calling for an eight-hour day suddenly turned violent after a bomb, thrown by person or persons unknown, exploded. Seven policemen and sixty-five others died or were wounded by the bomb or during the chaos that followed. Albert Parsons, a socialist and outspoken editor of the anarchist newspaper *The Alarm*, was one of seven workers wrongly accused of inciting the riot. He and three others were executed.

In 1905 the several hundred participants in attendance in Brand Hall took the first step toward the realization of the OBU by forming the Industrial Workers of the World (IWW), with the motto "An Injury to One is an Injury to All." Haywood told those assembled that they were there to emancipate the working class from the bondage of capitalism. The working class and the employing class, he said, have nothing in common.

Labor organizer Phil Cohen has written that the most significant improvement unions offer their workers is dignity and respect. Only in union facilities, said Cohen, does democracy penetrate the plant gate onto the shop floor. That is what the IWW set out to accomplish. The IWW held that the wage system must be replaced by an industrial society under the control of workers themselves; that workers' goals be accomplished by industrial action rather than political action; that a new moral code emphasizing human rights replace the capitalistic system, with its emphasis on property rights; and that those rights must be shared by all workers without regard to their sex, skills, race, creed, or national origins.

In addition, the IWW stressed that labor unions be organized along industrial lines rather than craft lines. Craft unions, which could trace their origins to the guilds of the Middle Ages, held that unions should represent only workers of a particular trade or skill. The Wobblies, on the other hand, envisioned a larger umbrella. Separation of craft from craft renders industrial and financial solidarity impossible, they said. They believed in the concept of an industrial union that would represent workers across entire industries. The IWW insisted that industrial unions encouraged solidarity and could wield more influence in negotiations than could craft unions. No less prominent an activist than civil rights leader W.E.B. Du Bois agreed with the IWW, writing in 1919 in *The Crisis* that he respected the Industrial Workers of the World as one of the social and political movements that draws no color line.

Haywood knew that the only ideas worth living for were those that inspired action. He also understood that he had to address the little details as well as the big picture, and that to achieve the goal of universal human dignity he had to begin with the particulars of employment and satisfaction of human hunger.

Haywood said that the IWW was going to bring the mass of workers up to a decent plane of living. This was a key concept: union leaders were not going to talk down to workers, they were going to go to where the people were and lift them up to a level of dignity and help them discover their own empowerment, where they would no longer be at the mercy of corrupt job sharks who charged them fees for job leads that most often led nowhere. And to the IWW they came: the loggers, haulers, seamstresses, and ranch hands, the miners, sawyers, pile butts, bindle bums, and floaters. They were white, black, Chinese, Scandinavian, Indian, Italian, Irish. They came from everywhere and in the IWW they were all Americans.

In San Francisco, Joseph Hillstrom ran into an acquaintance from Sweden. The two later rode the rails up to Oregon. The IWW had established a local there, and when sawmill workers went on strike the Wobblies joined in solidarity. Hillstrom contributed an article to the *Industrial Worker*, the IWW newspaper, with a new byline: Joel Hägglund and Joseph Hillstrom were no more. He was now Joe Hill, a card-carrying member of the Industrial Workers of the World.

The Power of Song

By 1910 JOE HILL was working on the docks in San Pedro, California, at the Port of Los Angeles, the busiest container port in the country. It was there that he came into his own as a songwriter and cartoonist for the union. He was not the first IWW songwriter, but he would become the best.

The Wobblies recognized that songs and singing could propel a movement. (At a time when poets were often parodied as effeminate and effete, no less imposing a figure than Big Bill Haywood, steeped as he was in Shakespeare and Milton, dabbled in poetry and understood the power of song.) Joe Hill became an indispensable voice toward that end. Hill biographer William M. Adler has written that Hill had "an artist's compulsion to create and a propagandist's need to incite."[2] That is perhaps the most accurate single-sentence appraisal of Joe Hill. His songs could wind up workers and belittle bosses in the same breath. "The Preacher and the Slave (Pie in the Sky)," "There is Power in a Union," "It's a Long Way Down to the Soup Line," "The Rebel Girl"—these and other Hill songs express the harsh and combative lives of itinerant workers, often with bitingly satirical humor, while celebrating those workers and calling on them to organize.

Music journalist and artist agent Josh Dunson has identified two traditions that went into Wobbly songs: Methodist/Baptist revival music as employed by evangelists and, ironically, by the Salvation Army, and the singing of hobo jungle camps, songs about railroad "bulls" and "John Farmer" that readily lent themselves to the Wobbly tradition.[3] These elements were key ingredients for songs destined for picket lines or union gatherings: simple, familiar melodies and simple, uncomplicated words—tunes and lyrics that even those with a limited grasp of the English language could easily absorb. These factors ensured that people could pick up the songs right away. Joe Hill became a master at this.

While Joe Hill developed into the IWW's most renowned songwriter, he was no simple parlor parodist. He actively participated in several strike actions, notable among them the 1911 Wobbly attempt to assist in the Mexican revolution against the American government-backed dictatorship of Porfirio Diaz. Though the effort ultimately proved unsuccessful, at one time Hill shouldered a 30–30 rifle and, with other volunteers, engaged Mexican Federal troops in gunfire.

In 1912, Hill befriended two fellow Swedes in San Pedro, the brothers John and Ed Eselius. The following year the brothers returned to their adopted hometown of Murray, a working-class suburb of Salt Lake City. They invited Hill and another Swede, Otto Appelquist, to join them. Both accepted. Hill, fresh from a near brush with deportation in Los Angeles, looked forward to a new start in Utah. It proved to be a fateful decision.

The Murders

ON THE NIGHT of January 10, 1914, John G. Morrison, a Salt Lake City grocer and former policeman, and one of his sons were shot and killed in their store by two men. That same evening Joe Hill arrived at a doctor's office with a gunshot wound, and briefly mentioned a fight with another man over a woman. He refused to explain further even after, on the basis of his injury, he was accused of the Morrison murders. Hill's booking photographs from January 14 identify him as Joe Hillstrom, 32 years old, 6 feet tall, weighing 143 pounds, with light complexion and hair, blue eyes, and no beard, a description quite similar to that of the initial suspect the police identified, a known criminal who had been observed that night near the Morrison store. Hill is further identified as "Danish" and his occupation "lumberman."

The case against Hill was weak and the evidence circumstantial, but the incident became a feeding frenzy for the anti–IWW media. Utah was up in arms about the presence in the state of the so-called revolutionary and subversive Wobblies. In a classic fake news campaign, local newspapers fed the public continuous tales of Wobbly misdeeds and of Joe Hill's supposed criminal record, among them a January 24 piece in the *Deseret Evening News* with the misleading headline "Hillstrom's Criminal Record in California Sent Here." The stories followed the standard steps of a negative spin offensive: First, establish a clear "we" and "they." Next, apply such terms as "revolutionary," "radical," and "subversive" to "they," so as to stoke fears in readers' minds that "they" seek to undermine and destroy "we" and our way of life. This is what the Utah press undertook to do in the case of Joe Hill.

The lawyer representing Hill declared that the main thing the state

A photograph of Joe Hill taken upon his arrest in Salt Lake City on January 14, 1914.

had against Joe Hill was that he was a member of the Industrial Work-ers of the World. That may have been enough. Hill biographer Adler has described the Salt Lake City of that day as an insular town, the ruling elites of which—among them the judge and prosecutor in Hill's trial—routinely shared club memberships and owned shares in each other's businesses. It was an atmosphere that did not take kindly to disruption of the status quo, particularly from the IWW, a union considered an anti-capitalistic, subversive, even anti–Christian organization. The lurid and false stories of supposed Wobbly transgressions created more ani-mosity regarding the union that was already a thorn in the side of local industry. Factory owners and civic authorities wanted the union out of the state, and the case against one of its best-known, Joe Hill, became hostage to that objective.

"The main and only fact worth considering however, is this," Hill wrote to the editor of the *Salt Lake Telegram* on August 15, 1915: "I never killed Morrison and I do not know a thing about it." In conclu-sion, he wrote, "Now if the people of the State of Utah want to shoot me without giving me half a chance to state my side of the case, then bring on your firing squads—I am ready for you. *I have lived like an artist and I shall die like an artist.*"[4]

A month later, writing to the Utah Board of Pardons in a letter enti-tled "A Few Reasons Why I Demand a New Trial," Hill explained that on the night of January 14, 1914, he was lying in bed in the Eselius house in Murray suffering from a bullet wound in the chest. Where or why I got that wound is nobody's business but my own, he said, adding that he was not shot in the Morrison store and all the so-called evidence that is sup-posed to show that he was is fabrication, pure and simple.

Hill never revealed the identity of the woman he had his confron-tation over. Some sixty years later biographer Adler discovered a letter the woman, named Hilda Erickson, had written in 1949 to a professor who planned to write a novel about Joe Hill. That novel never did get written, but the letter, which languished forgotten in the attic of the professor's daughter, revealed that Erickson saw Hill the night he was wounded, and that it was Hill's friend Otto Appelquist who had shot him in a quarrel over her. Hill did not testify in his own defense, despite the fact that the records of his preliminary hearing, which he read, had been tampered with and were filled with inaccuracies.

Did Joe Hill have faith that the wheel of the American judicial sys-tem would eventually turn in his favor? Did Hill's lawyers want to put Hilda Erickson on the stand, but Hill overruled them? (She was a regu-lar attendee during the trial, and visited Hill in jail.) Did he see no rea-son to involve her because he never expected to be convicted? Did local authorities, intent on railroading Hill, intimidate the Erickson family into silence? Adler and other commentators have asked these questions, but the answers remain elusive.

In the vehemently anti-union atmosphere stirred up by the fake news barrage Joe Hill was found guilty and sentenced to death. In a statement released through his counsel on September 19, 1915, Hill declared that if his life would help some other workingmen to a fair trial, he was ready to give it, and if by giving his life he could aid others to the fairness denied him, he would not have lived in vain.

President Woodrow Wilson sent a single-sentence telegram to Utah Governor William Spry asking, respectfully, if it would not be possible to postpone Hill's execution until the Swedish Minister had an opportunity to present his view of the case. Utah politicians and press pilloried Wilson for interfering in state matters. "The governor practically told him to go you know where."[5] IWW member Helen Keller, the Swedish ambassador, and the Swedish public all became involved in a bid for clemency. Thousands of people took to the streets to protest Hill's verdict, not only in America but also in England and Australia, all to no avail.

From the time of his arrest, on January 14, 1914, to the time of his execution, on November 19, 1915, Joe Hill spent almost two years in prison. He wrote constantly—songs, poems, essays, and letters. One of his regular correspondents was a ten-year-old girl named Katie Phar. The daughter of a Wobbly in Spokane, Washington, a city that was the site of a victorious union free speech fight in 1909–10, Phar was known as the IWW songbird because she led a union children's choir and sang regularly at the local IWW hall. Phar struck up a correspondence with Hill, who encouraged her to pursue her singing and musical studies.

Another regular correspondent was the legendary union organizer Elizabeth Gurley Flynn. Daughter of a socialist father and a feminist and Irish nationalist mother, with generations of rebels in her family, Flynn was born in New Hampshire and raised in New York. She became politically active and delivered her first public address, on women under socialism, when she was in her teens. She became a full-time organizer for the IWW, variously known as "the red flame" and the "Joan of Arc of the working class," and was involved in organizing textile worker strikes in Lawrence, Massachusetts, and Paterson, New Jersey, the same strike on which John Reed reported. Flynn was one of the most visible and effective members of the IWW as well as an outspoken advocate for birth control and women's suffrage. She later helped found the American Civil Liberties Union (ACLU). Joe Hill dedicated his song "Rebel Girl" to her.

Hill once wrote to Flynn that all the notoriety he was receiving was making him dizzy, and that he was afraid of getting more glory than he was entitled to. He despaired of becoming a martyr, claiming instead to be only a drop in the bucket of a fight where individuals don't count. To another friend he wrote that he did not have much to say about himself, only that he had always tried to do what little he could to advance freedom's banner.

Many commentators suggest that Hill may have come to see himself as worth more to the labor movement dead than alive, and that this may have influenced his decision not to testify at the trial. While that remains unresolved, Joe Hill had become the center of two conflicting characterizations: on the one hand, he was depicted as an immoral criminal member of a trouble-making union. On the other hand, he may have become more martyr than man, a sacrificial lamb on the altar of hatred and injustice.

On September 30, 1915, Hill wrote to Ben Williams, the editor of *Solidarity*, that he had nothing to say for himself "only that I have always tried to make this earth a little better for the great producing class, and I can pass off into the great unknown with the pleasure of knowing that I never in my life double-crossed a man, woman or child."[6]

On November 18, the day before his execution, Hill sent a telegram to Haywood at IWW headquarters in Chicago:

> "Goodby Bill. I will die like a true-blue rebel. Don't waste any time in mourning—organize!"
> It is a hundred miles from here to Wyoming. Could you arrange to have my body hauled to the state line to be buried? I don't want to be found dead in Utah.

Haywood replied by telegram:

> Goodbye, Joe: You will live long in the hearts of the working class. Your songs will be sung wherever the workers toil, urging them to organize.[7]

Haywood would later famously truncate Hill's comment into a memorable union rallying cry, "Don't Mourn—Organize!"

On Hill's last day alive, a reporter from the *Salt Lake Herald-Republican* visited him and asked him how he was going to dispose of his possessions. Hill sat down on the edge of his cot and scratched out his last will. The newspaper published it the next day, the day of Joe Hill's execution:

> My Will is easy to decide
> For there is nothing to divide
> My kin don't need to fuss and moan
> Moss does not cling to rolling stone

My body? Oh—If I could choose
I would to ashes it reduce
And let the merry breezes blow
My dust to where some flowers grow

Perhaps some fading flower then
Would come to life and bloom again
This is my Last and Final Will
Good Luck to All of you

　　　　　　　　　　　　—Joe Hill

On November 20, 1915, the day after Hill's execution by firing squad, a *New York Times* journalist wondered whether Hill's martyrdom might make him more dangerous to social stability than he was when alive. The next day the *Herald-Republican* printed the headline

"REBEL FUNERAL" FOR HILLSTROM ARRANGED

I.W.W. Songs, Including Executed Man's Own Composition,
"There is Power in a Union," Are to Be Sung
BODY WILL BE SENT TO CHICAGO

His body was delivered to that city where, after a funeral that drew tens of thousands of mourners, it was cremated. His ashes were placed into hundreds of small envelopes and, according to Wobbly folklore, sent around the world and released to the winds on May Day 1916. Fellow worker and songwriter Ralph Chaplin ("Solidarity Forever") concluded a written description of Hill's funeral by saying that the murdering of martyrs has never made any tyrant's place secure, and the death orgy by that heartless bunch of Mormon murderers, in spite of protests by the President and many noted men and women and thousands of working people all over the land, has done more to cement the forces that are about to overthrow the Capitalist system than anything that has happened in decades.[8]

Scores of eulogies praising Joe Hill appeared in the years following his execution, prominent among them comments made by Helen Keller and Carl Sandburg.

In the February 1918 issue of the socialist newspaper *The Call*, Keller underscored the need for union solidarity, writing that whether the IWW increases its power or is crushed out of existence, the spirit that animates it is the spirit that must prevail if the labor movement is to have a revolutionary function. Sandburg, who included Hill's "Preacher and the Slave" in his 1927 folk song collection *The American Songbag*, referred to Hill as the IWW's star songwriter and the only outstanding producer of lyrics widely sung in the militant cohorts of the American labor movement.

In his 1931 novel *Nineteen Nineteen* John Dos Passos devoted a whole chapter to Hill, saying he had a knack for setting rebel words to tunes. Ralph Chaplin, who wrote the first biography of Hill in a 1923 issue of *The Industrial Pioneer: An Illustrated Labor Magazine* later said that Hill came as close to being the poet laureate of labor as any poet the working class movement has yet produced.

Chaplin made that claim in 1926. Ten years later Alfred Hayes and Earl Robinson met at Camp Unity.

⇒ 3 ⇐

Strange Fruit

"A pamphlet, no matter how good, is never read more than once. But a song is learned by heart and repeated over and over."—Joe Hill

THE CAMP UNITY sing-along was over, the campfire damped down, the ashes spread. Everyone had joined in on the familiar union standards, like "Solidarity Forever." The debut of "Joe Hill" drew polite applause but did not create any overwhelming response. Its future hung in the balance. Would it be learned by heart and repeated over and over, or would it, like a pamphlet, quietly vanish into the distant dim? This was the song's pivotal moment: would it endure or would it be lost?

Songwriters know that once a piece of music becomes public it takes on a life of its own. The initial applause may have been nothing more than polite, but that night of the campfire something stupendous was born. The next morning a few people sought out Earl Robinson, telling him that's a pretty good song you have there, and asking if they could copy the words and music. Robinson gladly obliged.

It *was* a good song, with good words set to a good tune. And whether or not Alfred Hayes had it in mind when he wrote them, the first two lines of the song catch a listener's attention:

> I dreamed I saw Joe Hill last night,
> alive as you and me.

It is almost a sleight-of-hand maneuver. The song doesn't begin with "last night," it begins with "I," with immediate involvement. Then there is the dream—something perhaps otherworldly is coming, and then that someone "I" saw in the dream is alive, as alive as you and "I." After only those opening lines, the listener has to lean forward, has to know what comes next. And what comes next is a startling combination of the real and surreal. The narrator is in a dream, but the subject of the dream

33

is standing by his bed, alive as you and me. And unlike many songs that rely on a dream motif, this dream—this song—names names. There is Salt Lake City. There are copper bosses. These are concrete nouns that unfailingly snag a listener's attention and remain there after the song has gone silent.

It was the beginning of the "Joe Hill" diaspora that has spread throughout the world. Robinson would later write that only a true clairvoyant could have foreseen anything like its subsequent popularity.[1]

Soon enough "Joe Hill" began to spread to labor unions and affiliated organizations around the country. By the end of that summer the new song was being performed by the New Orleans Labor Council and on a San Francisco picket line. The song then found its way overseas for the first time, carried by volunteer members of the Abraham Lincoln Brigade who had joined in the fight against Franco's Fascists in Spain. So the song made connections, and connections produce more connections. From three stanzas to six, from six stanzas to a song. From one individual to another. From that individual to a group. From one group to the members of other groups, all of which took the song with them when they went their separate ways and used it to support their particular causes.

Prisoners of the Good Fight

> "We went because we were alarmed about what was happening both in our country and in Europe, as well as in Spain."—Carl Geiser

ONE OF THOSE who volunteered to go to Spain was Robert Steck, the Camp Unity director who had brought Earl Robinson in as musical director. Steck heard the debut performance of "Joe Hill" that summer night in 1936. In December of the same year the first contingent of American volunteers left New York City to fight in the Spanish Civil War. In February of 1937 Steck himself sailed aboard the *Île de France* for Spain, and through him and others the song "Joe Hill" took its first step beyond the context of an American topical labor song and toward becoming an international anthem for freedom and democracy.

Volunteering to fight in Spain was a logical move for Robert Steck. Born in Rock Island, Illinois, in 1912, he gained an early sensitivity to society's injustices from his father, a produce wholesaler who was also a member of the Freethinking Society. The Freethinkers were a group that espoused racial, social, and sexual equality as well as the abolition of slavery. Under his father's influence Steck developed a commitment to political activism and public service that continued throughout his life. At Ambrose College in Iowa, Steck discovered the theater, which he recognized for its potential use in the struggle for social equality and betterment. Eventually he moved to New York City, where, through the Theatre of Action, he met Earl Robinson.

Twenty-three years old when he went to Spain, Steck once described volunteering as a combination of selfless idealism, romanticism and historical foresight. His own service almost cost him his life. In April 1938 Italian Fascists captured Steck near the Ebro River. While imprisoned he endured frequent beatings. Despite the cruel treatment, Steck and other prisoners managed to put out a daily handwritten newspaper, a single sheet they dubbed the *Jaily News* to boost morale, discipline, and dignity among those incarcerated. Drawing on his New York experience at the Workers Laboratory Theatre and on the *New Theatre Magazine*, Steck arranged a Christmas Eve entertainment for fellow prisoners held in the San Pedro de Cardena Concentration Camp near Burgos. Singing in the camp was forbidden, but the resident major agreed to lift the ban if no revolutionary songs were sung. The program opened with Christmas and folk songs from many countries, representing the international make-up of the prisoners. The American contingent presented renditions of two labor ballads: one was "Casey Jones." The other was "Joe Hill," which from that moment on became a revolutionary song.

Ultimately Steck, on the verge of execution, was released in April 1939 when word came from Mussolini ordering a prisoner exchange of Fascist captives for international brigadiers. He returned to New York aboard the same ship on which he had sailed to Spain. Years later, from 1979 through 1986, he assisted a fellow volunteer veteran named Carl Geiser, who had also been captured and almost executed in Spain, in amassing biographical information on the Americans and international veterans who had been imprisoned in Spain to solicit their reminiscences of the war. He also visited archives in several countries.

The result was the book *Prisoners of the Good Fight: The Spanish Civil War 1936–1939*, a monument to the many volunteers who had risked their lives for the cause of democracy. Steck joined the Veterans of the Abraham Lincoln Brigade, which had been formed in 1939 to provide assistance and support to American veterans of the war as well as to Spanish refugees. He also served as chair of the Committee for the Release of the International Prisoners in Spain.

Abel Meeropol

ANOTHER PERSON who was present that June evening at Camp Unity for the debut of "Joe Hill" was a New York City public school teacher named Abel Meeropol. Born into a Jewish family in The Bronx in 1903, Meeropol graduated from DeWitt Clinton High School and earned degrees from the City College of New York and Harvard University. He later returned to DeWitt Clinton, where he would teach English for many years. Among his students were future writers James Baldwin, Paddy Chayefsky, and Neil Simon.

Meeropol was also a poet and social activist who wrote as Lewis Allan, the names of his two stillborn children. The use of that pen name allowed Meeropol to conduct himself not only as a writer but also in a second parallel life, as a political activist. In addition to his teaching Meeropol, as well as his wife, Anne, was a member of the Communist Party USA from 1932 to 1947, and donated a portion of his earnings to the party.

Meeropol was deeply disturbed by the continuing inhumanity of anti–Semitism and racism in the country, particularly the gruesome practice of lynching. It was a photograph of a particular lynching that inspired Meeropol to create one of the most memorable—and disturbing—songs ever written.

On August 6, 1930, four young black men, J. Thomas Shipp, Abraham Smith, Robert Sullivan, and James Cameron, were arrested in Marion, Indiana, for allegedly robbing and murdering a white factory worker and raping his companion. Sullivan was released and Cameron later spared. The next evening a mob broke into the jail where the Shipp and Smith were being held, pulled them from their cells, and lynched them. A local studio photographer, Lawrence Beitler, took what became a grisly iconic photograph of lynching in America—the bodies of two black men hanging from a tree in the center of town, surrounded by a crowd of white men, women, and children. Beitler spent many hours printing hundreds of copies of this photograph and sold them as postcards. Meeropol said that the photograph haunted him for days.

As Alfred Hayes had written "Joe Hill" in response to a travesty of justice, Abel Meeropol responded in kind. This racially motivated murder inspired him to write a poem entitled "Bitter Fruit." It was first published in the January 1937 issue of *The New York Teacher*, a union publication, and later in *New Masses*. His reasons for writing it were the following: "I hate lynching," said Meeropol, "and I hate injustice and I hate the people who perpetrate it."[2]

Meeropol later changed the title of his poem to "Strange Fruit" and composed music for it himself. He played the song for Barney Josephson, the proprietor of Café Society, a progressive nightclub that was open from 1938 to 1948 in a former speakeasy on Sheridan Square in New York City's Greenwich Village. At Café Society blacks and whites mixed, both on stage and off. The bartenders were said to include veterans of the Abraham Lincoln Brigade. "Strange Fruit" had been performed before in progressive circles around New York City, even by Anne Meeropol herself, who sang it in 1938 at Madison Square Garden with Laura Duncan, the prominent black vocalist and political activist who would perform with Paul Robeson, Pete Seeger and others during her career.

It was when Josephson passed the song on to Billie Holiday, who debuted it at the nightclub, that "Strange Fruit," like "Joe Hill," became one of the most iconic songs in American history. Because she sang the song in such an understated way some questioned whether Holiday understood the lyrics. She did. Fellow singer Tony Bennett once remarked that Holiday didn't sing anything she hadn't lived. The impact of Meeropol's song, speaking as it does of Southern trees bearing the strange fruit of black bodies hanging from poplar trees, was immediate and powerful. After Holiday recorded it in 1939—on the small, progressive Commodore label; Columbia wouldn't touch it—*Time* magazine denounced "Strange Fruit" as NAACP propaganda.

Lynching

> "Pull at the rope!
> O, pull it high!
> Let the white folks live
> And the black boy die."
> —Langston Hughes

LYNCHINGS—during which victims were maimed and murdered with unspeakable brutality, often in a carnival-like atmosphere and then, with the acquiescence if not the complicity of local authorities, hung from trees as a spectacle for all to see—were rampant in the South and elsewhere for many years following the Civil War. According to figures kept by the Tuskegee Institute between 1889 and 1940, more than 3,800 people were lynched in America. These numbers are probably conservative. In October 2019 *New York Times* columnist Jamelle Bouie wrote that more than 4,000 African American men, women, and children were lynched—burned, beaten, drowned, shot or hanged, with body parts often mutilated and discarded or even distributed as souvenirs—between 1877 and 1950. Whatever the actual numbers, lynching was the most blatantly vicious outgrowth of America's original sin—slavery. More than ninety percent of these victims were murdered in the South, the overwhelming majority of them black. Officially, there were only three lynchings in 1939, the year Billie Holiday first sang Meeropol's song. Nonetheless, there were signs that many more than that occurred but were hushed up.

LYNCHING WAS FAMILIAR to members of the Industrial Workers of the World, many of whom considered the execution of Joe Hill to be nothing less than an orchestrated lynching. In the years immediately following Hill's death two more prominent incidents drove home the Wobblies' awareness of lynching.

One notorious incident involved fellow worker Frank Little. Little was born in Illinois in 1879 to a Cherokee Indian mother and a Quaker father. The family later moved to Missouri and, finally, Oklahoma to become homesteaders during the 1889 Land Rush, Little's father having given up his medical practice. The Panic of 1893 meant poverty for the family, and in 1903 Frank Little moved to California, where he became a miner. He then became an organizer for the Western Federation of Miners before joining the Industrial Workers of the World. He was elected to the IWW executive board in 1914.

Frank Little was not only an effective organizer, he was a fearless agitator, renowned for his indomitable spirit and tireless activism. He was a veteran of many IWW free speech fights, among them confrontations in Missoula, Montana, in 1909; Spokane, Washington, in 1909–1910; Fresno, California, in 1910–1911; and Denver, Colorado, in 1913.

On the night of August 1, 1917, in the historic mining town of Butte, Montana, where the Western Federation of Miners had been founded in 1893 and where he had been organizing copper workers against Anaconda Mining, Little was hauled from his bed, beaten, tied to the rear bumper of a car and dragged through the streets, then hanged from a railroad trestle on the outskirts of town. A note was pinned to his thigh, "First and last warning," a clear message to other labor activists. No one was ever prosecuted for the murder.

Little's murder was the first hanging of a union organizer since the wrongly executed martyrs of the Haymarket riots. It would not be the last.

In November 1919 in Centralia, Washington, after four American Legionnaires were killed in a confrontation with Wobblies, union member and World War I veteran Wesley Everett was dragged from his cell by a mob that cut off his genitals, lynched from a bridge over the Chehalis River, his body riddled with bullets. The American Legion claimed that Wobblies had fired on them during an Armistice Day parade. IWW members said that the Legionnaires had attacked its union hall, and they fought back in self-defense. Everett's body, with the noose still around his neck, was returned to his cell, in full view of the other Wobblies who had been arrested with him. As in the case of Frank Little before him, Wesley Everett's murderers were never punished.

With his violent death Wesley Everett joined Joe Hill and Frank Little as three Wobblies who would be remembered for the sacrifice they made on behalf of all IWW members. That sacrifice should not be made light of, but throughout the years of the Industrial Workers of the World thousands of union men and women had been beaten, some to death, for their struggle to build the One Big Union. These are the unnamed heroes of the movement.

Woody

LYNCHING WAS FAMILIAR as well to an aspiring guitar player, singer and songwriter who was cutting his musical eyeteeth in Pampa, Texas, in the summer of 1936. This was Woodrow Wilson Guthrie, who would forever be known, by everyone everywhere, simply as Woody. Born on July 14, 1912, in Okemah, Oklahoma, he was named after the man who only twelve days earlier had become the Democratic Party presidential nominee, and who would win the White House later that year.

Oklahoma was a state whose politics aligned it with the Southern states where Jim Crow ruled. As Guthrie biographer Ed Cray has written, in the aftermath of World War I the solid citizens of Oklahoma transformed militant patriotism into fervent self-righteousness.[3] The *Tulsa World* even urged citizens to get out the hemp and strangle any member of the IWW, just as they would any snake—as did the Salt Lake City press in the case of Joe Hill.

One year before Woody was born, a mob had burst into the Okemah jail and seized a black woman named Laura Nelson and her fourteen-year-old son, Lawrence. The Nelsons had been arrested following a confrontation with a deputy sheriff, who reportedly had been searching their farm for a stolen cow. A struggle over a gun ensued, resulting in the death of the deputy. The Nelsons were dragged from the jail by a crowd of white men and lynched on a railroad bridge across the Canadian River outside of town. A photograph of the incident became a postcard, as had the Shipp-Smith lynching in Indiana that inspired

"Strange Fruit." Woody's father, Charley Guthrie, a hotheaded Democrat fully in line with segregationist views, was almost certainly a member of the mob.

Woody's Guthrie forebears have been described as fervent Confederates, and his father did not deviate from that label. Woody himself, though raised in that atmosphere of racial segregation and violence, did not adhere to it, but would make a personal journey away from that background to become a progressive activist and outspoken advocate for racial equality. He would later learn about the Nelson incident and would write songs about lynching, including the unrecorded "Don't Kill My Baby and My Son" and "High Balladree" as well as at least one he would record, "Slipknot," also known as "Hangknot." On a handwritten sheet of the lyrics to "Slipknot," dated February 29, 1940, in New York, Woody wrote that the song was dedicated to the many negro [sic] mothers, fathers, and some alike that were lynched under the bridge of the Canadian River, seven miles south of Okemah and to the day when there would be no more such hangings.[4]

But in the summer of 1936 Woody, at 24, was busily improving his musical skills. He would later write that virtually his first memory as a child was the sight and sound of a Negro minstrel jazz band marching in a street. Later, when he was around fourteen, he heard a young black man, who shined shoes in front of a local barbershop, playing a harmonica. Woody was enthralled, and soon enough he was playing the harmonica himself. To that first instrument he would add varying levels of ability on the mandolin, fiddle, and banjo, while the guitar became and remained his main instrument. He was also starting to write his own songs, beginning his journey to becoming America's foremost folk balladeer, a trajectory that would bring him into direct contact with "Joe Hill."

Pete

THAT SAME SUMMER, when participants at Camp Unity were singing "Joe Hill" and Woody Guthrie was getting his musical chops together, a young man back East was looking to find his own way. Seventeen-year-old Pete Seeger was on the road with his father to visit Bascam Lamar Lunsford at the Ninth Annual Folk Song and Dance Festival in Asheville, North Carolina. Pete's father, Charles Seeger, was a classical ethnomusicologist who at one time had been the youngest full professor in the history of the University of California. The elder Seeger was relatively apolitical until 1914, when he visited a migrant camp in

California's San Joaquin Valley and witnessed first-hand the deplorable conditions under which agricultural workers labored and lived.

Charles Seeger began frequenting the IWW headquarters in San Francisco and expressing anti-war views, which were deemed unpatriotic after the outbreak of World War I. The University of California placed him on what it termed a sabbatical, with the understanding that he would not return. Seeger and his family left California for New York. There he linked up with Marc Blitzstein, Aaron Copland and others to found the left-wing Composers Collective, the group Earl Robinson later joined.

Pete Seeger was born on May 3, 1919. As a teenager he accompanied his father to May Day demonstrations in New York City, and there he heard protest marchers singing union songs, among them originals by Joe Hill. In high school Pete identified journalism as the career path he intended to follow, but music soon began to capture his attention. He tried the autoharp and the ukulele, but they didn't engage him. He tried plucking out Tin Pan Alley tunes on a four-string banjo, but remained unsatisfied and frustrated. On a visit to his father in Washington, D.C., when he was seventeen, Pete brought with him a four-string banjo. Why do you play that wretched thing, his father asked? What should I play, said Pete? You should play a five-string banjo, his father said. Never heard of it, Pete said. Come with me, said Charles Seeger.

So it was that Pete Seeger accompanied his father to North Carolina to talk with Lunsford, an accomplished banjo player, folklorist, and performer of traditional folk and country music who was known as the "Minstrel of the Appalachians." Lunsford hailed from Mars Hill, North Carolina, a hamlet tucked up north of Asheville near the state's convergence with Tennessee, Virginia, and Kentucky. This was mountain country: the Bald Mountains, the Great Smoky Mountains, the Unicoi— all part of the Appalachians. This *was* Appalachia, another America, a geographical and metaphorical part of the country that Pete Seeger had never seen and knew nothing about—an America with deep-seated traditions of hardscrabble living and biblical fatalism. Only nine years had passed since record producer Ralph Peer "discovered" the Carter Family and Jimmie Rodgers during his historic sessions in Bristol, Virginia, on the Carolina border.

Much of this mountain music remained insular, and during his visit there Pete Seeger became obsessed with it and with the five-string banjo. He became absorbed in folk music, what he called the melodies time-tested by generations, songs with the meat of human life in them, the real music of rural people that did not simply present endless variations on "Baby, I need you." The five-string banjo, folk music and his growing commitment to leftist politics became the foundations upon which Pete Seeger would chart the course of his life.

Harvest Gypsies

BY 1936 JOHN STEINBECK, a thirty-four-year-old native of Salinas, California, had written several books but had achieved critical success only one year earlier, with *Tortilla Flat*. It was his 1936 novel *In Dubious Battle* that established his reputation not only as a novelist but also as a champion of workingmen and women. Steinbeck had met an organizer for the Cannery and Agricultural Workers Industrial Union, which in 1933 had launched an ambitious, though ultimately unsuccessful, attempt to unionize California's farm laborers. Steinbeck used the organizer's experiences as the basis for *In Dubious Battle*. Impressed by the novel, George West, chief editorial writer for the progressive *San Francisco News*, approached Steinbeck to write for his paper about the waves of migrant workers then pouring into the state.

From 1931 to 1939 more than one million people would emigrate from other states to California. Like Joe Hill before them, many of these migrants encountered opposition to their very presence as well as an over-abundance of aspiring workers like themselves that contributed to low wages, labor strife, and workers' camps with deplorable living conditions. These people would often be labeled refugees, but they were not. They were American citizens, one-time hard-working homeowners now essentially homeless people in flight after being driven out by the Dust Bowl that ravaged their farms and turned out by bankers repossessing their property.

Technology was another factor that would have a negative impact on workers. The use of farm machines, which reduced the importance of all migratory workers, would also contribute to the eventual decline of the Industrial Workers of the World. The heyday of the IWW may be roughly dated from its founding in 1905 to its post–World War I decline in 1924, spurred further by the union's unpopular anti-war stance.

Steinbeck began touring the state's agricultural valleys in an old bakery truck, immersing himself in the migrant experience. His epiphany came with visits to camps such as those in Visalia, in the San Joaquin Valley, where he encountered 5,000 migrants in flooded conditions; Nipomo, north of Santa Barbara, where he witnessed stricken families sometimes on the verge of starvation; and Weedpatch, a camp in Kern Country near Bakersfield. There he met Tom Collins, manager of the camp. With Collins he visited farms and migrant settlements, talked to residents, and attended camp meetings and dances.

The resulting articles, which benefited from reports compiled by Collins and Sharon Babb of the Farm Security Administration, were published in the newspaper from October 5 to 12, 1936. In 1938 they were collected in a pamphlet called *Their Blood Is Strong*, with photographs by Dorothea Lange and a newly written epilogue by Steinbeck, and later published as a small book, *The Harvest Gypsies*, which would provide the writer with material that he would later incorporate into his masterpiece, *The Grapes of Wrath*. Steinbeck's novel became, and remains, the dominant fictional statement of the Dust Bowl.

Steinbeck and Collins viewed these migrants as displaced Jeffersonians who needed and deserved their own plots of land. This ideal ran counter to the tyranny of the state's large agricultural farms. In California, Steinbeck wrote, there is a curious attitude toward a group that makes our agriculture successful—the migrants are needed and yet they are hated. On one side the entrenched authorities regularly violated the rights of the migrants; on the other side were the powerless victims of such abuse, willing to work but mired in poverty and bound by a system that denied them dignity and opportunity. Those who disliked migrants often considered them carriers of disease, unwanted people who increased the need for additional police and schools, meaning increased taxes for those already in residence in affected areas.

While the big landowners needed transient labor they feared one thing above all else, and that was union organizing. Many who despised the migrants considered their camps to be breeding places for strikes. The growers associations consistently used this argument to justify harsh and brutal means of control, stamping out any indication of unionization.

Woody Sez

DURING HIS OWN TRIPS up and down California, Woody Guthrie witnessed conditions in the migrant camps that were similar to those that John Steinbeck had experienced. He observed desperate, hungry people who had been stuck sometimes for years on what he called the dirty edge of California's green pastures. Some growers hired armed guards to protect ripe fruit, while migrant workers and their children went hungry. Some growers even torched fruit lying on the ground to prevent migrants from gathering it. Guthrie also saw organizers visiting the camps and promoting the formation of unions.

"There is a crime here that goes beyond denunciation," Steinbeck would write in *The Grapes of Wrath*. "There is a sorrow here that weeping cannot symbolize ... in the eyes of the hungry there is a growing wrath. In the souls of the people the grapes of wrath are filling and growing heavy...."[5]

At radio station KFVD in Los Angeles, Woody had a series of unpaid shows, the first being the popular *Woody and Lefty Lou from Old Missou* ("Lefty Lou" was a nickname he gave his singing partner Maxine Crissman). Their audience was largely composed of Dust Bowl veterans. There Woody met Ed Robbin, whose news program regularly reported on unions and the struggle of workers. Robbin also served as the local editor for *People's World*, a communist newspaper. Woody never became a Communist Party member. ("I'm not a communist," he once quipped, "though I've been in the red all my life.") He was far too unpredictable and impatient to sit through political study meetings or adhere to any strict party doctrine. He was interested, however, in this movement that seemed to offer some alternative to what appeared to be a failing capitalist system, much as Alfred Hayes and Earl Robinson had been.

The experiences Woody had in and around Los Angeles, seeing near-starving people in wretched camps or in tents along the Los Angeles River or homeless on Skid Row, affected him deeply. These were his people—the Okies and Arkies and Mizzous struggling to find a better life than the broken ones they had left behind. After his experiences in California, Woody the populist became Woody the radical.

It wasn't long before Woody was writing a column for *People's World* called "Woody Sez," where he displayed his down-home, Will Rogers type of humor. Through his writing and his frequent appearances singing for political rallies, fund-raisers, and unions, Woody championed equal rights for all races and railed against billionaires, greedy landlords, and what he termed "punk politicians." He also echoed one of the founding objectives of the Industrial Workers of the World when he advocated for a United States where everybody belonged to the same big union.

Woody's genuine anger resonated with his audiences because his message was clear: out here in America's pastures of plenty people were starving and being exploited. Woody's songs would have been music to Joe Hill's ears—they could fan the flames of discontent. He had become, as James Forester wrote in *The Hollywood Tribune* on July 3, 1939, the troubadour of those who are condemned to the other side of the fence.

Abel Meeropol and Robert Steck knew the song "Joe Hill" from its debut around a campfire. Woody Guthrie, Pete Seeger, and John Steinbeck all had a rendezvous with the song, though none of them knew it yet.

Ballad of Uncle Sam

THROUGHOUT THE 1930s Earl Robinson wrote music for a number of shows that were sponsored by the Works Progress Administration (WPA), a cornerstone of President Roosevelt's New Deal. Among the projects that he worked on was a 1939 revue called "Sing for Your Supper," with lyrics by John LaTouche, a poet whose work as a librettist and lyricist would include collaborations with Duke Ellington, Leonard Bernstein, and fellow poet Richard Wilbur. The show's finale was called "The Ballad of Uncle Sam," The theme of the show positions Uncle Sam as the producer of a musical that puts unemployed performers back to work. After his production, Uncle Sam is buttonholed by ushers, costumers, and others who ask him who he is and where is he from.

Uncle Sam's answer is a thirteen-minute cantata that paints a musical history of the United States. In seventy-six the sky was red and Bad King George couldn't sleep in his bed, he says. "Am I an American?" he asks, rhetorically. He then proceeds to rattle off a list of some sixteen nationalities and ethnic origins and religious orientations, from Irish to Jewish to Hungarian to Swedish (a nod to Joe Hill?) to Greek to Czech. Years later the New York City Labor Chorus would add African, Jamaican, Dominican, and Native American. Now you know who I am, Uncle Sam concludes: America!

After the revue closed Robinson spoke with Norman Corwin of CBS and suggested that the song might be incorporated into Corwin's new network series *The Pursuit of Happiness*, a single-season showcase that celebrated Americans and their heritage. The program followed its tagline of "Life, Liberty and the Pursuit of Happiness" through patriotic acts by America's greatest performers, writers, and authors. Robinson sang "The Ballad of Uncle Sam" at the piano for Corwin, who liked it and asked him to repeat his performance for the CBS brass. When company vice president Bill Lewis heard it he was impressed and responded, "Wouldn't Robeson knock the hell out of this!"[6]

═ 4 ═

Paul Robeson

"The artist must elect to fight for freedom or slavery.
I have made my choice."—Paul Robeson

BY 1939, WHEN CBS vice president Bill Lewis mentioned him, Paul
Robeson was firmly established as an international star of stage and
screen. Strikingly handsome at 6 feet 3 inches and over 200 pounds, he
also possessed a rich bass-baritone singing voice that made him one of
the most famous and in-demand concert artists in the world.

The man who would do more than anyone else to promote and per-
petuate the song "Joe Hill" was born in Princeton, New Jersey, on April
9, 1898. One month earlier, the journalist and anti-lynching crusader
Ida B. Wells had joined a group of congressmen who met with President
William McKinley to seek federal action against the continued practice
of lynching. That coincidence would not be lost on Robeson when, half a
century later, he would meet with President Harry Truman for the same
reason—and receive the same lukewarm reception as did Wells.

Robeson's parents were the Reverend William Drew Robeson and
Maria Louisa Bustill. William Robeson had been born a slave on a plantation in Martin County, North Carolina, but in 1860, at the age of fifteen, he escaped by way of the Underground Railroad. He served as a
laborer for the Union Army during the Civil War, and later obtained an
elementary school education and studied for the ministry at all-black
Lincoln University, near Philadelphia. By 1881 he was the minister of
Witherspoon Presbyterian Church in Princeton.

Princeton and Rutgers

PRINCETON AT THAT TIME has been described as the northernmost
reach of the Confederacy, a Jim Crow town with its own entrenched tradition of hostility toward black people, as evidenced by a caste system

of rigid segregation of schools, transportation, and restaurants. So Paul Robeson was born into and grew up surrounded by a racial atmosphere similar to that experienced by Woody Guthrie—except, of course, Robeson was black, and while he was warmly embraced by the black community he would soon enough become all too familiar with the treatment afforded his people by white America. As he would later write in his autobiography, Princeton "was spiritually located in Dixie.... Like the South to which its heart belonged, Princeton's controlling mind was in Wall Street. Bourbon and Banker were one in Princeton, and there the decaying smell of the plantation Big House was blended with the crisper smell of the Counting house. The theology was Calvin; the religion—cash.... Rich Princeton was white; the Negroes were there to do the work."[1] Segregation had been effectively endorsed two years before Robeson's birth by the Supreme Court's ruling in Plessy v. Ferguson, which accepted so-called "separate but equal" facilities as constitutional.

In 1900 a disagreement between William Robeson and the white financial supporters of his church led to his resignation. After working a series of menial jobs and losing his wife, Paul's mother, in a freak kitchen fire, he was able to re-establish himself at St. Luke African Methodist Episcopal (A.M.E.) Zion Church in Westfield, New Jersey, and then at the St. Thomas A.M.E. Zion Church in Somerville, New Jersey.

Paul attended high school in Somerville, where he performed in *Julius Caesar*, played the lead role in *Othello*—a role he would come to define in his professional career—sang in the glee club, and excelled at sports. Before his graduation he took a statewide competitive examination and won a four-year scholarship to Rutgers College.

In the fall of 1915, at the same time when Joe Hill was enduring his final days in prison, Paul Robeson became only the third African American student ever to enroll at Rutgers—and the only one at that time. "As I went out into life," he later wrote, "one thing loomed above all else. I was my father's son, a Negro in America. That was the challenge."[2]

The challenges came early. When he tried out for the football team he was severely tested by his own teammates, who engaged in racially motivated excessive play during which Paul's nose was broken and his shoulder dislocated. Once, after a ball carrier stamped on his hand, Robeson lifted the player up over his head, as if to smash him to the ground. He was never again roughed up by his own teammates.

He continued to endure racism from other schools. One college, Washington and Lee, agreed to play Rutgers only after it was confirmed that Robeson could not participate. Robeson ultimately prevailed and was named first team All-American in his junior and senior years.

Walter Camp, a former player and later coach and sportswriter who is often called "the father of American football," considered Robeson the greatest end he ever saw. Paul would finish his university career with fourteen varsity letters in different sports.

His bass-baritone was the prominent voice in the university's Glee Club, though only at home concerts. Due to his race he was not invited to travel with the club, and even at Rutgers could not attend post-performance social functions. But the Glee Club was not his only outlet for singing. As Geraldine Neale, a young black woman with whom Robeson had a romance at the time, recalled, if Paul was asked to sing at friends' gatherings he sang everything from spirituals to love songs. He also brought his voice to the varsity debating team, which was a natural for him. Growing up, his father, who had a passion for the spoken word, often gave Paul speeches to memorize and deliver back to him, coaching him on his enunciation and inflection.

Robeson was as brilliant in the classroom as he was on the athletic field. In his senior year he was accepted into Phi Beta Kappa and Cap and Skull honor societies. His senior thesis was entitled "The Fourteenth Amendment: The Sleeping Giant of the American Constitution." That amendment, which followed the 1865 Thirteenth Amendment that abolished slavery, was ratified on July 9, 1868. Its opening statement declares:

> All persons born or naturalized in the United States, and subject to the jurisdiction thereof, are citizens of the United States and of the State wherein they reside. No State shall make or enforce any law which shall abridge the privileges or immunities of citizens of the United States; nor shall any State deprive any person of life, liberty, or property without due process of law; nor deny to any person within its jurisdiction the equal protection of the laws.

For the rest of his life, in everything he did, Paul Robeson would fly the flag of the Fourteenth Amendment.

During Robeson's junior year his father died unexpectedly at the age of 73. The glory of my boyhood days was my father, Paul would always say. There was no hint of servility in his makeup. From Paul's earliest days the Reverend Robeson had insisted on a central aspect of character—the courage to remain true to one's convictions. "Unbending. Despite anything."[3] William Robeson had taught his children that black people were in every way equal to white people and that they had a responsibility to their race. At the same time, he insisted that they reject bitterness or unkindliness. Paul referred to these as the core texts of his father's life. These were the concepts that he himself became imbued with as a youth and would maintain thereafter.

Robeson's Rutgers classmates elected him class valedictorian, and in his valedictory address Paul urged them to work for equality for all Americans until there would be equal opportunities for all throughout the country, until black and white would realize that they are brothers, and until an injury to the meanest citizen would be recognized as an insult to the whole constitution.

The Sorrow Songs

ROBESON ENTERED New York University School of Law in the fall of 1919 but soon transferred to Columbia Law School. In 1921 he married Eslanda "Essie" Goode, a chemistry student at Columbia who would go on to become the first black woman to head a pathology laboratory. That same year Robeson postponed school to act in Mary Hoyt Wiborg's play *Taboo*. He then sang in the chorus in a production of *Shuffle Along*, an all-black Broadway show written by the comedy duo of Flournoy Miller and Aubrey Lyles and featuring music and lyrics by Eubie Blake and Noble Sissle. It helped launch the careers of Josephine Baker and Adelaide Hall, as well as Robeson's own, and is credited as being a seminal milestone in the Harlem Renaissance. He later rejoined *Taboo* in London, where he briefly lived in a room in the flat of the black American singer John Payne. There he met another black American musician.

THIS WAS LAWRENCE BROWN. The meeting between the two men could not have been more auspicious, and would shape their professional careers for the rest of their lives. Brown was born in 1893 in Jacksonville, Florida, the son and grandson of former slaves. Brown had displayed exceptional musical talent as a child, which ultimately led him to study in Boston, where he worked as an elevator operator to cover the expenses of his musical studies. A classically trained pianist, he made his debut as an accompanist for the tenor Sydney Woodward. He later became the pianist for the renowned tenor Roland Hayes, with whom he toured from 1918 to 1923, during which they had performed before the king and queen of England.

Now at London's Trinity College, he was working on a volume of transcriptions of African American spirituals, research for which had taken him deep into the American South. Hearing Robeson sing, Brown was convinced that Paul had a great future ahead of him as a vocalist. The result of their meeting was that Brown became Robeson's chief accompanist for more than thirty-five years, during which he would provide not only his piano, but also occasionally his tenor voice.

Robeson returned to Columbia Law and graduated, but soon renounced a career in law due to the continued racism he encountered. (I don't take dictation from a nigger, one secretary said.) In December 1924 he landed the lead role of Jim in Eugene O'Neill's *All God's Chillun Got Wings.* When that production was delayed, he took the lead role in a revival of O'Neill's *The Emperor Jones.* Reviews declared him an unequivocal success, thereby firmly igniting his stage career.

It was a heady time for Robeson. In addition to launching his stage career, in 1925 he starred in his first movie, *Body and Soul,* a silent film by the pioneering black American author, film director, and independent producer Oscar Micheaux. As important as these two milestones were to Robeson, a perhaps even more significant development occurred in his professional life in 1925. This was his embrace of the African American spiritual.

Early in the year Lawrence Brown had returned to New York. In the intervening time since the two men met in London, Brown had sent Robeson a draft of the book of spirituals on which he had been working. (It would be published as *Negro Folk Songs* in 1930.) Now Brown began visiting Robeson on a regular basis, and would play the piano while Robeson sang. Within weeks they decided to work together. The two men assembled a set of spirituals and booked the Provincetown Playhouse in New York's Greenwich Village for a concert.

ON APRIL 19, 1925, Robeson and Brown presented their program, consisting solely of Negro (as they were known then) spirituals and secular songs, many of them arranged by Brown. Their performance was a resounding success. As Eslanda Robeson remembered in her 1930 book *Paul Robeson, Negro,* the audience greeted Robeson and Brown with roar after roar of enthusiasm even as the two walked on stage, and at the conclusion of the performance clamored for encores. Many years later labor historian Philip S. Foner would write that the critics hailed both the songs and the singer, and it was acknowledged that Robeson had shattered the concept that Negro music was inferior and that the Negro song could not be considered as art.[4]

Spirituals, along with work and jubilee songs, had been part of black life since the mid–1600s, particularly on the forced work camps known as plantations. In 1801 a freed slave named Richard Allen, who founded the African A.M.E. Church with which Paul Robeson's father and brother Ben were affiliated, published a hymnal entitled *A Collection of Spiritual Songs and Hymns.* In 1867 Northern abolitionists William Francis Allen, Lucy McKim Garrison, and Charles Pickard Ware published the book *Slave Songs of the United States,* consisting of 136 songs they transcribed from the Gullah Geechee people of Saint Helena Island in South Carolina. That collection included such now widely known songs as "Roll, Jordan, Roll," "Michael Row the Boat Ashore," "The Old Ship of Zion," and "Nobody Knows the Trouble I Had."

In the wake of that publication, in 1871 the *a cappella* Jubilee Singers of Fisk University, the historically black college in Nashville, Tennessee, was formed as a gospel ensemble to tour and raise funds for the struggling five-year-old university. The Singers introduced spirituals to audiences through their many concerts in the United States and Europe. A handbill announcing their 1873 performance in Manchester, England identifies them as ex-slave students who have appeared and sung their slave melodies before many illustrious audiences. The original group continued to tour until disbanding in 1879, due to its grueling schedule and the racist ill treatment it sometimes endured.

What was significant about Robeson's recital of African American spirituals was that it was the first time that a black soloist, rather than a choral group, had performed a program devoted to them. Among those who responded favorably to Robeson's concert was James Weldon Johnson, lawyer, writer, NAACP executive secretary, and author of "Lift Every Voice and Sing," often referred to as the black national anthem. In the same year as Robeson's concert Johnson published *The Book of American Negro Spirituals*, in which he compiled 120 of these songs, with arrangements by his brother, J. Rosamond Johnson, as well as five by Lawrence Brown. Robeson, Johnson claimed, feels the spirituals deeply and pulls at the heartstrings and moistens the eyes of his listeners.

The *New York World* called Robeson's performance a turning point, one of those moments when a star is born, adding that Robeson's voice is one in which deep bells ring. A critic for *The New York Times* wrote that Robeson's spirituals hold in them a universal humanism that touches the heart. And in the *New Republic*, Elizabeth Shepley Sergeant wrote that she hoped that men like Paul Robeson and Lawrence Brown are establishing a classic spiritual tradition that will long live in American music.

Joining Johnson in his praise of Robeson's concert was NAACP co-founder W.E.B. Du Bois. Twenty-two years earlier, in 1903, Du Bois had approached the subject of the spiritual in his seminal book *The Souls of Black Folk.* There he refers to black folk song as the most beautiful expression of human experience. Calling spirituals "sorrow songs," because they speak of death and suffering and longing for a better world, Du Bois noted that such songs often had been neglected, misunderstood, even despised, but that they remained the spiritual heritage of the nation and the greatest gift of his people. He would later write that Robeson, more than any other living man, has spread the pure Negro folk song over the civilized world.[5]

One of the reasons that the spirituals had been neglected and misunderstood lies in their origin—the brutal and inhuman conditions of slavery, and the desire of black people to move beyond that legacy. While the songs may have been born out of that tragedy, and clearly reflected the reactions of slaves to their lot—for example, "Nobody Knows the Trouble I Had," which would evolve into "Nobody Knows the Trouble I've Seen"—as early as 1845 the renowned abolitionist and former slave Frederick Douglass recognized another aspect of the spirituals. Many were code songs that contained hidden messages to slaves who were planning to escape their plight of forced labor. The spirituals spoke of much more than a desire to reach heaven in the afterlife. They spoke of a desire to reach freedom in this life.

A prominent example of a code song is "Follow the Drinking Gourd." The gourd is a reference to the Big Dipper, and the lyrics of the song contain coded instructions for slaves escaping from southern Alabama to cross the Tombigbee River and continue north to the Tennessee River to where that waterway meets the Ohio River and the free states beyond.

Many years later Maurice Jackson, an associate professor of history and African American Studies and an affiliated professor of performing arts at Georgetown University, underscored this function of the spirituals. Professor Jackson suggested that while Du Bois referred to the spirituals as "sorrow songs," they likewise carried a message of hope, a faith in the ultimate justice of things. Jackson further proposed that these songs contained another dimension. Referring to so-called experts who try to give meaning to the spirituals in strictly religious terms, Jackson writes, "By doing so they emphasized the despair of slaves and later free blacks with their conditions in this world and their hope for a better life in the next. However," Jackson continues, "a close reading of many of the texts of the spirituals shows that these were not songs of despair, but songs of struggle. Not all believed that only in heaven would freedom come. In other words, the songs were otherworldly, but also of this world."[6] They were not, then, simply a way to avoid dealing with this world. They were freedom songs, songs fully engaged *with* this world.

When slaves sang "Steal away, steal away home, I ain't got long to stay here," they weren't singing just about going home to Heaven: they were singing about escaping on the Underground Railroad.

Writing in the book *American Roots Music*, Grammy-nominated music critic Claudia Perry agreed. She argues that slaves found in the Christianity that their white owners practiced a worldview that spoke to their own plight. But when they sang the same hymns that white overseers sang, those songs took on a different meaning—a way to communicate plans for escape or rebellion.

Robeson and Brown presented a second concert on May 3, 1925, to a similar overwhelming response. The *Evening Post* commented that once more the singer and pianist had revealed their mastery of the songs of their people. It is noteworthy to recognize that not all of the songs Robeson sang in his concert program were spirituals. A song that remained one of his favorites throughout his career was "Water Boy," a black secular song that was written by the white composer Avery Robinson and performed or recorded by many artists including Roland Hayes, Fats Waller, Earl "Fatha" Hines, Odetta, and Harry Belafonte, and as recently as 2015 by Rhiannon Giddens, on her first solo recording after her tenure with the Carolina Chocolate Drops.

On the strength of these concerts Robeson signed a contract with Victor Records. His first recordings were issued both in the United States and England late in 1925, four double-sided records that sold fifty-five thousand copies within four months. Harlem Renaissance poet and writer Langston Hughes wrote to Robeson, saying that the great truth and beauty of the singer's art struck him as never before. In January 1926 Robeson and Brown embarked on an extensive concert tour across America, during which they performed their program of spirituals to packed houses. The following year they gave a similar series of concerts in Europe. In an interview later published in London, Robeson said the spirituals have the same value as other folk songs, and there are excellent melodies amongst them.

It's not that Paul Robeson had never heard these songs before. While he did not grow up forced to work under the sweltering sun of Southern cotton fields, he did grow up in his father's church and there heard spirituals or songs much like them. His family, his father's church, and his supportive black community formed the solid basis of Paul Robeson's character. "I've got a home in that rock," he would later sing. As he later noted in his autobiography:

> I heard my people singing ... from choir loft and Sunday morning pews—
> and my soul was filled with their harmonies.... I heard these songs in the
> very sermons of my father.... The great, gospels we love are merely sermons
> that are sung.[7]

And, as has been noted, he sang them at informal gatherings while at Rutgers. But now, embarking on a professional singing career, Robeson credited Lawrence Brown with having guided him to the beauty of black folk music and to the music of all other peoples so like his own. Robeson also began the study of folk songs of many cultures and many struggles, among them the songs of working men and women, a quest that would lead him to "Joe Hill."

Ol' Man River

IN APRIL 1928 Robeson appeared in the London stage production of the American musical *Show Boat*, based on Edna Ferber's 1926 novel of the same name. *Show Boat* would be revived on stage many times over the years and would spawn three films, but the highlight from all of its versions remains Paul Robeson's rendition of "Ol Man River." Composed by Jerome Kern with lyrics by Oscar Hammerstein II, it is the show's most famous song, and is so because of Paul Robeson. His performance of it remains the benchmark against which all performances of the song are measured.

Some critics were not pleased with the play's use of the word *nigger*. Robeson himself once included that word in a 1930 recording of "Ol' Man River." By the time he appeared in the 1936 film version of *Show Boat*, Robeson had further reworked the lyrics, moving away from any use of the words *niggers* or *darkies* to refer simply to an old man called the Mississippi. It was what his son, Paul Jr., would later call the symbolic equivalent of the raised black fist: Robeson's rendition of the song was a showstopper.

His changes to the song didn't stop there. Over the years, for the demeaning lines about blacks getting a little drunk and landing in jail Robeson substituted "you shows a little grit and you lands in jail." Finally, he dispensed with the lines about getting weary, sick of trying and being tired of living and scared of dying in favor of

> But I keeps laughin' instead of cryin'/
> I must keep fightin' until I'm dyin'.

That final change solidified a line—I must keep fightin' until I'm dyin'—that might be called Paul Robeson's personal motto, a commitment from which he would never waver.

Paul Robeson and "Ol' Man River" became inseparable, and his renditions of it a cultural landmark. Edna Ferber herself described a 1932 performance in a letter to writer Alexander Woollcott; as Martin Duberman recounts, she said that "the ovation given Robeson on opening night exceeded any she had ever heard accorded 'a figure of the stage, the concert hall, or the opera.'"[8] The audience stood up and howled, she wrote; they applauded and shouted and stomped. The show stopped and they called him back to sing it again.

I Want to Be African

IN 1934 ROBESON enrolled in the School of Oriental and African Studies in London, where he studied African dialects. His growing interest in African history and its impact on culture coincided with his essay "I Want to Be African." Robeson wrote that in his music, plays, and films he wanted to carry the central theme of being African, that it is from this concept of being African that black people will make their real contribution to the culture of the world. Robeson's growing embrace of things African further indicated that he was expanding his artistic and personal quest, and would not be stifled by any racial limitations.

Years later, when introducing Robeson to an audience at a forum in New York, Helen Rogers Reid, publisher of the *New York Herald Tribune*, identified Robeson's period in London as the beginning of his political radicalism. While performing in that city he became interested in the African people, she said, and through his study of the plight of colored peoples in other parts of the British Empire as well as the rest of the world, he reached the conviction that the problems of all backward people, white or colored, were interrelated. After that, she further commented, he plunged into the struggle for freedom in earnest.

To his repertoire Robeson began to add progressive songs of his own day. He was becoming the voice of the international working class. Philip Foner would later write that so far as the United States is concerned we may consider Paul Robeson the father of the American political song of the contemporary era.

In 1934, on an invitation from film director Sergei Eisenstein (*Battleship Potemkin*), Robeson visited the Soviet Union for the first time. Responding to his warm reception there, he said he felt that he was welcomed not simply as a Negro but as a human being for the first time in his life. His affection for the Soviet Union would continue for the rest of his life, as would the trouble that affection would cause him in his own country.

Spain

> I must drive the bombers out of Spain!
> I must drive he bombers out of the world!

I must take the world for my own again—
A worker's world
Is the song of Spain.
                —Langston Hughes

THE CIVIL WAR in Spain, which had erupted one month after the Camp Unity sing-along where "Joe Hill" was debuted, was becoming an ever-increasing concern for Robeson. In December 1937 alone he spoke and sang at four concerts in support of the Spanish Republican cause. One of those events was a huge benefit concert, in London's Royal Albert Hall, sponsored by the National Joint Committee for Spanish Relief to raise funds for victims of the war. Robeson followed a succession of speakers who lashed out at the Western democracies who were following a hands-off policy regarding the war. When his time came to address those assembled, he sang "Strike the cold shackles from my leg," lines that Lawrence Gellert had included in his book *Negro Songs of Protest*, that had so influenced Earl Robinson. He then sang "Ol' Man River," with his altered lyrics, and the audience went wild. He also declared:

Every artist, every scientist, must decide NOW
where he stands.... The artist must take sides.
He must elect to fight for freedom or slavery.
I have made my choice. I had no alternative.

In January 1938, after Robeson had spent an afternoon recording songs from *Porgy and Bess* at London's Abbey Road Studios, which years later would become world-renowned as The Beatles' studio, he and Eslanda traveled to Spain. She had hesitated at first, but he insisted that the fight in Spain was their fight as well. Robeson was recognized everywhere he went by those who had seen his movies or read about or heard his recordings. And suddenly there he was—they could hardly believe it. Brigade fighters had grown weary and somewhat jaded at the parade of VIPS who would swoop in for brief visits with British and American troops in the trenches and then just as quickly depart, but by all accounts Paul Robeson was welcomed wherever he went, from barracks to hospitals, and his renditions of "Ol' Man River" and "Joe Hill" brought wild cheers from Americans and Spaniards alike.

Robeson referred to his trip as a major turning point in his life, saying that he had never met such courage in a people. Returning from Spain, Robeson stopped in Paris to sing for the exiled delegates of the Spanish Parliament. When asked by an interviewer what brought him to Spain, Robeson answered, "My devotion to democracy ... and it is not only as an artist that I love the cause of democracy in Spain, but also as a black. I belong to an oppressed race, discriminated against, one that could not live if Fascism triumphed in the world."[9]

In 1940 the Veterans of the Abraham Lincoln Brigade made Paul Robeson an honorary member, a rare recognition from that organization. Milt Wolf, a founding member of the VALB, said that when he stood next to Robeson to pin the star on his lapel, he felt that Robeson was not so much becoming a member of the Brigade as that we were becoming a part of Paul Robeson. Later, in 1943, Robeson told the *Herald Tribune* that his heart was filled with admiration and love for the white volunteers and that he had a sense of pride to see in his own people in the ranks of the Brigade—a strong statement given the then-current segregated U.S. Army.

Robeson had only recently returned from Europe and his visit to Spain when he and Earl Robinson met in late October 1939 in New York and set to work on *The Pursuit of Happiness*. Robeson was clearly pleased to be working with Robinson, and when they first got together in Robeson's apartment the singer told the composer, "I already know one of your songs."

⇒ 5 ⇐

Where You'll Find Joe Hill

"[Joe Hill] is a kind of Arthurian figure of the proletariat, who will return from the grave to help working men everywhere beat the boss."—Rick Renshaw

THE SONG, OF COURSE, was "Joe Hill." For the rest of his professional life Paul Robeson would refer to it as his special favorite, and "Joe Hill" joined "Ol' Man River" as Robeson's signature songs. The song from *Show Boat* was Robeson's crowning moment from the musical stage and screen, while "Joe Hill" was his lasting connection to the international labor movement. Both songs, particularly after Robeson's changes to "Ol' Man River," would forever reflect his defiance in the face of opposition to human rights.

He had learned "Joe Hill" earlier in the decade while in England, when he was acting in a play staged by a theater group that called itself Unity (no relation to the camp where "Joe Hill" debuted). Robeson was attracted to the play *Plant in the Sun* by its story line that showed black and white workers joining together in a strike. He also identified with Unity's position as a people's theater that was dedicated to empowering people's lives and making them conscious of the need for united action. Robeson performed in the play without a fee.

Earl Robinson found it remarkable that Robeson knew "Joe Hill," because the song was only a few years old at the time. It had not been formally published until the firm of Bob Miller did so in 1938. At first the publisher refused to allow the song to be reprinted in any labor songbooks that appeared at that time. Pete Seeger complained about this to Robinson, calling it a blight upon working class culture. "Son of a bitch!" he said. "Well, it's the system!"[1]

Eventually, the song did begin to appear in print. Over the years artists who performed the song, beginning with Paul Robeson, would modify a word or a phrase here and there, as is customary in the folk song tradition. As author and cultural critic Louis Menand has written, the survival of any idea "depends not on its immutability but on its adaptability."[2] So it is with "Joe Hill." The liberties that performers have taken and continue to take with the song have only served to make it more powerful, timely, and gender inclusive, liberties that ensure its ongoing relevance in changing times.

Wales

BY THE TIME Paul Robeson and Earl Robinson got to work on "The Ballad of Uncle Sam" the singer had already performed the song in Spain and Wales. The occasion in Wales was particularly poignant. Nearly ten years earlier, before Robeson and Robinson met, the world economic downturn that would become the Great Depression had already struck the Welsh mining industry, particularly in the important coal mines of South Wales's Rhondda Valley. A failed strike in 1926 resulted in the blacklisting of union members. When a worker's council in the valley called for more direct action, a group of unemployed miners responded by walking more than 140 miles to London to protest their harsh working conditions and to seek help in feeding their families. On an impulse, Robeson, in London at the time, stepped in to march with these men, sang to them, and helped pay for their train ride home. This encounter, and his aforementioned growing interest in all things African, contributed to the beginning of Paul Robeson's political radicalization, as he himself admitted in a 1960 London interview when he said that came to England unshaped, and that great parts of his working class roots were there.

In December 1938 Robeson visited Wales for a memorial meeting to commemorate the Welsh members of the International Brigade who died in the Spanish Civil War. This occasion cemented Robeson's bond with the people of Wales, a mutual affection and respect that would remain strong throughout his life, sealed by his 1940 film about Welsh miners, *The Proud Valley*.

Body and Soul had launched Robeson's film career in 1925. He would follow it with ten more screen appearances, among them *The Emperor Jones, Sanders of the River, Show Boat*, and *Song of Freedom*. The movies helped make Robeson an international star, but he became dissatisfied with the stereotypical and degrading parts offered to him as a black man. He would eventually quit making films, referring to Hollywood's old plantation tradition as offensive to his people. "I made a decision," he wrote. "If the Hollywood and Broadway producers did not choose to offer me worthy roles to play, then I would choose not to accept any other kind of offer."[3] The one film he would continually stand by was *The Proud Valley*.

At the commemoration seven thousand people gathered to remember the thirty-three men from Wales who had sacrificed their lives to defend democracy. Robeson told the assembly that he was there because he knew that those fallen men had fought not only for Spain but also for him and the whole world, and he felt it was his duty to be here. Then he sang "Joe Hill." Years later historian Patrick Renshaw, son of one of those miners present, told Hill biographer Gibbs Smith that the audience was thunderstruck by the power and beauty of Robeson's rendition of the song. They gave him a standing ovation.

Thirty years later, while researching his book *The Wobblies*, Renshaw interviewed a number of IWW veterans, some of whom had been active in the union as far back as the 1910s. He encountered no old-timers who thought that Joe Hill was guilty of the crime for which he was executed.

Highlander

THE SAME YEAR that Robeson sang at the Wales commemoration Zilphia Horton, of the Highlander Folk School, published the first of many song compilations she would edit. Many of Joe Hill's own songs, as well as the Hayes-Robinson ballad, would regularly appear in Horton's songbooks.

Highlander was founded in 1932 by activist Myles Horton, educator Don West, and Methodist minister James Dombrowski. Originally located near Monteagle, Tennessee, the center was established to provide training for existing and emerging leaders of the labor and civil rights movements. Rosa Parks trained there before her historic act that helped launch the Montgomery bus boycott. Other civil rights leaders who received training at Highlander include Martin Luther King, Jr., and John Lewis.

The importance of Zilphia Horton, who arrived at Highlander in 1935, cannot be over-emphasized. Born Zilphia Mae Johnson in 1910 in Spadra, a coal-mining town in Arkansas, she trained as a classical pianist at the College of the Ozarks (now the University of the Ozarks). After graduating, she joined Presbyterian minister Claude Williams and the Progressive Miners Union in their efforts to unionize a local coal mine owned by her father—who subsequently disowned her. In 1935 she attended a workshop at Highlander, by then renamed the Highlander Research and Education Center, and later married Myles Horton.

Zilphia took note of how some of her favorite composers, Franz Liszt and Johann Sebastian Bach among them, incorporated simple folk melodies into their works. This led her to embrace the music of the common people and to learn other instruments, particularly the accordion. (Horton was one of several women accordionists, all trained pianists—among them Agnes "Sis" Cunningham, who sang with the Almanac Singers and cofounded *Broadside* magazine, and Jenny Vincent, a longtime New Mexico musician and political activist and friend of Earl Robinson—who helped confirm the accordion as a legitimate folk instrument.) She became an indefatigable collector of folk songs and a key figure in the development of some of America's most vital anthems, including "We Shall Overcome," "This Little Light of Mine," and "We Shall Not Be Moved." Her songbooks were repositories of labor songs. Musing once about why composers such as Bach and Liszt collected folk tunes, she concluded that folk songs grow out of reality, out of the everyday lives and experiences of people, which gives them vitality and strength and genuine musical merit.

Horton took some inspiration from Joe Hill when she began rewriting hymns and songs that people in her area of Tennessee knew. She referred to this practice as "parody singing," where new lyrics might be incorporated into a familiar tune to draw attention to a "new" song.

As Robeson and Robinson got down to work for *The Pursuit of Happiness* series, Norman Corwin suggested that "The Ballad of Uncle Sam" be renamed "Ballad for Americans." So it was, and with the inaugural broadcast, in November 1939, the cantata became a sensation. I represent the whole, says Uncle Sam in the piece. That's it! Commenting years later on the experience of working with Robeson, Earl Robinson said, "I never worked with such a cooperative person,"[4] adding that there was nothing of the prima donna about Robeson.

"Ballad for Americans" was the right piece at the right time. Americans were feeling optimistic about pulling out of the Depression and staying out of yet another European war. (Two months earlier, on September 1, Germany had invaded Poland.) It was also a welcome antidote to an event held earlier that year in New York City's Madison Square Garden, when more than 20,000 members of the German American Bund staged a pro–Nazi rally, complete with banners carrying such messages as Wake Up America! and Smash Jewish Communism! and bearing a three-story tall image of George Washington, referred to as the "first Fascist" because he allegedly distrusted democracy, while Bund leader Fritz Kuhn mocked President Franklin D. "Rosenfeld" and his "Jew Deal."

"Joe Hill" composer Earl Robinson, left, with singer, actor, and activist Paul Robeson at work in 1939 on Robinson's "Ballad for Americans." Robeson would refer to "Joe Hill" as his special favorite and become its first great champion.

The Grapes of Wrath

EARLIER THAT SAME YEAR, as Paul Robeson and Earl Robinson collaborated on "Ballad for Americans," John Steinbeck published *The Grapes of Wrath.* This was the conclusion of the writer's Dust Bowl trilogy, following *In Dubious Battle* (1936) and *Of Mice and Men* (1937). Steinbeck warned his publisher on the eve of the book's appearance that his novel was bound to be controversial. That prediction proved to be an understatement.

The book's reception was nothing short of tumultuous, revered by many as an instant American masterpiece and reviled by others as subversive to the American capitalist system. The book was banned and even burned in some places, proving that Fascist tactics were not the exclusive domain of Adolf Hitler and Benito Mussolini. A reviewer for the *London Times* named it one of the most arresting novels of its time, while *Newsweek* dismissed it as a mess of silly propaganda. Because of its depiction of the nation's economic woes, particularly those of poor farmers and migrant workers, the Associated Farmers of California denounced *The Grapes of Wrath* as a pack of lies, calling it communist propaganda. Some academic scholars even called it sentimental and unconvincing. On the other hand, among the prominent defenders of the novel was First Lady Eleanor Roosevelt, who said she could not put the book down.

Near the end of the novel Steinbeck has his main character, Tom Joad, deliver one of the more memorable speeches in American literature.

> I'll be ever'where—wherever you look. Wherever they's a fight so hungry people can eat, I'll be there. Wherever they's a cop beatin' up a guy, I'll be there.[5]

With this famous speech Steinbeck echoed a central theme of the song "Joe Hill": wherever people stand up for their rights, Joe Hill is at their side. Wherever workers organize and strike, that's where you'll find Joe Hill.

In a radio interview conducted shortly after the book's publication Steinbeck declared that he can only write about what he admires, and what he admires are the poor, adding that the present day kings are not inspiring and the gods seem to be on vacation. When the poor make a stand, he said, it is a heroic struggle. If they lose it means imprisonment, starvation, or death.

The Grapes of Wrath appeared in April 1939. That summer actor Will Geer introduced his friend Woody Guthrie to Steinbeck. As chronicled by Holter/Deverell in the aforementioned *Woody Guthrie L.A. 1937–1941*, Guthrie's years in and around that southern California city were formative in his development. His experiences on the radio, his "Woody Sez" column for *People's World*, and his own travels around workers' camps had crystalized his politics. Meeting Steinbeck further solidified his views. *The Grapes of Wrath*, said Guthrie, shows the men that broke us and the dust that choked us and it comes right out in plain English and says what to do about it.

One reaction Woody had to the book was a cartoon he drew that year: three figures stand under a flag covered with dollar signs. Below them is the caption in Woody's purposeful down-home spelling, "We plege our alegiance to our flag ... an to wall st., for which it stands ... one dollar, ungettable."[6] It is a drawing that the accomplished cartoonist Joe Hill would have appreciated.

Another Guthrie response to Steinbeck's book came a year later, when he summarized the novel in his long ballad "Tom Joad." When he heard the song Steinbeck is reported to have griped about that fuckin' little bastard who got in seventeen verses the entire story that took him two years to write!

Guthrie's lyrics echo not only Tom Joad's climactic speech but also a comment Joad makes two pages earlier about long-time family friend Preacher Casy's idea that we are all just a little piece of a great big soul, an idea that recalls the Wobbly theme of one big union. When RCA Victor records asked Guthrie to write twelve songs about the Dust Bowl, "Tom Joad" was joined in short order by "I Ain't Got No Home," "Vigilante Man," "Talking Dust Bowl Blues" and others that together became Woody's 1940 recording *Dust Bowl Ballads*.

As Dave Marsh notes in a 2000 compact disc reissue of the recording, Woody's ambition was to become the vernacular voice of his people, like the poets Alexander Pushkin, Walt Whitman, and Carl Sandburg. With *Dust Bowl Ballads* he succeeded. "This bunch of songs are really just one song,"[7] Guthrie wrote, and they are: they form a suite of an insider's view of the Dust Bowl. Taken together, *Dust Bowl Ballads* is an American masterwork.

This Land

IN THE WINTER of 1940 Guthrie was in in New York City. He had ridden buses and hitchhiked through a bitter weather to get to the city. On his way from Texas any bus that Woody was traveling in made occasional stops for passengers, fuel, and food. If there was a jukebox where the bus stopped, it seemed that "God Bless America" was playing on it.

Since Kate Smith premiered it on her radio show the previous November, Irving Berlin's song had become a national obsession, and it annoyed Woody. He knew the song was popular because it provided comfort to people, but in Woody's view it was a false comfort. If God was going to bless America, reckoned Guthrie, why was He waiting so long? So on February 23 in the Hanover House, a cheap hotel on West 43rd Street, he wrote a rebuttal initially entitled "God Blessed America."

Eventually, with title and text changes, "God Blessed America" became "This Land Is Your Land." While the song has today practically reached the status of America's unofficial national anthem, its complete lyrics are all too often ignored or repressed, particularly two verses about a "No trespassing" sign and about hungry people in a relief office. Is this land really made for you and me? Woody asked. Joe Hill would have identified with those two verses.

In March 1940 Guthrie, fresh from participating in a benefit for Spanish Civil War refugees, took part in another benefit performance in New York. Called "A Grapes of Wrath Evening," this was an event in support of the John Steinbeck Committee for Agricultural Workers, sponsored by Will Geer and the Theatre Action Committee. Woody was joined on the bill by, among others, Pete Seeger, musicologist Alan Lomax, activist and folksinger Aunt Molly Jackson, blues giant Huddie Ledbetter (Lead Belly), and singer Burl Ives, who performed "Joe Hill." It was on this occasion that Lomax introduced Guthrie to Seeger. Following in the footsteps of his father, Alan Lomax was on his way to becoming one of the most important, if not the most important, song collectors in America.

That same year Earl Robinson, who had been in the audience for the Grapes of Wrath Evening, met Woody at a Theater Arts Center gathering in New York. Robinson found Guthrie immediately riveting and authentic from head to toe. Woody's face lit up and he grasped Robinson's hand, thrilled to meet the composer of "Joe Hill."

On Record

PAUL ROBESON was not the first singer to record "Joe Hill." That milestone belongs to movie actor and vocalist Michael Loring, whose rendition of the song, accompanied by a group identified as the TAC singers, was released in 1939. The 78-rpm disc was notable not only as the first appearance of "Joe Hill" on record but for featuring its composer, Earl Robinson, on piano.

Before singing the song Loring recites, over Robinson's piano background:

> "Joe Hill was a migratory worker and labor organizer who composed songs which captured the militant spirit of men on the picket lines.

Like many of his fellow organizers Hill was convicted of murder on trumped up charges.

He was shot on November 19, 1915. His last words were 'Don't mourn for me—organize!'"[8]

"Joe Hill," credited to both Hayes and Robinson, was on the B-side of the record. On the A side was "Old Abe Lincoln," another Robinson collaboration with Hayes. *Time* magazine reviewed the recording as two crusty proletarian items. Loring would record the song one more time, on the Theme label with no credit for lyricist or composer. On January 8, 1940, Robinson recorded a version in New York's Reeves Sound Studio, with credit given to both Hayes and himself. Paul Robeson would soon follow.

Robeson had made significant changes to his version of "Ol' Man River." Now he made a subtle but equally significant alteration in his delivery of "Joe Hill": Robeson changed "What they forgot to kill" to "What they could never kill." Labor historian Franklin Rosemont wrote, "By replacing two little words with other words, Paul Robeson transformed a very good song into a splendid and extraordinarily powerful song."[9] The effect of Robeson's alteration to "Joe Hill," similar to what he did to "Ol' Man River," was nothing short of electrifying and was transformative for the song.

The year 1940 also saw the release of *Ballad for Americans* on Victor Records. By the end of the year the album had sold more than 40,000 copies. Piggybacking on that success, the leftwing Timely Records released Robinson's *Songs for Americans* at the same time as *Ballad for Americans*. The album includes a number of traditional songs as well as "Joe Hill."

Wo-Chi-Ca

IN THE SUMMER of 1940 Paul Robeson visited Camp Unity's sister camp, Wo-Chi-Ca, in New Jersey's Washington Township. It was his first visit in what would become an annual summer event for many years.

According to a memoir by June Levine, who had spent many childhood days at the camp, and her husband Gene Gordon, Camp Wo-Chi-Ca was founded in 1934, when a progressive farmer named Lanz and his wife, who could no longer make a go of their farm, donated the 127-acre property to Camp Unity. Wo-Chi-Ca was born, taking as its name a contraction of Workers Children's Camp.

Wo-Chi-Ca was a multi-racial camp whose attendees proudly sang:

Where the children of the workers
Live as one big family,
Black and white we are united
In a true democracy.[10]

In 1940 campers immediately took Robeson to their hearts and celebrated his every visit as Paul Robeson Day. Campfires and group sing-alongs were parts of life at Wo-Chi-Ca, and campers never failed to ask Robeson to sing "Joe Hill."

Students at Highlander Folk School likewise kept the "Joe Hill" flame burning. Visiting the school over the Labor Day weekend in 1941, photographer Edward Weston and his wife, Charis Wilson, joined in an after-dinner sing-along. Wilson later recalled that the students sang a round of labor songs that she and her husband joined, as they knew most of them, including "Joe Hill."

Talking Unions

IN THE SUMMER that Paul Robeson first visited Camp Wo-Chi-Ca, Woody Guthrie and Pete Seeger hit the road heading west. At the Grapes of Wrath benefit, where they met, Pete, in his first solo appearance, had bungled a version of "John Hardy," while Woody had wowed the crowd with his combination of down-home banter and original songs. Not long after, Woody asked Pete if he would like to come west with him. It's a big country out there, said Guthrie, and you should see it. Seeger, who at that time had seen little of the country, jumped at the chance. He had watched Guthrie at the benefit performance, and knew he was looking at the real thing. Now he was ready to learn more from the man who had seen much, much more. The two hitched and jumped trains across parts of the Midwest and West, playing where they could.

The two men could hardly have been more different. The tall, lanky Seeger and the small, wiry Guthrie were vastly different in personality and worlds apart in terms of a sense of responsibility. But they complemented each other, and during their on-again off-again relationship they became one of the most important duos in American musical history.

Woody stayed on the in Pacific Northwest, where he had been hired by the Bonneville Power Administration to write songs about the building of the Grand Coulee Dam. In thirty days he churned out twenty-six songs, including some of his best such as "Pastures of Plenty" and "Hard Travelin.'" As writers Greg Vandy and Daniel Person point out, Woody did not sell out and become a business hack. He was drawn to the project by the prospect of affordable and accessible power for working people, and the songs he produced "attest to the worth and aspirations of the American workingman."[11]

IN 1941 ELIZABETH GURLEY FLYNN, the prominent union activist who had visited Joe Hill in prison, brought some of his papers to the Almanac Singers, a New York–based folk music group that had been founded by Lee Hays, Millard Lampell, and Seeger, after Pete's return from his trip with Guthrie. Passing in and out of the Almanac picture were such varied talents and styles as Agnes "Sis" Cunningham, Richard Dyer-Bennett, Tom Glazer, Peter and Baldwin Hawes, Cisco Houston, Burl Ives, Huddie Ledbetter (Lead Belly), Bess Lomax (Alan Lomax's sister), Brownie McGhee, Earl Robinson, Arthur Stern, Sonny Terry, and Josh White, as well as Guthrie, who joined after returning from his stint with the Bonneville Power Administration. Active from 1940 to 1943, the Almanac Singers' repertoire featured union songs as well as anti-war songs, before Pearl Harbor, and anti–Fascist songs after America entered the war. The Almanacs dedicated their *Talking Union* album to the memory of Joe Hill.

Perhaps the first mention of the Almanac Singers in print appeared in the *Daily Worker* of March 24, 1941. Written by George Lewis, the article drew attention to the group's performance for the League of American Writers, during which the audience repeatedly called for Woody Guthrie's recent peace song "Why Do You Stand There in the Rain?" as well as "Joe Hill."

In the summer of 1941 Seeger, Guthrie, Hays, and Lampell hopped in a beat-up Buick and headed west. Starting in Pittsburgh, the Almanacs traveled to cities across the country, singing in union halls and other venues in support of the Congress of Industrial Organizations (CIO). One particularly memorable stop was in San Francisco, where they played for the International Longshore and Warehouse Union (ILWU) and its embattled president, Harry Bridges.

A native of Australia, Bridges served as a merchant seaman and a member of that country's sailors' union before coming to the United States in 1920. In America he joined the IWW and then the ILWU. As president of the ILWU he guided the union through the notorious and bloody—but ultimately successful—1934 strike on the San Francisco waterfront, during which several union members were shot dead. Vilified by company owners and threatened with deportation by the United States government for supposedly subversive activities, Bridges prevailed and led the ILWU for forty years until his retirement in 1977. The Almanacs created a song, "Harry Bridges," in his honor.

AT THIS POINT in the journey of "Joe Hill" it was Paul Robeson who almost single-handedly transformed the song from a labor ballad into a universal anthem of protest against any form of oppression. Everywhere Robeson traveled "Joe Hill" traveled with him. In this manner Robeson was himself becoming the Joe Hill in the song. Wherever people stood up for their rights, that is where you would find Paul Robeson.

The same year that the Almanac Singers traveled across the country the Fourth Annual Congress of the League of American Writers met at the Commodore Hotel in New York. Among the headliners were novelists Richard Wright and Dashiell Hammett. The closing event of the convention was a panel entitled "Poets, Songwriters & Folksingers." A featured participant on that panel was Earl Robinson, who ended the session by performing "Joe Hill."

IN DECEMBER 1941, shortly after the Japanese attack on Pearl Harbor, Robinson was invited to Washington, D.C., by his friend Adrian Dornbush to participate in a concert being staged by First Lady Eleanor Roosevelt for the people of the Office of Civil Defense. Dornbush also happened to be a friend of Mrs. Roosevelt, and during a rehearsal he popped a question to Robinson: "How would you like to go to the White House for dinner tonight?"

Off they went, to an occasion that included not only Mrs. Roosevelt but also President Roosevelt and British Prime Minister Winston Churchill. Following dinner Robinson performed a few patriotic songs that he felt were more appropriate than his left-leaning material. "But Mrs. R crossed me up," he later recalled. "I was totally unprepared when from her front row seat in the audience she asked for 'Joe Hill.' Which I had not been performing since the war began because it talked about strikes with great approval."[12]

Of course, at Mrs. Roosevelt's request, Robinson sang the song. Sitting with her afterward, he apologized for the song's pro-strike slant, upon which Mrs. Roosevelt rose to her feet to address the audience. Mr. Robinson was worried about his song giving the wrong impression, she said, but we must remember that at the time "Joe Hill" was written it was right and necessary for workers to strike. That evening led to a friendship between Eleanor Roosevelt and Earl Robinson that continued until her death in 1962.

ONE OF PAUL ROBESON's regularly scheduled stops was the annual convention of the National Maritime Union. In 1936 Joseph Curran, a member of the International Seamen's Union, decided to leave that conservative organization and form a new union affiliated with the Congress of Industrial Organizations, which Paul Robeson favored. This was the

National Maritime Union. Robeson appeared at the union's conventions in 1941, 1943, and 1947. On each occasion he sang songs requested by members of the audience, requests that invariably included "Joe Hill."

In September 1945, after returning home from singing for troops in Europe—while he opposed war on principal, he remained devoted to the men and women who served in the armed forces—Robeson and pianist Lawrence Brown undertook the longest tour they had ever made, 115 engagements across America. Despite the overwhelmingly positive reception he received everywhere, Paul Robeson was becoming increasingly despairing of the future of race relations in his country. The Federal Bureau of Investigation (FBI) was now regularly following him, describing him as a communist functionary. This harassment by the bureau would continue for decades. In Toronto, Robeson appeared at a gathering of the Labour Progressive Party where, according to the FBI, he sang the American left-wing song "Joe Hill."

Joe Hill, the man and the song, were being remembered in other media as well. The 1944 novel *The Timber Beast*, set in the Pacific Northwest where author Archie Binns grew up, tells the story of an old-school logging operator named Charley Dow, whose favorite song is "Joe Hill."

People's Songs

IN 1945, after his tour of duty in the Pacific, Pete Seeger returned to New York and, with a group of friends—among them Guthrie, Hays, Lomax, McGhee, and Terry—formed People's Songs, a progressive organization where like-minded individuals could stay in touch with each other and perform and promote political and topical songs. Editors at People's Songs wrote that if they were to choose some figure who best symbolized the work of the group, that person would be Joe Hill, for Joe Hill was sort of a one-man People's Songs outfit back in the days of the IWW, and he left a great singing and fighting tradition.

From 1946 through 1950 the organization published the quarterly *People's Songs Bulletin* that would serve as a template for future folk music magazines, *Sing Out!* and *Broadside* among them. The cover of its second anniversary issue featured a drawing of Joe Hill on its cover, with the caption "I Never Died."

The FBI promptly declared People's Songs to be a threat to national security. In Canada, the provincial government of Quebec agreed. It seized copies of the new *People's Songbook*, along with Tolstoy's *War and Peace* and Whitman's *Leaves of Grass*, and declared the song "Joe Hill" to be subversive.

≈ 6 ≈

No Quarter

"All races and religions, that's America to me."
—Abel Meeropol

ON APRIL 12, 1945, President Franklin Roosevelt was sitting for a portrait by the renowned painter Elizabeth Shoumatoff at his retreat in Warm Springs, Georgia. Noting that he only had fifteen more minutes to pose, he suddenly put his left hand up to the back of his head and complained that he felt a terrific pain. Moments later Roosevelt collapsed. Three hours later he died from a massive cerebral hemorrhage.

In an instant the man who had guided the country out of the Great Depression and through the Second World War was gone. He had been in the thirteenth year of his presidency. The man many of his detractors had first considered a lightweight had proven himself to be the most adroit politician in American history. Now he would not live to see the conclusion of the war in Europe, which took place less than a month later, on May 8. The war with Japan would continue for three months, until on August 6 and 9 when the United States dropped atomic bombs on the cities of Hiroshima and Nagasaki. Japan formally surrendered on August 15.

THE YEAR FDR DIED the composer of "Joe Hill" was collaborating with the creator of "Strange Fruit." In 1943 Abel Meeropol, writing as Lewis Allan, had produced a lyric called "The House I Live In," and now Earl Robinson was working with him to finish the song. Meeropol's words speak to what is wonderful about America, with its homey images of the butcher, the churchyard, the "howdys," and handshakes. But it also reflects how he thinks the country could be better, how it could be a place of racial and religious harmony and freedom of speech. Meeropol invoked people working side by side, individuals exercising the right to speak their minds, and all races and religions. As they had

71

with "Strange Fruit," some commentators denounced the song as left-ist propaganda.

Meeropol, who had heard Robinson debut "Joe Hill" at Camp Unity, would collaborate and remain friends with the composer for decades. Robinson said that Abel Meeropol possessed an inexhaustible ability to turn out topical lyrics.

That year Frank Sinatra sang it in a short film of the same name written by Albert Maltz, who was later blacklisted as one of the Hollywood Ten. In it Sinatra takes a break from a recording session and steps outside the studio to smoke a cigarette. He sees a group of boys chasing one smaller boy. Sinatra stops them and asks why, and they tell him it's because of the boy's religion. Sinatra talks to them about America, that we are all Americans, that one American's blood is as good as another's and that all our religions should be respected. The film won a special Academy Award, but when he saw it Meeropol is said to have become so incensed that it did not use his verse that included a reference to "my neighbors white and black" that he had to be removed from the theater. Paul Robeson would later add the song to his repertoire and restore Meeropol's original verse.

Tensions Home and Abroad

Meeropol's appeal for racial and religious tolerance came at a time of growing tensions between the United States and the Soviet Union. This wariness between the two former allies was exacerbated on March 5, 1946, by a speech that Winston Churchill delivered at Westminster College in Fulton, Missouri. Churchill, who was in between his two stints as British Prime Minister, warned of Soviet expansion, saying that from Stettin in the Baltic to Trieste in the Adriatic an iron curtain was descending across the European continent.

Churchill's speech came in the aftermath of the Potsdam (Germany) Conference of July 17 to August 2, 1945, when Roosevelt's successor Harry Truman, Churchill (then just days before leaving office), and Soviet Premier Stalin met to discuss postwar issues focusing on Europe in general and Germany in particular. The Western powers hoped to continue working with their Soviet ally, but Stalin had other goals in mind—the domination of Central and Eastern Europe.

There were tensions at home as well. Black veterans of the war were coming home expecting to enjoy the rights for which they had fought overseas, including the right to vote. The reaction in the South was an increase in lynching and other racial violence. One notorious such incident took place in February 1946, when returning Sergeant Isaac Woodard, one of more than 900,000 black men who had served during the war, was beaten and left permanently blind in Batesburg, South Carolina. President Truman ordered a federal investigation into the incident, but the local police chief, who had participated in the attack, was acquitted.

Four months later, on July 25, two black couples—George and Mae Dorsey and Roger and Dorothy Malcolm—were murdered along a dirt road near Moore's Ford Bridge in Walton County, Georgia. George Dorsey was a five-year veteran of the war in the Pacific, and had been back in the United States only nine months. Isaac Woodard had been honorably discharged from the Army just hours before he was attacked.

It was in this atmosphere that Paul Robeson, joined by W.E.B. Du Bois and others, decided to launch an American crusade against lynching. They planned a conference and rally in Washington, D.C., for September 23, 1946, to coincide with the 84th anniversary of Abraham Lincoln's signing the Emancipation Proclamation on September 22, 1862. Several thousand black and white delegates gathered for the rally, which also drew support from such prominent figures as Albert Einstein, who wrote a letter to President Truman endorsing the crusade's call for every American citizen to be guaranteed protection against such acts of violence.

Robeson then joined a ten-member delegation in an ill-fated attempt to enlist Truman's support of an anti-lynching bill. Forty-eight years had passed since Ida B. Wells had joined a similar delegation to meet with President McKinley about the same subject, and six years since the prominent educator and activist Mary McLeod Bethune, a friend of Eleanor Roosevelt, had approached President Roosevelt to gain his support. Bethune was a member of FDR's so-called "black cabinet," a group of black men and women whom the president had named to relatively minor positions in his administration in recognition of the growing importance of the black vote, but to whom he paid little attention in the end, so as to appease the Southern voting bloc. Robeson and his colleagues had not finished their opening statement when Truman interrupted them, declaring that while the government opposed lynching, enacting legislation in that regard was a political as well as a moral issue, and the time was not right for such a measure.

Truman would later order his attorney general to bring charges against the officers who had beaten and blinded Isaac Woodard. And on July 26, 1948, he signed Executive Orders 9980 and 9981, racially integrating the U.S. military and the federal government workforce.

Soon after the American crusade against lynching rally Robeson was called to testify before a Joint Fact-Finding Committee on Un-American Activities in California. Asked by committee chairman State Senator Jack Tenney if he was a communist Robeson replied that Tenney might just as well have asked if he was a member of the Democratic or Republican Party, since the Communist Party was no less legal in the United States, but added that he was not a communist. The nature of the inquiry was polite, almost cordial. As Robeson biographer Duberman wrote, Robeson was not yet the pariah to be vilified. That would come later.

IN 1946 PETE SEEGER recorded his own version of "Joe Hill," with Hally Wood, Lee Hays, Lou Kleinman, and Dock Reese. He and Alan Lomax and Woody Guthrie had included the music and lyrics to "Joe Hill" in an anthology they compiled back in 1940, *Hard Hitting Songs for Hard Hit People*. Unfortunately, the book, with an introduction by John Steinbeck, was not published until 1967. But with his recording, Seeger added "Joe Hill" to his repertoire, a major milestone in the journey of the song.

"Joe Hill" was now into its tenth year. The little poem that had become a song sung around a campfire was now a militant labor anthem, a freedom song, and a rallying cry against Fascism. It wore all these labels easily, and would acquire more.

What I Sing and Where

IN MARCH 1947, speaking to 2,000 people who had just heard his rendition of "Joe Hill," appropriately enough in Salt Lake City, Paul Robeson surprised the audience by announcing that they had just heard his final concert for at least two years. He said that he would continue to sing for his trade union and college friends—in other words only at gatherings where he could sing what he pleased. Robeson had reached this decision a few weeks earlier, while he was participating in an NAACP picket line at an auditorium in St. Louis to protest segregation. It was a stunning declaration at the moment, but one that could have been foreseen.

In 1939, at the outset of World War II, Robeson had returned to the United States after being based in London since 1927. He felt his responsibility was to be with his own people at that time. Upon his return, he announced that he would no longer sing for segregated audiences. He did give concerts for war relief efforts and war bond rallies, and for this service he received official recognition from the Secretaries of War and Treasury.

Paul Robeson singing to dock workers in Oakland on September 20, 1942. In March 1947 Robeson stunned a Salt Lake City audience who had just heard him sing "Joe Hill," for the first time in the city where Hill was executed, by announcing that he was retiring from formal concert work to sing for his trade union and college friends, "in other words only at gatherings where I can sing what I please."

Robeson's announcement to the audience in Salt Lake City signified more than his decision about where and to whom he would now sing. It stood as his unspoken but complete alignment with the growing civil rights movement of the 1940s. From this point on Robeson would be recognized as a forerunner of that movement. The man who had become radicalized and despairing of the progress of civil liberties and racial equality in his country was throwing down the gauntlet and taking his talent to the front lines for freedom. And with him he would always take his two signature songs, "Ol' Man River" and "Joe Hill."

His increasingly outspoken political statements quickly drew fire. In 1942 Congressman Martin Dies of Texas accused Robeson of being a communist. At that time Dies was chairman of the Special Committee Investigating Un-American Activities, later the House Un-American Activities Committee (HUAC). Despite his numerous successes during the 1940s, Robeson sensed the growing threat of anti-democratic forces, and so in Salt Lake City made it clear that he was turning away from much of his successful career to take a more prominent stand in the fight against racism and Fascism.

The next month Robeson sat down in Chicago for a conversation with Edward Robb Ellis, the journalist known for his books on the Depression as well as his diary which, at twenty-two million words, was the largest in existence at the time. Robeson had just been refused permission to appear in Peoria, Illinois, because of his supposed communist affiliations. Angered by the continuing bigotry he faced on tour, Robeson told Ellis that what was at stake was more than just a personal issue. Robeson told Ellis he needed to know what had happened in Peoria in the past two or three years—three railroad workers and a railroad president had been murdered there. Robeson said that he was going to Peoria as a friend of labor. When Ellis asked if he was going to sing "Joe Hill," Robeson answered that he has sung "Joe Hill" on every one of his programs for the past six years.

NOT EVERYONE agreed with Paul Robeson that Joe Hill was a martyr, worthy to being memorialized in song. Back in 1919 Zane Grey had published *The Desert of Wheat,* an anti–IWW novel set in the Pacific Northwest that imagines German agents using the Industrial Workers of the World to disrupt the wheat supply that was vital to the American war effort.

In the same spring when Robeson announced his future intentions to a Salt Lake City audience, author Wallace Stegner published an article questioning Hill's innocence. Entitled "I Dreamed I Saw Joe Hill Last Night," and published in the *Pacific Spectator,* the piece put forth Stegner's conclusion that Hill was probably guilty of the Morrison murders. The following year Stegner would further advance his belief, this time in the *New Republic.* Stegner's research in Salt Lake City had led him to conclude that Hill was guilty, that there was little evidence that Hill was an effective strike leader, and that his martyrdom was merely an image tailored by the IWW—an image enhanced by the Alfred Hayes and Earl Robinson song about him. A group calling itself the Friends of Joe Hill Committee picketed the magazine's offices in protest. Stegner's 1950 novel *The Preacher and the Slave,* later reissued as *Joe Hill: A Biographical Novel,* would reflect the same conclusions.

Henry Wallace

IN DECEMBER 1947 Henry Wallace formally declared his candidacy for the presidency on the Progressive Party ticket. Paul Robeson immediately pledged his support, and in January joined a newly formed Wallace-for-President Committee. Former Minnesota Governor Elmer Benson chaired the committee, and Robeson joined Rexford Tugwell, a former advisor to President Roosevelt, and prominent sculptor Jo Davidson as co-chairs. Wallace's supporters included such other notables as Aaron Copland, Albert Einstein, Edna Ferber, Dashiell Hammett, Lillian Hellman, Eugene O'Neill, and Earl Robinson.

Born in Iowa in 1888, Henry Wallace became and would remain deeply influenced by the agrarian lifestyle of his home state. After studying agriculture at Iowa State University, he wrote and edited his family's farm journal, *Wallace's Farmer,* which the family had founded in 1894 and which made them wealthy and politically influential. He later started a successful hybrid corn company. His father had served as secretary of agriculture under presidents Warren G. Harding and Calvin Coolidge, and after entering politics and supporting the New Deal, Henry Wallace was named to that same position by President Roosevelt. After serving as secretary of agriculture from 1933 to 1940, Wallace was picked by Roosevelt to be his vice presidential running mate as the president prepared to run for an unprecedented third term.

In 1944 Democratic Party conservatives, particularly those representing the Southern states, opposed Wallace's renomination as vice president, ostensibly due to his increasingly progressive politics. Yielding to this internal pressure in an effort to keep the Southern voting block solidly Democratic, Roosevelt opted for Harry Truman as his vice presidential running mate, appointing Wallace as secretary of commerce. Contributing to this shift in vice presidents was Wallace's idealism and his somewhat tenuous grasp of Washington politics.

Hawaii

WITH THE PROGRESSIVE PARTY Nominating Convention looming in July 1948 Paul Robeson first made two important stops in the spring.

In March he undertook a tour of Hawaii. Because Lawrence Brown intensely disliked flying, Earl Robinson agreed to accompany Robeson on the trip that took them to six of the islands. Robinson later recalled those ten days as the most exciting, the most educational, the most fulfilling time of his life, adding that the love Robeson gave out to the islanders was beyond belief.

His concert repertoire on the tour showcased the full breadth of

Robeson's interests and abilities. He sang Mendelssohn's "Lord God of Abraham." He sang from Mussorgsky's *Boris Godunov.* He sang such spirituals as "On My Journey" and "Swing Low, Sweet Chariot," and, of course, his signatures, "Ol' Man River" and "Joe Hill." With his ability to grasp different languages, Robeson also included a few songs in Hawaiian, having apparently managed to learn them on short notice. He had gone to Hawaii in support of the Longshoremen's and Warehousemen's Union, the parent union of the sugar cane and pineapple workers. Like the IWW before it, the ILWU in Hawaii worked to amalgamate smaller locals into a larger organization. As recalled by Earl Robinson, Robeson told his union audiences that he stood by them and with them. "But to those who run things, those higher-ups symbolized by the Big Five"—the companies that controlled sugar production in the islands—"from them I ask, and give, no quarter."[1]

In a March 22, 1948, article titled "Robeson in Honolulu Backs Wallace, Denies Communist Peril," the *Honolulu Star-Bulletin* quoted Robeson as telling reporters that his trip to the Hawaiian Islands was one of the most stirring he had ever made. According to the newspaper report Robeson appeared at a surprise press conference at the conclusion of his visit and said he was very much impressed by the island people, and that there was a lesson in racial matters to be learned here. It would be a tremendous impact on the United States, he said, if Hawaii was admitted as a state. He scoffed at the idea that Henry Wallace was a communist, calling him instead a progressive capitalist, and himself an advanced New Dealer. If anybody can continue the New Deal traditions of Franklin Roosevelt, said Robeson, that person is Henry Wallace. The trip held a special added element for both Robeson and Robinson: decades earlier Joe Hill himself had worked on the docks at Hilo on the big island.

The local FBI agent who shadowed Robeson and Robinson during their entire week in the islands had to report back to J. Edgar Hoover in Washington that there was no evidence that Robeson was in Hawaii for any Communist Party purpose.

Robeson followed up his trip to the Hawaiian Islands with an appearance at the International Fur and Leatherworkers Convention in May, where he promoted the candidacy of Wallace and sang "Joe Hill."

Early in 1948 some newspapers across the country carried a scandalous story about how for some twenty years communists had been infiltrating the Young Men's Christian Association. While sources were not identified, the chief evidence for this claim appeared to be the organization's official songbook, *Sing Along the Way*, which included "Joe Hill."

The Campaign

THE 1948 PRESIDENTIAL conventions were unlike any before or since: For the first and only time they were all held in the same hall in the same city, and for the first time television brought the proceedings to the American public. The city was Philadelphia, and Philadelphia was suffering through a heat wave that made the non–air-conditioned Convention Hall a sauna for Republicans, Democrats, and Progressives alike. Republicans met from June 21–25, followed by the Democrats from July 12–15 and, one week later, the Progressives. At the Democratic convention Southern Senator Strom Thurmond became so incensed at President Harry Truman's policies regarding race that he (and many followers) abdicated from the party, forming their own States Rights Democratic Party, known as the Dixiecrats, and holding their own convention in Birmingham, Alabama, where Thurmond was nominated to run for the presidency.

AT THE PROGRESSIVE Party nominating convention in Philadelphia, Robeson joined Pete Seeger, New Mexico activist Jenny Vincent and others to sing on behalf of their candidate. The event also drew such future notables as H.L. Mencken, Norman Mailer, and George McGovern, as well as numerous FBI agents. The convention ratified Wallace's platform of a foreign policy that would ease Cold War tensions and end Jim Crow.

The Progressive Party convention proved to be what Pete Seeger biographer David King Dunaway called "probably the singingest one in U.S. history."[2] An unofficial theme song of the convention, performed by Michael Loring, was "The Same Merry-Go-Round," written by Ray Glaser and Bill Wolff and published by People's Songs. The song portrayed the Democratic donkey and Republican elephant as bobbing up and down on the same old merry-go-round, espousing the same old tired blather because in spite of their yelling and fussing they are sisters under the skin.

The singing continued in the subsequent campaign, as did the FBI surveillance, which had dogged the convention. Laura Duncan performed "Strange Fruit" at some rallies. At many stops on the campaign Seeger sang with Loring, who also performed "Ballad for Americans" with a high school choir in Portland, Oregon, for Wallace's visit there. Loring also released a record entitled "Great Day," with Wallace's photograph on the label and "The Same Old Merry-Go-Round" on the B-side. Loring would later became a longtime cantor at Temple Beth Israel in Fresno, California.

Robeson continued his efforts on behalf of the Progressive campaign, including a stop at the Longshore, Shipclerks, Walking Bosses & Gatemen and Watchmen's Caucus in August, where his rendition of "Joe Hill" drew a loud and sustained standing ovation. But the campaign was plagued with accusations of communist infiltration, and the press inflamed voters much as the Utah press had years ago against Joe Hill and the Oklahoma press did against the IWW.

HENRY WALLACE: He was sixty years old at the time of his nomination, described as a vigorous but somewhat rumpled man whose lofty idealism was later captured in the title of his biography by John C. Culver and John Hyde: *American Dreamer.*

As Commerce Secretary first under Franklin Roosevelt and then Harry Truman, Wallace had begun to speak out against the administration's foreign policy, arguing for a more flexible attitude toward the Soviet Union in order to maintain peace. This brought a backlash among hard-liners, who accused Wallace of being soft on communism, and ultimately led to his being fired by Truman.

Wallace himself addressed this issue during a campaign speech in February, insisting that any communist who supported his independent ticket will be supporting his program, not the communist program. He steadfastly denied being a communist or ever having been one, at the same time repudiating accusations that the Progressive Party was controlled by communists or that its convention or program was dictated by them. When Wallace added that he found nothing criminal in advocating different economic and social ideas, it only increased suspicions about the extent of communist influence on his campaign, suspicions that continue even to this day.

His clarifications fell on deaf ears that were impervious to nuances of thought. Wallace rallies often were met with violence. Seeger recalled that at a rally in Winston-Salem, North Carolina, the police let some people throw eggs at Wallace. As soon as they found they could get away with that kind of hazing, Ku Kluxers showed up at each rally, armed for business. Wallace, who had refused to speak before segregated audiences, was in real physical danger. At no small risk to himself, Paul Robeson campaigned for Wallace in the Deep South, where he participated in voter registration drives.

In August he addressed a West Coast meeting of the longshoreman's union, which he concluded by singing "Joe Hill" to a standing ovation. Union President Harry Bridges reminded members that Robeson had donated the proceeds of his recent Hawaii concerts to the union.

IN THE END Henry Wallace received only a little more than a million or 2.4 percent of the popular vote, placing him a distant fourth behind Truman, New York Governor Thomas Dewey, and Dixiecrat Strom Thurmond. Following his defeat Wallace remained only sporadically active in politics, continued to co-own his Pioneer Hi-Bred (formerly Hi-Bred Corn) Company, and wrote on agricultural subjects before gradually slipping into obscurity. He died in 1965 of amyotrophic lateral sclerosis (ALS, known as Lou Gehrig's disease) at the age of 77.

Earl Robinson thought the poor showing of the Progressive Party signaled the last gasp of the New Deal. Demoralized by Wallace's poor showing in the election, equally discouraged Pete Seeger turned away from New York City, bought a parcel of land up the Hudson River in Beacon, and prepared to build his own house. His decision reflected the influence of Ernest Thompson Seton, the outdoor individualist and one of the founders of the Boy Scouts, whose books had fascinated Seeger as a boy. (Chop some wood, Joe Hill had written in "The Preacher and the Slave," it'll do you good.)

Paris Controversy

IN THE AFTERMATH of the election, Paul Robeson continued his relentless schedule. What also continued was the growing pressure on him from the government, the business community, and the public sector that opposed his politics. His staunch refusal to denounce the Soviet Union, his continued ties with left-wing labor and similar organizations, and his stubborn insistence on equal rights for black people brought increased government surveillance, the cancellation of recording contracts, and dwindling concert appearances.

One particular incident that incensed those already angered at Robeson occurred in Paris in April of 1949, when he attended the Congress of the World Partisans of Peace. It was a time when Cold War tensions were escalating. The Soviet Union was accelerating its nuclear weapons research, and would detonate its first such device in August. Mao Tse-tung (now Mao Zedong) was on the brink of establishing the communist People's Republic of China. At home a number of defendants were on trial, accused of violating the Smith Act, which forbid any activity designed to overthrow the United States government.

The State Department denounced the Paris meeting in advance as a communist effort to convince people that warmongers governed all Western powers. Speaking before Robeson, British left-wing leader Konni Zilliacus said British workers should not be dragged into fighting the Soviet Union. When it came his turn at the podium, Robeson sang "Joe Hill" and then made brief remarks. An Associated Press dispatch, purporting to quote from Robeson's remarks, sent out these words:

> We colonial peoples have contributed to the building of the United States and are determined to share its wealth. We denounce the policy of the United States government, which is similar to that of Hitler and Goebbels.... It is unthinkable that American Negroes would go to war on behalf of those who have oppressed us for generations against a country [the Soviet Union] which in one generation has raised our people to the full dignity of humankind....[3]

In fact, what Robeson said was:

> We in America do not forget that it was the backs of white workers from Europe and on the backs of millions of Blacks that the wealth of America was built. And we are resolved to share it equally. We reject any hysterical raving that urges us to make war on anyone. Our will to fight for peace is strong.... We shall support peace and friendship among all nations, with Soviet Russia and the People's Republics.[4]

What Robeson actually said didn't matter. The Associated Press dispatch, which apparently was released even before Robeson finished speaking, was reprinted across the nation. Even though Robeson had been grievously misquoted, few bothered to check the report for accuracy. The outcry was immediate, the denunciation fierce.[5] The white press vilified him, and much of the black leadership hastened to say that he did not speak for them.

The question lingers as to why Robeson did not receive more support from the liberal press at this time. He continually argued against the suppression of free speech and in favor of a free press. He was in the forefront of the burgeoning civil rights movement. He symbolized everything that liberals and their press stood for—tolerance for all peoples. But the misquoted Paris remarks would haunt him.

Only one issue continued to plague Robeson in terms of his acceptance by many liberals (and probably all conservatives), and that was his stubborn refusal to speak against the Soviet Union, even in the wake of that country's so-called "purge trials" of the mid- to late 1930s. In hindsight it is easy to question why any intelligent person would support Soviet communism. But it is important to remember that Paul Robeson came of age during the Great Depression, when capitalism appeared to have failed and left many nations in dire economic straits. At that time the new Soviet Union might have been viewed as a promising experiment.

Robeson apparently remained enamored of that vision of the Soviet

Union as an egalitarian society of the future, even when its current status, under the dictatorship of Joseph Stalin, indicated otherwise. Americans, including liberals, were swept up in anti–Communism, and Robeson found himself called the Kremlin's voice of America and the Black Stalin. Some called him a traitor. Some in the press called for his execution.

No Quarter

FOLLOWING THE PARIS conference Robeson continued on a concert tour of Europe. On June 14, 1949, he performed in Moscow's Tchaikovsky Hall, where he received a rapturous welcome, a reception for which he was further vilified back in America. When he sang "Water Boy" the applause was so strong that he sang it again. In his introduction to "Joe Hill" Robeson referred to the song as an important one for the American working class, and Joe Hill as a brave man who died in the struggle for the rights of working men and women. When he finished singing it the applause continued so long that, like "Water Boy" before it, he sang "Joe Hill" again.

The audience response was the same at another concert Robeson gave, this one in Stockholm at a gathering place for Swedish workers. According to *Ny Dag*, the Swedish Communist Party newspaper, Robeson drew intense interest from the huge audience with a poignant rendition of "I Dreamed I Saw Joe Hill Last Night." It was a fitting reception in Joe Hill's native country.

TWO MONTHS after the Paris conference Paul Robeson flew back to the United States. Speaking to an assemblage of reporters and friends—an assemblage that included police and FBI agents, as well—he reiterated his love for America, but not for Wall Street and the press. He spoke of his love for the working classes of Britain and France and the people of the Soviet Union, emphasizing that he loved them for their struggles for the freedom of his people and the working white people. It was a simple, straightforward, and noncontroversial statement of his fundamental position. But it was too little too late. The distorted words attributed to Robeson in Paris had done their damage. In Hawaii, Robeson had asked workers to show the big companies no quarter. Now, in America, many people were prepared to show him the same.

⟹ 7 ⟸

Peekskill

"As we held the line at Peekskill we will hold it every-where."—Pete Seeger and Lee Hays

In March 1947, the same month that Paul Robeson made his surprise announcement in Salt Lake City, President Truman issued Executive Order 9835, which authorized the search for "disloyal persons" in the government. The setting was now ripe for an expanded Cold War abroad and a resurgent Red Scare at home. As former Secretary of State Madeleine Albright has written:

> There is a tendency in the United States to romanticize the years after World War II—to imagine a time of sky-blue innocence when everyone agreed that America was great and each family had a reliable breadwinner, the latest appliances, children who were above average, and a rosy outlook on life. In fact, the Cold War was a period of unceasing anxiety....[1]

By 1949 the United States and the Soviet Union had slipped deeper into that Cold War. In the few years following the conclusion of World War II Americans had heard Winston Churchill warn of an iron curtain descending across Europe; they had witnessed the Berlin airlift; they had watched as the Soviet Union took over Czechoslovakia; they had participated in the founding of the North Atlantic Treaty Organization (NATO), designed to resist Soviet expansion, and they had read Paul Robeson's misquoted remarks from Paris.

Created in 1938 from several precursor committees dating back to 1918, the House Committee on Un-American Activities (HUAC) became a standing (permanent) committee in 1945. Its nine representatives were charged with investigating suspected threats of subversion or propaganda that attacked the American form of government. In the end this made-in-America inquisition would serve almost no legislative function, but would contribute to the wave of hysteria that would grip the country for years while at the same time stifling free speech and free opinion, in violation of the First Amendment to the Constitution, and damaging or outright ruining the careers and livelihoods of many citizens. The HUAC's activities peaked in the 1950s alongside Senator Joseph McCarthy's Senate-based witch-hunts, until its decline in 1960s and ultimate abolishment in 1975, when its functions were transferred to the House Judiciary Committee.

COLD WAR storm clouds may as well have been gathering over Paul Robeson's head when, in July 1949, the New York–based left-wing theatrical agency People's Artists announced that it would present a concert on Saturday, August 27 at the Lakeland Acres picnic grounds in Cortlandt, a few miles outside of Peekskill, a town some forty miles north of New York City. The concert was billed as "A Summer Musicale," a benefit for the Harlem Chapter of the Civil Rights Congress, which was raising funds for the defense of several black men who were on trial in New York City.

The concert headliner was to be Paul Robeson. The concert never happened.

Robeson's previous appearances in the Peekskill area had been successful, including a 1946 performance hosted by the nearby Mohegan Colony, a cooperative community dedicated to egalitarian living. However, in 1947 the Albany Board of Education had denied Robeson permission to hold a concert at a local school. State Supreme Court Justice Isadore Bookstein subsequently ordered that the school be made available and the concert went forward with one condition, that Robeson make no political speeches. Robeson agreed, but skirted that restriction by giving brief introductions of each song, thereby placing each in context. Only for the last song did he make no introduction, later declaring that it wasn't necessary. This was "Joe Hill," the song of an ordinary worker who was killed on trumped-up charges. Its words summoned the unfortunate people to organized struggle. Joe Hill, Robeson said, is immortal, as a just cause is immortal.

This was a time when Cold War hysteria was at its peak. The Soviet Union had recently tested its first nuclear bomb. Mao Zedong had just declared the communist People's Republic of China. On the home front, in 1946 a then little-known politician from Wisconsin named Joseph McCarthy used Red scare tactics to defeat his Democratic rival for the Senate. It would be another year before McCarthy made the national headlines he so desperately aspired to, but in fact communism as an issue had been a Republican Party staple for some time.

Upon the announcement of Robeson's pending concert local newspapers jumped in with a campaign of inflammatory fake news, just as

Utah papers had done thirty-five years earlier during the trial of Joe Hill. *The Peekskill Evening Star* published an editorial on August 23 saying that the illustrious name of Paul Robeson was now tarnished by his questionable politics. A later front-page story carried the headline: "Robeson Concert Here Aids 'Subversive Unit, '" noting that it was the U.S. attorney general who had called the Civil Rights Congress subversive. The newspaper referred to Robeson as violently and loudly pro–Russian, adding that while it advocated a peaceful demonstration the time for tolerant silence was running out. On an inside page the newspaper printed a letter from an American Legion officer headlined "Says Robeson and His Followers Are Unwelcome," declaring further that weaker minds may be susceptible to communist teachings unless something is done by loyal Americans in the area. The *Star* continued its inflammatory editorials for the next few days.

The concert announcement also drew attacks from the American Legion post in nearby Verplanck, the Veterans of Foreign Wars, the Peekskill Chamber of Commerce, and the Cortlandt town supervisor. The Catholic Veterans and the Jewish War Veterans announced that they would picket the concert. The local Ku Klux Klan joined in. Anti-communist anger in America was growing exponentially, as was anti–Robeson rage in the wake of his misquoted comments from Paris. It was a field day for hard-liners: a benefit concert for accused black men, supported by Jews and other outsiders from New York City. And worse, a concert headlined by a black man, a prominent black man whose very professional success and political outspokenness made him the object of envy—and bitter animosity.

The atmosphere in Peekskill was set for a perfect storm.

Commies! Jews!

PEEKSKILL, ON THE EAST BANK of the Hudson River in New York's Westchester County, was a blue-collar working class town, named for an early Dutch trader, Jan Peek. Many of its residents held a growing resentment for the well-to-do weekenders and summer residents, some of whom were Jewish and left wing progressives, who owned houses in the area. Among those weekenders who were the objects of scorn were Sam and Helen Rosen, who were close friends of Paul Robeson. Sam was a renowned ear specialist at Mount Sinai Hospital in New York City, and Helen was a political activist. Robeson had first met the Rosens when he was playing Othello on Broadway and Helen was volunteering with the Independent Citizens Committee for the Arts, Sciences and Professions, a forerunner of the Progressive Party. He and the Rosens became intimate friends, and Robeson was a frequent guest at their Upper East Side apartment in Manhattan

On August 27 Helen arranged to have Robeson met at the Peekskill train station, when they heard that protestors were gathering at the picnic grounds. As they approached the concert site they could see that a brawl was ensuing. Helen saw a burning cross on a hill. Mobs of young men were stopping vehicles, searching the occupants inside, and dragging some out of their cars and beating them. Helen ran back to the car were Robeson sat and screamed to the drivers, "Get him the hell out of here." Their friends managed to turn the car around and drive Robeson away.

In the meantime, as concertgoers attempted to enter the grounds for the program they were turned away and forced to run a gauntlet of rioters, many of whom were drunk, throwing rocks and screaming, "Go back to Moscow! Kikes! Nigger-lovers!" while police stood on the sidelines, some smiling, none making any move toward curbing the riot. Some in the mob were shouting anti–Semitic epithets—"We're Hitler's boys" and "We'll finish Hitler's job!"—this just four years and four months since VE Day and the conclusion of a war in which thousands of Americans of all races and religions had given their lives to defeat Fascism. As in the Oklahoma of Woody Guthrie's early years, militant so-called patriotism had morphed into fervent self-righteousness.

If there had been an afterglow of tolerance following America's vital role in the defeat of the Axis powers, that aura was now dispelled. The rioters were in the firm grip of mob mentality, with no time or inclination for rational thought. The anti–Semitism and racism that seems ever present just below the surface in American life boiled over. "Give us Robeson," the mob yelled. "We'll lynch the nigger up!" (He was hanged in effigy.) Then the mob attacked the concert staff and others already on the grounds.

One of the concert's organizers, the writer Howard Fast, later recounted what happened that night. Fast and his fellow attendees had to physically fight off repeated charges by mobs wielding clubs and throwing rocks. Camp Wo-Chi-Ca teenager Issar Smith recalled that the grounds became completely surrounded by the mob, preventing any further entrance or exit. As the situation grew uglier, with the rioters chanting "Kill a commie for Christ!" Fast organized a defense line.

Backed up against a truck, Fast and his colleagues, who numbered fewer than fifty, locked arms to stand against the onrushes of the drunken attackers. It was a classic Wobbly maneuver—no violence but a standoff with folded arms. "When we fold our arms, the world will stop," wrote Barrie Stavis in his play *The Man Who Never Died*.[2] Then Fast and his colleagues broke into song, another Wobbly trademark, with "We Shall Not be Moved." The attackers stopped short of the group but continued to pelt them with rocks. Fast and his colleagues defended themselves by charging directly into the mob and repelling it. The lights went out and the mob, frustrated by Fast and his group, turned to smashing the stage and burning chairs. At long last, some three hours after the melee had begun, state troopers showed up to disperse the crowd. Wobbly tactics and the power of song had saved the day.

IN THE WAKE of the incident, some in the press portrayed the riot as being one of veterans against Robeson and his followers, notwithstanding the factor that many of Robeson's so-called "followers" were themselves patriotic veterans, including a decorated World War I pilot named Eugene Bullard. A hero to black people, Bullard had flown for France during that war because he had been rejected by the United States due to his race. At Peekskill police beat him to the ground with nightsticks.

Following the aborted concert, applications to the Ku Klux Klan reportedly swelled by more than seven hundred, and burning crosses appeared as far away as Tallahassee, Florida, with signs on them reading "We protest Paul Robeson and Communism."

We Won't Be Frightened!

THE NEXT DAY, at a press conference in New York, Robeson called for a Justice Department investigation of the incident. That afternoon the Rosens opened their weekend home in the village of Katonah, some twelve miles from Peekskill, for a protest meeting. Fifteen hundred people showed up. The Rosens also received so many death threat phone calls that union men bedded down on their front porch to guard the family.

The denials began pouring in: the Joint Veterans Council of Peekskill disclaimed any involvement in the riot. The Peekskill police chief said the picnic grounds were outside of his jurisdiction. A spokesman for the state police said he had not received a request for troopers. But the commander of the Peekskill Post of the American Legion said their objective was to prevent the concert, and their objective had been accomplished.

On August 30 a crowd of 3,000 attended a meeting in Harlem to protest the Peekskill riot. Despite calling the Peekskill incident a preview of American storm troopers in action, Robeson displayed his characteristic positive attitude by declaring the riot a real turn in the anti–Fascist struggle in America. He vowed to return to Peekskill, promising that he and his people would not be frightened by crosses burning there or anywhere else.

In a message to members and friends of the Council on African Affairs, Robeson said the would-be American Fascists were becoming bolder, and that what they did in Peekskill was just what Hitler's Nazis did to German anti–Fascists. They were not merely attacking me personally, he said. They were attacking the Negro people, the Jewish people, and all who stand for peace and democracy in America.

TENSIONS HAD BEEN running high in Peekskill since the announcement that Robeson would return to the area. The Associated Veterans Group declared that it would stage a protest parade on the day of the concert. Signs and car bumper stickers appeared with the slogan "Wake Up America/Peekskill Did," an echo of the Nazi slogan *Deutschland erwache!*—Wake up Germany! Other signs and stickers declared, "Communism is Treason: Behind Communism Stands the Jew!" phrases reminiscent of the anti–Semitic slogans of the 1939 German American Bund rally in New York.

On September 4 more than 2,500 members of various unions began arriving at the concert site at 6 a.m. to set up defense lines. They were met by the veterans' protest parade, 8,000 strong, marching and shouting anti–Semitic and racist threats: "Get going, red bastards!" "We'll kill you!" "You'll get in but you won't get out!" There was no violence on the picnic grounds, but union security guards flushed two snipers out of the overlooking woods.

The concert began at two o'clock, with some 25,000 people in attendance. At four, Robeson, accompanied by a terrified Lawrence Brown, took the stage and sang, encircled by some fifteen or more union men. When he completed his program Robeson was taken out of the grounds in a convoy of cars whose windows were shaded with blankets. Robeson himself lay on the floor of one car while two union bodyguards covered him with their own bodies. When the remaining concertgoers tried to leave they had to drive through a gauntlet of enraged locals.

For Pete Seeger, it must have been like *déjà vu* of the Wallace campaign. As he later recalled, he and all others exiting the concert were directed to turn in one direction where rock throwers awaited them. Orderly piles of rocks along the road were clear evidence that this was no spontaneous protest, but an organized attack. Cars were overturned and their riders dragged out and beaten. "Go back to Jew town," some yelled. "If we catch you up here again we'll kill you." Local and state police not only did nothing to stop the violence, some were even seen administering beatings.

Some 150 people suffered injuries during the riot. Lawsuits filed by concertgoers and Robeson proved futile. Veterans groups and the police were exonerated of any wrongdoing.

Never Forget

IN OCTOBER the Council on African Affairs announced that sixty church, labor, and other leaders throughout the country had signed a letter that Robeson sent to President Truman, demanding a federal investigation and prosecution. The letter warned that what happened at Peekskill demonstrated that mounting anti–Negro violence and contempt for human rights may develop unless something was done and done quickly to prevent such riots. In December, Robeson, Fast, the Civil Rights Congress, and twenty-five victims of the mob violence filed federal suits asking a total of $2,02,000 for personal injuries, property damage, and deprivation of civil rights. Nothing came of the letter or the lawsuits.

There is no recording of Robeson's program that day, but a typewritten schedule in the Tamiment Library & Robert F. Wagner Labor Archives at New York University, bearing the words "From Pete Seeger" penciled in at the top, outlines the concert in six steps. Miss Sylvia Kahn opened the program with "The Star-Spangled Banner." Seeger appears fourth in the schedule, listed as performing a selection of American folk songs, followed by pianist Leonid Hambro performing works by Chopin, Mendelssohn, and Bartok. Robeson was the sixth and final performer.

The list does not mention the song "Joe Hill" by name, but years after the riots Cortlandt residents Marilyn Elie and Abby Luby tracked down and interviewed several witnesses of that concert for a video and spoken word presentation they were preparing. Librarian Elie had become interested in the riots as a member of Pete Seeger's Walkabout Chorus, a nonprofit ecologically oriented group, where she learned the Seeger and Hays song "Hold the Line."

Among those they contacted was Lloyd Brown in Manhattan, who had just completed a book, *The Young Paul Robeson*. Brown was one of the volunteers who guarded Robeson at the infamous concert. The singer's voice, he recalled, was as strong and moving as ever. He sang "Ol' Man River," the protest song "Joe Hill," and others that roused the crowd. The concert went fine, Brown said, but afterward all the trouble started. As concertgoers got on buses to go back to New York City rocks started flying through the windows. It was scary, said Brown, but the truly frightening thing was that the police were just standing by there condoning what the protestors were doing.

Pete Seeger kept two of the stones that ended up in his car. He later incorporated them into the fireplace he built in his house, telling a journalist that he thought if he put them there he would never forget what happened. Woody Guthrie responded to the riots with a group of songs that focus on burning crosses, mobs throwing stones, and his friends being beaten by police and getting "Kueklucked."

At Peekskill, Robeson would later say, he saw some men he had seen on the frontlines in Spain, ready to give their lives for democracy. I saw them a few days ago, facing Fascist hoodlums, saw them standing shoulder to shoulder once again, he said, and these are the kind of people the government, federal and state, is persecuting.

At a speech in Detroit, one month after Peekskill, Robeson said, "I don't get scared when Fascism gets near, as it did at Peekskill.... The spirit of Harriet Tubman, Sojourner Truth, Frederick Douglass fills me with courage and determination that every Negro boy and girl, yes and every white boy and girl, shall walk this land free and with dignity."[3]

The fact that black and white workers had come together to protect the performers at Peekskill underscored Robeson's confidence that, despite racist influences of long standing, white workers would come to understand how black workers had faced exploitation for so long and would join in the fight for freedom for those black workers—and all workers. His experience at the second Peekskill concert fully convinced Robeson that his optimism was justified.

Two months later, at a banquet sponsored by the National Council of American-Soviet Friendship, Robeson returned to the events of the Wallace campaign and of Peekskill. "On my southern tour for Henry Wallace I recall our stops in Memphis, Tennessee, where the fighting organization of the Mine, Mill, and Smelter Workers joined hands with my people to guarantee that progressive thought and action could find a channel for expression. In Winston-Salem, North Carolina, I saw tobacco workers. I saw progressives and liberals ... all fighters who are leading a valiant struggle for liberation. It was during Peekskill that this unity was most sharply put forward. There, trade unionists, Jewish people, foreign born, Negro and white, stood side by side, fighting off the Fascist attack of gangs."[4]

The Deadly Parallel

IN THE WAKE of the Peekskill riots a group calling itself the Westchester Committee for a Fair Inquiry into the Peekskill Violence issued a document entitled *Eyewitness: Peekskill U.S.A. Aug. 27; Sept. 4, 1949.* In an introductory statement, "To You Who Believe in Democracy," the authors wrote,

> We who submit this report to you are residents of the area.... We send you this report as a warning. Please don't delude yourselves with the thought that what happened in our communities could never happen in your town.... We send you this report in the fervent hope that you will never close your eyes and ears to the truth; that you will never permit this vicious thing called Fascism to degrade and brutalize the people of our land.[5]

The document contains full accounts of the tense days leading up to the concerts, the incendiary news articles attacking Robeson, the concerts themselves, and the so-called investigations that followed.

The report also reprinted statements from various newspapers, among them *The New York Times* and *The New York Herald Tribune.* The *Times* commented that on the roads near Peekskill there occurred a series of incidents that were a disgrace to the community and a reminder that as great violence can be done to democracy by a gang of hoodlums in Westchester County as by a lynch mob in darkest Georgia. The *Herald Tribune* piece concluded that it is up to law-enforcement agencies, veterans' groups and the citizenry at large to see to it that there is no repetition of the Peekskill rioting, no condonation of the violence. The episode is inexcusable.

The *Eyewitness* document also contained firsthand accounts of the riots, including one by a refugee from Nazi Germany who came to America in 1940. Identified only as Kurt J., to protect him and his family, the man wrote,

> I saw in Peekskill a repetition of the day in November of 1939 when I was finally driven from my home in the Rhineland town of Andernach. I was not yet thirteen years old on that day, which saw the final outburst of anti–Semitic violence throughout Nazi Germany prior to the wholesale massacre of my people in that unhappy land.... The howling mobs came in the evening with great piles of rocks which they threw into our homes.... There was that same rock throwing with intent to kill at Peekskill as there was at Andernach. But even more striking for me was the psychopathic hatred, the hysteria of the hoodlum mob. Both acted and looked exactly the same.[6]

The report concluded with a statement from Paul Robeson, as told to Dan Burley, managing editor of the *Negro Weekly, New York Age,* in that publication's issue of September 17, 1949.

Where will the next Peekskill be, he asked? What new battleground has the reactionary police and those behind them selected? Where will they demonstrate further the old Southern custom of beating in the heads of Negroes and all those identified with the struggle to free the shackles of the greedy exploiters of his labor and his talents? "I shall take my voice wherever there are those who want to hear the melody of freedom or the words that might inspire hope and courage in the face of despair and fear."[7]

The Peekskill riots stand today as a continuing reminder of how quickly a populace with no tolerance for differing opinions or inclination to investigate inflammatory misinformation can become a violent mob. They stand as a classic example of how any stratum of society that feels itself being squeezed out, left behind, and in danger from others can aggressively seek out a scapegoat to blame for what they perceive as their failing fortunes—and that scapegoat all too often results in violent anti–Semitism and racism.

It is small wonder that after his experience at Peekskill, while later imprisoned for refusing to cooperate with HUAC investigations, Howard Fast wrote his famous novel *Spartacus.* The novel showcases how oppressive political systems can strip away the most basic values of freedom, hope, and life itself. He published the novel in 1951, the same year he wrote *Peekskill USA: Inside the Infamous 1949 Riots.*

Years later, folksinger and guitarist Bob Gibson told Pete Seeger that he knew the whole story behind that riot. Gibson, who was raised in Peekskill and whose father was on the Peekskill police force, said that the Ku Klux Klan was behind the riots, and the Klan was in cahoots with the police.[8] They had that place surrounded with walkie-talkies, just like a battlefield, Gibson told Seeger. You didn't have a chance.

⇒ 8 ⇐

On Their Journeys

"Everybody knew 'I Dreamed I Saw Joe Hill Last Night.'"
—Gary Snyder

THE PEEKSKILL CONCERT and the riots that ensued were over, but the controversy over what happened there and who was responsible raged on for months throughout the country. Robeson was the subject of accolades and accusations from both the white and black press, and his planned concerts closely following the Peekskill incidents met both with applause and protests, as well as outright cancellations. Regardless of the increasing pressures upon him, Robeson did not back down, but continued, as his father had counseled him years before, to remain true to his convictions.

Change of Direction

AT THE TIME of the Peekskill riots, the author of the original Joe Hill poem and subsequent lyric had changed directions. Thirteen years had passed since Alfred Hayes handed his poem to Earl Robinson at Camp Unity. In the interim he had moved away from his earlier political affiliations. As a versatile writer with serious literary ambitions—he wrote for radio, produced film criticism, and saw at least two of his plays make it to Broadway—Hayes chafed under any restrictions on writing that might be applied by a political party. At thirty-eight, his radical days were behind him.

Drafted into the Army during World War II, Hayes was assigned to a special services unit in Italy. There he met film director Roberto Rossellini and, being a quick study in the Italian language, subsequently worked, along with Federico Fellini and others, on the script of Rossellini's *Paisan*, for which he received an Academy Award nomination.

Paisan reflected the neorealist movement of the current Italian cinema, which attempted to deal with the difficult conditions in the country after the war. Hayes also contributed to Vittorio di Sica's *The Bicycle Thief* (apparently uncredited).

Hayes had published his first full-length volume of poetry, *The Big Time*, in 1944 and in 1946 completed his first novel, *All Thy Conquests*. The book, organized into a series of alternating vignettes of Italians and Americans in post-war Rome, exhibits none of the determined optimism that characterizes "Joe Hill." Instead, the book presents portraits of existential angst through the lives of people grappling with disillusion, confusion, and grief, *All Thy Conquests* reflects some lingering influence that the modernist writers of the preceding generation had on Hayes: the opening paragraph of the book contains the phrase "One would not have thought there would be so many people," to describe those at sea in the post-war world, a phrase that echoes T.S. Eliot's "unreal city" lines from "The Waste Land" about death having undone so many. Rome, in *All Thy Conquests*, is indeed an unreal city, and the strength of the book is Hayes's unsparing insight into human behavior. *The New Yorker* proclaimed it to be beautifully written and expertly constructed, an expose of the hollowness of victory. John Hersey (*Hiroshima*) praised the novel's depiction of failure to purge the Fascists or their ideas as well as a failure of those in the story to embrace the new demands of democracy. The somber mood of the book is consistent with the description of the younger Hayes by those who knew him and worked with him—a dark cynicism on one hand and romanticism on the other.

The central theme of *All Thy Conquests*—that at the dawn of the Cold War peace had not settled in as expected—dovetails with the neorealist films that Hayes worked in, as does its epigram, a line from Shakespeare's *Julius Caesar* that lends the book its title: "Are all thy conquests, glories, triumphs, spoils / Shrunk to this small measure?"

Hayes followed his debut novel with *Shadow of Heaven* (1947), a story about a burned-out forty-year-old union organizer named Harry Oberon. Reflecting on his youth, Oberon recalls that when he was nineteen his choices had seemed simple, his opportunities unlimited, and his energy and passion inexhaustible. Now, disillusioned and unfulfilled, he leaves his radical past behind. The name recalls the king of the fairies in Shakespeare's *A Midsummer Night's Dream*—a king with a tenuous grasp on reality—as well as C.M. Wieland's later poem using the same character.

When Hayes returned to the United States he received an invitation to work in Hollywood, thus igniting his career as a writer for the movies and for television. Among his film credits are *Act of Love*, based on his third novel *The Girl on the Via Flaminia (*with collaborators including Irwin Shaw, known for *The Young Lions* and *Rich Man, Poor Man)*; *Clash by Night*, on which Hayes collaborated with Clifford Odets, based on Odets's original play; *Teresa*; *The Lusty Men* (uncredited); *The Left Hand of God*; *A Hatful of Rain* (with collaborators including Carl Foreman, the Academy Award winner for *High Noon* and *The Bridge on the River Kwai* who went uncredited as he was blacklisted at the time); *Joy in the Morning* (collaboration); *The Double Man* (collaboration); and *Human Desire.*

The first Hollywood blacklist had been instituted in 1947, when the HUAC began to summon people from the film industry on suspicion that their work was inspired by or supportive of communism. New in town at that time, Hayes could not have wanted his early politics or his affiliation with "Joe Hill" to become known. In any event he considered the song less important than his mature fiction and poetry.

IN 1947, THE YEAR Hayes had his protagonist Oberon appear disillusioned with his radical past, Margaret Bradford Boni included "Joe Hill" in her well-received volume the *Fireside Book of Folk Songs*. A musicologist with an academic background that included the Juilliard School of Music, Boni compiled an anthology of what she termed some of the best-loved songs in the world. The book may stimulate interest in our cultural history and in so doing it will do well, she wrote in its preface, "but its primary purpose, as the title implies, is to encourage the domestic performance of the songs of long ago that are still the songs of today."[1]

"Joe Hill" is included in the section labeled Ballads and Old Favorites, despite the song's being only eleven years old at the time. An introductory statement to the song identifies Joe Hill as a great labor organizer and poet who was executed in 1915 on a murder charge that union circles have always considered a frame-up. Earl Robinson is credited as the composer; Alfred Hayes's name does not appear.

Wobblies and Beats

THE SAME YEAR that Boni published her songbook an aspiring poet enrolled at Reed College in Oregon. Gary Snyder remembered hearing his grandfather's stories of the Industrial Workers of the World, of which he had been a card-carrying member. Interviewed for Bruce Cook's book *The Beat Generation*, Snyder said that the IWW mythology had been important to him as he was growing up, and that Joe Hill was one of the first names he heard. Now it would be through the young Snyder, as he developed into one of America's leading poets, that the song "Joe Hill" would make a connection between the IWW and the Beat movement. Labor historian and author Franklin Rosemont has referred to Snyder as "the strongest link between the hippest labor union in U.S. history and the most vibrant poetic ferment of the mid-twentieth century."[2]

Snyder remained at Reed College until 1951. There he was recognized as someone who knew a lot about the Wobblies and had a repertoire of Wobbly and other labor songs that he would play on his guitar. Years later Snyder would recall that at Reed everyone sang "I Dreamed I Saw Joe Hill Last Night." Hardly anybody knew Joe Hill's own songs, Snyder added. He used to talk about the Wobblies a lot, and sang Joe Hill's songs, but he ran into very few people who knew what he was talking about. But everybody sang "I Dreamed I Saw Joe Hill Last Night."[3]

While he established his own solid body of work, Snyder also came to the attention of his peers and the reading public in general as the model for Japhy Ryder, the hero of Jack Kerouac's novel *The Dharma Bums*, where he was depicted as a "mountain-climbing Zen poet whose interests include old-fashioned IWW anarchism and old worker songs."[4]

IN SEPTEMBER 1950 Earl Robinson was invited by the International Mine, Mill, and Smelter Workers Union to sing at its convention that month. For Robinson it was a pleasant surprise. While not officially blacklisted, he was on what he referred to as the "gray list," meaning that offers of any kind were few and far between. When he arrived at the Denver convention site, Robinson discovered the panels of the hall covered with Alfred Hayes's verses. He was told that "Joe Hill" was the union's official song, and then the whole union membership rose to its feet and sang it with him. The same thing happened to him at a similar meeting in Canada, where workers had adopted the song as their own.

Mother Bloor

PAUL ROBESON continued to be the song's main champion, but his freedom of movement was soon further curtailed. In 1950 the federal government enacted the McCarran Internal Security Act, supposedly to protect the country against un–American and subversive activities. Robeson was an easy target. The State Department revoked his

passport, and his concert bookings continued to dry up. The announcement of a pending appearance by Paul Robeson in any city would routinely bring on a backlash of opposition and protest. He continued to
make appearances for unions and similar organizations. In November
1950, while his passport case was held up in court, he attended the second World Peace Conference, this time in Warsaw, Poland, where he
sang "Joe Hill."

ON AUGUST 12, 1951 Robeson delivered the eulogy at the funeral of
Mother Bloor. Born on Staten Island in 1862, Ella Reeve "Mother" Bloor
was a legendary labor organizer who first embraced activism in support
of temperance and women's rights, and eventually developed ties to the
socialist and communist movements in America. She was renowned
for, among many causes, her lifelong advocacy of women's suffrage and
for organizing farmers and often leading their strikes. Poet Langston
Hughes recalled Mother Bloor as someone who was as sweet and full of
sunshine as she could be, but who battled the capitalists tooth and nail
for seventy years.

　　Mother Bloor was also the grandmother of Herta Geer, Will Geer's
wife. Herta had introduced Woody Guthrie to Mother Bloor when he
first arrived in California. It was Mother Bloor who told Guthrie about
the 1913 massacre in Calumet, Michigan, when strike breakers barred
the doors of a hall where members of the Western Federation of Miners and their families were holding a Christmas party, and yelled "fire!"
In the ensuing panic and confusion seventy-three children were smoth-
ered or trampled to death. Guthrie responded to this tragedy with his
song "1913 Massacre."

　　Further inspired by reading Mother Bloor's autobiography *We Are
Many*, Guthrie penned "Ludlow Massacre," recounting the 1914 killing of a number of men, women, and children by the Colorado National
Guard during a strike against John D. Rockefeller's Colorado Fuel and
Iron Company. In both instances, workers and their families had been
reduced to living in squalid conditions similar to those that gave rise
to the IWW back in 1905. Mother Bloor and Paul Robeson had shared
a great affection for Camp Wo-Chi-Ca, which they sometimes visited
together. At Bloor's memorial Robeson recalled a lad of five who insisted
time and time again on hearing him sing "Joe Hill."

　　Camp Wo-Chi-Ca had enjoyed the tolerance of its local neighbors,
who welcomed the camp's annual Fourth of July celebrations and who
frequently joined campers in friendly baseball games—tolerance, that
is, that evaporated when the political atmosphere in the country began
to change. In the growing atmosphere of the Cold War and after the

riots at Peekskill not far away, neighbors took increased notice of blacks and Jews at the camp. As June Levine and Gene Gordon recounted in their memoir, it all changed around 1950, only one year after Peekskill:

> Then, seething with hate from the Cold War and Red Scare, local "patriots" converted their playful bats to lethal clubs. They assailed campers verbally and physically. "Wo-Chi-Ca stands for integration, integration means Communism and Communism is un–American!" They invaded the grounds demanding removal of the PAUL ROBESON sign from the Playhouse. In the end the camp had to shut down.[5]

Sixty years later camp alumnus Jack Broitman remembered Wo-Chi-Ca as a phenomenon not only because of its leftist origins and persuasion. As quoted by Levine and Gordon, Broitman said, "Its significance as one of the few interracial experiences for white and black kids should not be understated."[6] It was, Broitman added, an idealistic foreshadowing of the kind of integrated loving world we all hoped would follow World War II.

IN 1951 JOE HILL was the subject of a play written by American playwright Barrie Stavis. Entitled *The Man Who Never Died*, the play is a companion to Stavis's earlier book, *Joe Hill: The Man and the Myth*. Act 1 opens with Hill declaring, "My name is Joe Hill. I am a member of the Industrial Workers of the World—the IWW. They call us the Wobblies; but we don't wobble; we stand firm—like a rock."[7]

Born into a Jewish family in New York in 1906, Stavis early demonstrated his ambition to become a writer. While his father had reservations about his son's choice of career, it did not cause the kind of rift that beset the family of Alfred Hayes. The Stavis family regularly attended plays together in the city.

In 1931 Stavis was working at 18th Street and Fourth Avenue in New York, and on his lunch breaks would go down to Union Square, just as Earl Robinson would do a few years later. There he witnessed hundreds of people marching for jobs and singing. Joe Hill's song "The Preacher and the Slave (Pie in the Sky)" made a particular impression on Stavis. It was all very vivid, he would recall in an interview in 1994. Stavis went to the library and looked up the poet who had written that song. He would return to Union Square and witness more protests and listen to more singing, experiences he credits as the beginning of his political awakening.

If the Great Depression launched Stavis's engagement in politics, the Spanish Civil War solidified it. Turning down a contract offer as a Hollywood screenwriter, Stavis left for Spain in 1937. He was deeply committed to the idea of social justice, what he sometimes referred to as a fair shake of the dice, but as yet did not know how to achieve it politically. He would later say that he went to Spain as an innocent liberal with socialist tendencies, and came out of Spain with the deep notion that one must act politically. He considered his time in Spain as the most important experience of his life.

Referring to *The Man Who Never Died*, Stavis explained that what was at stake was Joe Hill himself, who will have power over his life and, beyond that, the universal struggle for the rights of all working people.

In the same year that Stavis wrote *The Man Who Never Died*, novelist James Jones published *From Here to Eternity*. In the book Jones has an Army private tell another soldier who was too young to remember the Industrial Workers of the World that there has never been anything like the Wobblies. They were workstiffs and bindlebums like you and me, he says, but they were welded together by a vision that made them great. And nobody ever sang the way those guys sang!

The Peace Arch

IN 1952 PAUL ROBESON was scheduled to perform a concert in Vancouver, Canada, sponsored by the United Mine, Mill and Smelter Workers Union. At the border a representative of the U.S. State Department informed him that while no passport was required for an American citizen to enter Canada, a special order had come through forbidding him to leave the country. Robeson and Mine Mill solved the problem by using a long-distance telephone hookup relayed to a public address system. For seventeen minutes Robeson sang and spoke over the phone from Seattle. He began by singing "Joe Hill." According to a correspondent with the *Canadian Tribune*, some 2,000 Vancouver citizens heard Robeson sing, and at the conclusion of his performance gave him a thunderous ovation.

In 1952 and 1953, still forbidden to travel outside the United States, Robeson sang from a flatbed truck at the Peace Arch on the United States-Canadian border to tens of thousands of people on both sides. His selections included "Ol' Man River" and, of course, "Joe Hill."

Situated between Blaine, Washington, and Surrey, British Columbia, where Interstate 5 crosses the American-Canadian border, the Peace Arch is a sixty seven–foot structure, the construction of which was spearheaded by businessman, lawyer, and railroad executive Sam Hill (no relation to Joe Hill). It was dedicated in 1921 to symbolize the long history of peace between the two nations. The inscription on the American side reads "Children of a common mother," while on the Canadian side it reads "Brethren dwelling together in unity."

Robeson recalled the Peace Arch event in a 1954 letter to Soviet writer Boris Polevoi. I might mention, he wrote, that the Mine, Mill and Smelters Union has a rich heritage of working class struggle, for it grew out of the old Western Federation of Miners and the heroic strike struggles led by "Big Bill" Haywood.[8] From the early struggles of this union, he added, came the martyred organizer Joe Hill, killed by the copper trust in Utah—the same Joe Hill of whom I sing, and who himself was the greatest writer of songs for the American working people.

Labor's Troubadour

IN 1954 singer and songwriter Joe Glazer released two albums of songs associated with the Industrial Workers of the World—*Songs of Joe Hill* and *I Will Win: Songs of the Wobblies.* The Joe Hill album features Hill's own songs as well as the Hayes-Robinson ballad, using the lyrics as they appeared in the *Fireside Book of Folk Songs*, and credits Alfred Hayes as lyricist. These two recordings were among the more than thirty that Glazer would release during his long career.

Born in June 1918 in New York City, the son of a tailor in the International Ladies Garment Workers Union, Joe Glazer grew up in the Bronx and started his musical career as a boy when he bought a $5.95 mail order guitar. What began as an infatuation with Gene Autry and other cowboy crooners evolved into six decades as a writer and singer in support of unions and their representation in mines, mills, factories, and offices. A graduate of Brooklyn College, Glazer served as a civilian radio instructor in the Army Air Force during World War II. His working experiences included time with the Textile Workers of America and the United Rubber Workers. In 1961 he joined the Foreign Service of the United States Information Agency, then headed by Edward R. Murrow, and served in Mexico before returning to Washington.

Over his long life and career Joe Glazer rubbed shoulders with American presidents—once performing on the White House lawn—and foreign dignitaries, but he never forgot his roots in the labor movement. He came to be known as "labor's troubadour," but self-deprecatingly referred to himself simply as a musical agitator for good causes. Before he turned to writing his own songs Glazer assembled a repertoire of labor and protest material, including an early version of "We Shall Overcome" that he learned from his friend Agnes Douty, a singer and labor educator—"She knew a good labor song when she heard it"[9]—who had learned it from Zilphia Horton at the Highlander School.

Glazer's laws for communicating musically with audiences who don't understand your language could have come straight from Joe Hill's own working methods: Keep songs short. Variety is the key. Learn a song in the local language. Translate an American song into the local language. Keep introductions short and sweet; skip them now and then. Sing along.

On December 5, 1954, Glazer performed at the convention in New York for the historic merger of the American Federation of Labor and the Congress of Industrial Organizations into the AFL-CIO. At one point CIO President Walter Reuther joined him for a duet of "Joe Hill," which was Reuther's favorite song.

Joe Glazer, left, and United Auto Workers President Walter Reuther sing "Joe Hill," Reuther's favorite song, in December 1954 at the historic merger of the American Federation of Labor and the Congress of Industrial Organizations. During his long career Glazer recorded many of Hill's original songs as well as Hayes and Robinson's "Joe Hill," which he called the most important factor in perpetuating Hill's memory.

On Their Journeys

FOR TWO YEARS, 1953–55, Paul Robeson, Jr., ran Othello Recording Company, which he and Lloyd Brown set up to provide an artistic outlet for Paul Jr.'s father after other recording studios closed their doors to him. Actor Adolph Menjou snidely commented that one of the best ways to spot a communist is if that person is seen applauding at a Paul Robeson concert or owns a Paul Robeson recording. The records made at Othello are available today as *On My Journey: Paul Robeson's Independent Recordings*, and of course they include "Joe Hill."

With his passport impounded, Robeson's travels were severely limited. He must have been heartened to some degree by two developments in 1954, though they did little to relieve his personal circumstances. On May 17 the United States Supreme Court, ruling on *Brown v. Board of Education of Topeka, Kansas*, unanimously stated that racial segregation in public schools violated the Fourteenth Amendment of the Constitution, which guarantees equal protection of the laws to all citizens. Robeson, of course, had written his senior thesis at Rutgers on that amendment. And on December 2, the U.S. Senate, by a vote of 67–22, formally censured Wisconsin Senator Joseph McCarthy, stating that McCarthy had acted contrary to Senatorial ethics and had brought dishonor and disrepute upon the Senate.

McCarthy had been an undistinguished senator until February 9, 1950, when he delivered a Lincoln Day address to local Republicans in Wheeling, West Virginia, declaring that he had in his hand a list of Communist Party members who were working and shaping policy in the State Department. With that bogus claim McCarthy was vaulted into the national headlines that he so cravenly desired. The censure effectively ended McCarthy's four-year campaign of lies and baseless allegations that caused incalculable damage to many individual Americans and to the country itself. Now censured and disgraced, he died three years later, a powerless, embittered alcoholic.

ONE OF THE PROJECTS Earl Robinson managed to complete in the 1950s was a 1957 collaboration with former Almanac Singer Millard Lampell on music for the film *A Walk in the Sun*. Lampell had earlier written lyrics for Robinson's "The Lonesome Train," a ballad opera on the death of Abraham Lincoln, and would go on to write movie and television scripts and be blacklisted for refusing to testify before the HUAC.

The film *A Walk in the Sun* was adapted from a 1944 novel by Harry Brown, who would later enjoy some success as a screenwriter working on *The Sands of Iwo Jima, Ocean's 11,* and *A Place in the Sun,* for which he was co-recipient of an Academy Award. His novel is a fictional account of the Allied invasion at Salerno, Italy, and Lampell and Robinson's songs were intended not to underline the action in the picture but rather to add a further dimension to the scenes.

That same year Robinson released *A Walk in the Sun*, a recording that included some songs that were not used in the final film, among them "The House I Live In" and "Joe Hill." The printed lyrics to "Joe Hill" adopt the changes made by Paul Robeson, but, oddly enough, Robinson's repeated last lines appear only after stanzas one, two, and seven. Alfred Hayes's name is not included anywhere in the liner notes.

Here I Stand

IN 1957 the State Department unexpectedly made its first concession to Paul Robeson in seven years. Though still refusing him a passport, State announced that henceforth he would be permitted to travel to Alaska, American Samoa, Guam, Hawaii, Puerto Rico, and the Virgin Islands, places in the Western Hemisphere where a passport was not required of U.S. citizens.

Slowly, offers began to come in. In July alone he appeared in California five times, singing to thousands in sold-out venues. The concerts received no notice or reviews by the commercial press. And what's more, said Robeson, I don't care. Adhering to his 1947 announcement in Utah, he was continuing to sing for audiences he believed in, not, he said, for well-to-do snobs. My labors in the future, he said, will remain the same as they have in the past. They will be based on my whole experience—in the anti–Fascist struggle that saw its finest expression in Spain, in the worldwide struggle of working people against their oppressors.[10]

Early in 1958 Robeson performed successful concerts not only in California but also in Portland and Chicago. But nothing did more toward refurbishing his image than the publication that same year of *Here I Stand*, his manifesto-autobiography co-written with Lloyd Brown, who had previously collaborated with Robeson on speeches and other writings and who had witnessed the Peekskill riots. While he did not apologize for his earlier activities, in the book Robeson made a clear declaration to black America that he viewed his primary allegiance as being to his own community and not to international communism. "The truth is," he wrote, "I am not and never have been involved in any international conspiracy or any other kind, and do not know anyone who is."[11] *Here I Stand* is a powerful document in which Robeson underscores his unflinching commitment to the liberation of his own people, and of all people. He refers to the words of Frederick Douglass, in that following this commitment he will feel himself discharging the duty of a true patriot; for he is a lover of his country who rebukes and does not excuse its sins.

VANGUARD RECORDS put Robeson back into a studio in April of 1958—the first time in seven years—and on May 9, one month after his 60th birthday, Robeson achieved a major milestone on his road to restoration with a concert at New York's Carnegie Hall. He had been absent from the city's concert stages for more than a decade. The audience cheered Robeson on his arrival, stood several times during the concert to cheer him again, and at the conclusion shouted and whistled its approval. He was accompanied by pianist Alan Booth, a graduate of the Oberlin Conservatory of Music, who became Robeson's pianist in concert and on the independent recordings when Lawrence Brown stepped aside after the violence at Peekskill. At Carnegie Hall Robeson presented spirituals, international songs, a monologue from Othello, and a memorable rendition of "Joe Hill," his special favorite that he had been singing now for twenty years.

The reviews were unanimous: Robeson was back. Irving Kolodin of the *Saturday Review* wrote the Robeson remained a man of magnificent vocal endowments with a power of articulation second to none. Harriet Johnson wrote in the *New York* Post wrote that Robeson's characteristic dignity had left its unforgettable mark.

Buoyed that success, Robeson scheduled a second concert, this time ensuring a more integrated audience by seeing that more tickets were available through outlets in Harlem. That concert, too, sold out. Two weeks later he delivered a concert at his brother Ben's church, Mother A.M.E. Zion in Harlem. While Alan Booth had been accompanying him for many of his recent appearances, for this concert Robeson was reunited with Lawrence Brown. "I want the crowd to know," he told his overflow audience, "that a lot of the hard struggle is over and that my concert career has practically been reestablished.... I've been waiting for this afternoon just to come back to give my thanks...."[12]

Soon after that performance the news came regarding something else he had been waiting for a long time. The Supreme Court announced that the Secretary of State had no right to deny a passport to any citizen based on his or her political beliefs. In particular, the ruling added that the Passport Division had no right to demand that an applicant sign an affidavit regarding membership in the Communist Party.

After these many years, Robeson's passport was restored. He

followed his Carnegie Hall concerts with a successful return tour of Europe, where he was welcomed everywhere with tumultuous applause.

The previous two decades had been years of increasing turmoil for the great man, with growing opposition to his political stances, the threats to his life during the Henry Wallace campaign and at the riots in Peekskill, and the impounding of his passport that cut severely into his very livelihood. But with his Carnegie Hall concerts and successful return to the international scene, he closed out the decade of the 1950s on a note of personal triumph.

⚌ 9 ⚌

Carry It On

"Freedom's a thing that has no ending."
—Millard Lampell

IN 1952 EARL ROBINSON had been denied a passport by the State Department, but by 1959 it had been restored, and in May of that year he and his wife visited Europe. Their trip included an unannounced visit to East Berlin in the German Democratic Republic.

Ten years earlier, following the end of World War II and in the ensuing Cold War, the Soviet-occupied zone of Germany had been formally founded as the German Democratic Republic. Relations between the United States and the GDR were hostile, and American citizens at the time of Robinson's visit were prohibited from entering that zone. The local GDR authorities cooperated by not stamping the Robinsons' passports.

Robinson was scheduled to present a concert and to conduct a performance of his cantata "The Lonesome Train." Composed back in the early 1940s, with a libretto written by Millard Lampell, the 27-minute piece centers on the death of Abraham Lincoln and the funeral train that carried his body back to Illinois. Lampell concludes with the unforgettable lines, ""Freedom's a thing that has no ending / it needs to be cared for, it needs defending."

Once, speaking with a small gathering of international participants, Robinson was asked to sing "Joe Hill." He sang a verse in English, which members of the group then translated into German, next into French, and finally into Vietnamese for the understanding of all assembled. Verse by verse, Robinson later recalled, the song made its way into the ears of four nations.

That is music: the international language. And that is "Joe Hill": an international song. It was later printed in a Russian publication, *Erl Robinson Pyesni*, "Earl Robinson Songs," a thirty-five-page collection that included Abel Meeropol's "The House I Live In" as well as "Joe Hill." The same two songs, along with other selections by Robinson and Paul Robeson were issued that year as *Das ondere Amerika: Paul Robeson und Earl Robinson singen* (The Other America: Paul Robeson and Earl Robinson sing) on the Berlin label Deutsche Schallplatten.

On June 19, 1953, Julius and Ethel Rosenberg were executed on charges of espionage. Their two orphaned sons, Robert and Michael, were subsequently shuttled from one home to another among relatives, friends, even shelters. This was during the McCarthy period, when many people were terrified of being associated with the Rosenberg name, and were afraid to take care of their children.

Eventually Abel and Anne Meeropol adopted them, an act of great courage, and the boys took the Meeropol name.

Robert has confirmed that Meeropol remained familiar with "Joe Hill." "I'm pretty sure we sang it as a family at home in the 1950s," he said.[1]

Work and Protest

IN 1960 JOE GLAZER and Edith Fowke published *Songs of Work and Freedom*, later renamed *Songs of Work and Protest.* Glazer had first presented the idea for the book five years earlier to the National Labor Advisory Committee of the Labor Education Division of Roosevelt University in Chicago. At the time of its publication Glazer was serving as the education director of the United Rubber Workers of the AFL-CIO. For the book he and Fowke, a Canadian folklorist, assembled one hundred songs of American workers, providing music and historical notes for each. The book had two aims, they wrote in its introduction: to provide a collection of songs that could be sung by trade unions and other interested groups, and to show how these songs reflected mankind's struggle for a better life.

In the Preface to the book, Frank McCallister, director, and Agnes M. Douty, assistant director of the university's Labor Education Division, write, "This is no book for resting on a quiet library shelf. It will be in constant use—well-thumbed—as union men and women and their children sing to piano or guitar at home, at union meetings, at summer schools in this country, and, we predict, in other countries of the world."[2] A song is learned and repeated over and over, said Joe Hill.

Songs of Work and Protest includes many of the most well-known of labor's songs, among them "Solidarity Forever" (Ralph Chaplin),

"Union Maid" (Woody Guthrie), "We Will Overcome" (before Pete Seeger changed "will" to "shall"), "Sixteen Tons" (Merle Travis), "Which Side Are You On" (Florence Reece), and Joe Hill's "The Preacher and the Slave." Included as well are several Glazer originals, "The Mill Was Made of Marble" being one of his best known.

Over a third of the songs in the book represent the American trade union movement. "Joe Hill" is one of them. Glazer and Fowke credit both Hayes and Robinson, and in accompanying text tell the story of Joe Hill, alluding to the controversy over Hill's guilt or innocence that was still being debated. Joe Hill has become a symbol of the hundreds of men and women who have been killed while battling for labor's rights, Fowke and Glazer write, concluding that "perhaps the most important factor in perpetuating his memory is the song which was written by Earl Robinson and Alfred Hayes some twenty years after his death."[3]

In 1961 *American Folksong* magazine published "Joseph Hillstrom," a poem written some years earlier by Woody Guthrie. In its fourteen stanzas Guthrie recounts the entire story of Joe Hill's arrest and execution, concluding that Joe Hillstrom had done a pretty good job.

Dylan

IN THE BITTER cold of January 1961 a young aspiring folk singer arrived in New York City from the Midwest to pursue his future, just as Woody Guthrie had done twenty-one years earlier. Foremost on the 19-year-old Bob Dylan's agenda was to meet Guthrie, his idol.

Born Robert Zimmerman in Duluth, Minnesota, in 1941, Dylan grew up in nearby Hibbing, where he absorbed music ranging from the country of Hank Williams and the blues of Robert Johnson to the rhythm and blues of Little Richard and the early rock 'n' roll of Buddy Holly. In high school he played guitar and piano in several bands, and it was during his brief attendance at the University of Minnesota that he discovered folk music in general and Woody Guthrie in particular. Guthrie became an obsession. Years later, writing in his memoir *Chronicles*, Dylan recalled his first encounters with Guthrie's music made his head spin, as if the land had parted. After reading Woody's autobiographical book *Bound for Glory*, Dylan became determined to travel east to meet his idol.

Since 1954 Woody had been wasting away from Huntington's disease, a progressive degeneration of the nervous system for which there was no known cure. Soon after arriving in New York Dylan hitchhiked his way out to Greystone Park Hospital in Morristown, New Jersey, where Guthrie was housed, and began what would become a series of regular visits. Trapped in the grip of his disease, Woody could hardly communicate with his young admirer, but Dylan would sing to him and the two struck up a bond.

On one of those visits Dylan met a man called Ramblin' Jack Elliott. Born Elliott Charles Adnopoz in Brooklyn in 1931, Ramblin' Jack as a child had been inspired by rodeos staged in Madison Square Garden. Wanting to be a cowboy, he ran away from home at age fifteen, but was brought back by his parents. He taught himself to play guitar and began busking on the streets. In 1950 he met Woody Guthrie, with whom he would become both student and friend, and a confirmed Guthrie acolyte before Dylan. He toured England and Europe, and by the time he met Bob Dylan he was an established figure on the American folk music scene with a driving guitar style that would influence other artists, among them Dylan, Phil Ochs, and Woody's son, Arlo. Dylan once referred to Ramblin' Jack as the king of the folksingers.

Soon Dylan was finding his way in Greenwich Village, as Woody had done years before, meeting people and soaking up songs. There he kept hearing a song called "I Dreamed I Saw Joe Hill," so he set about finding out who Joe Hill was. What he discovered led him to recognize Joe Hill as the forerunner of his idol, Woody Guthrie.

The presence of "Joe Hill" in Greenwich Village at that time is further testimony that the song was continuing to expand its relevance beyond its original context. Through the efforts of Paul Robeson and others, the one-time labor anthem was now part of the repertoire of the folk revival of the early 1960s, recognized as a song of general protest against all forms of oppression.

Moscow Mystery

Two months after Bob Dylan arrived in New York a bizarre incident occurred in Moscow, where Paul Robeson was staying. Around 2:00 or 3:00 a.m. on the morning of March 27, during a noisy party in his hotel suite, Robeson was discovered in the bathroom, his wrists slashed with a razor blade. A team of Soviet doctors diagnosed depression and paranoid psychosis, perhaps related to a form of arteriosclerosis.

Under the care of Soviet doctors Robeson appeared to recover and, after some time resting in a sanatorium, traveled to London. There he suffered a relapse of mood swings, agitation, and depression. Doctors decided on a course of electroconvulsive therapy (ECT), or brain seizures triggered by electric currents. More commonly referred to as electric shock treatment, this procedure was accepted practice in the Sixties, and while it may still be administered today, many medical professionals question its possible culpability in memory loss or even brain damage.

Electro-shock in combination with psychoactive drugs was also a technique used by the CIA at that time. Paul Jr., who arrived in Moscow a few days later, and who himself suffered a subsequent breakdown, long suspected that the United States government had a hand in his father's incident. He would later write that the raucous party and his father's so-called suicide attempt remain unexplained, and accused the U.S. government of withholding relevant documents. For decades Paul Jr. investigated the circumstances surrounding this mystery, all the while suspecting that his father had been slipped a synthetic hallucinogenic by U.S. intelligence operatives at the party—a party that may have been hosted by anti–Soviet dissidents funded by the CIA—causing his father's uncontrolled reaction.

This incident did come eight years into the CIA's illegal human experimentation program called MKUltra, which was undertaken to develop procedures and drugs that could be used to weaken people during interrogations, as well as for manipulating a subject's mental state.

The timing of the incident remains suspicious. Robeson had planned to visit Havana to meet Fidel Castro and Che Guevara. The United States was on the brink of its Bay of Pigs invasion of Cuba, and Robeson's intended visit could have been seen as undermining that effort.

In the weeks preceding his trip to Moscow Robeson had expressed to friends that he was feeling weary. Had he been suffering emotional turmoil and depression? Had he become disillusioned with the Soviet Union? Was he suffering from exhaustion? Was it really attempted suicide, or had he been poisoned? So much of this matter remains unknown.

Whatever the actual circumstances surrounding the incident, it came at a time when Paul Robeson had been pursuing a schedule of personal, professional, and political commitments that would have worn out a lesser man much sooner. Now, at the age of sixty-three, after enduring years of relentless harassment by his own country's government, Robeson's health was beginning to falter. Some family members also pointed to the series of electro-shock treatments, saying that whatever happened to Paul Robeson in Moscow and during the treatments afterwards, he was never quite the same man again.

So Long, It's Been Good to Know Ya

BACK IN 1927 the poet, biographer, and folksinger Carl Sandburg had praised Joe Hill in his collection of American folk songs, *The American Songbag*. After reading Sandburg's poetry book *The People, Yes*, Earl Robinson contacted the poet with the idea of setting some of his work to music. While that project never came to complete fruition, Robinson did produce a work entitled *In the Folded and Quiet Yesterdays*, its title taken from one of his favorite lines from *The People, Yes*. Robinson and Sandburg remained in contact for many years.

Sandburg's daughter Helga would immortalize the composer's visits with her father at Connemara, the poet's farm in Flat Rock, North Carolina, when she published *Sweet Music: A Book of Family Reminiscence and Song*. Helga included two of her favorite Robinson compositions in the book, "Black and White," which would become a hit for the rock vocal group Three Dog Night, and "Joe Hill."

Carl Sandburg died on July 22, 1967. On October 1, his ashes were buried at his Galesburg, Illinois, birthplace. Two days later, Woody Guthrie died.

PETE SEEGER received the news of Woody's death while on tour in Japan. "Finally," Seeger later wrote, "he could no longer walk nor talk nor focus his eyes nor feed himself, and his great will to live was not enough and his heart stopped beating."[4] Seeger said that all he could think of at first upon hearing of Guthrie's death was that Woody will never die—as Joe Hill will never die—as long as there are people who like to sing his songs—and there always will be.

"Woody Guthrie was, is, America's balladeer," the renowned radio host and author Studs Terkel would later write. "During the epoch of our deepest despair, the Great Depression, his were the songs that lifted the lowly spirits of the 'ordinary,' the millions of dispossessed. Woody did that through the thousand or more songs that he wrote, songs that looked American life right in the eye and told it like it was, songs that have nothing to do with bombs bursting in air nor with sanctimonious blessing, but have to do with what this country is about. And in so doing he became the greatest folksinger and folk song writer in American history. There will never be another Woody."[5]

Born on the brink of World War I, Woody Guthrie had come of age during the dark days of the Depression and, in particular, the Dust Bowl, an experience that marked him for the rest of his life. Incurably restless, he could be a loving but unreliable husband and father while at the same time deeply feeling the suffering of others.

He was not an accomplished instrumentalist, consciously preferring a musical simplicity to support his words. That is where his genius lay—in the torrent of songs and other writings that flowed out of him, songs that continue to have a profound influence on succeeding generations of singers and songwriters and anyone who really listens.

One year before he died Woody received a citation from Stewart Udall, Secretary of the Interior, honoring him for the songs he wrote in May 1941 for the Bonneville Power Administration. At the same time Udall announced that a small power station along the Columbia River would be named for Guthrie, the two honors "in recognition of the fine work you have done to make our people aware of their heritage and the land."[6] It was a well-deserved if largely symbolic gesture of the type that too often is made only after the recipient is past the prime of life or dead. Some of Woody's followers objected to it, complaining that the recognition was turning the radical Guthrie into conservationist. This true son of America accomplished more than only a very few ever do, before wasting away in hospitals from an incurable disease for the last thirteen years of his life. Woody Guthrie was fifty-five years old.

Alive as You and Me

THREE MONTHS AFTER Guthrie's death, Bob Dylan released *John Wesley Harding*, his first album since suffering a motorcycle accident one year earlier.

Dylan had made his mark writing memorable protest songs—"finger-pointing songs" he called them—among them "Blowin' in the Wind," "Masters of War," "A Hard Rain's Gonna Fall," and "The Times They Are a-Changin'." He then plugged in with electric instruments and, to the dismay of folk song purists, released several albums that steered away from protest into more personal statements, some featuring abstract, even surrealistic, lyrics.

As author Ted Anthony has written, the notion that purists are romantic and necessary is ultimately unrealistic. "In music and culture, what matters is the journey, and purists allow no journey. They are consumed with beginnings, and they are always frozen in the past."[7] Bob Dylan was a student and connoisseur of folk music and the past from which that music came, but no purist in the sense of letting tradition interfere with his artistic vision and development. Nevertheless many commentators saw *John Wesley Harding* as a signal that Dylan was returning to acoustic music, when it was just as likely that he was simply following another of his ever-changing musical directions.

One song on the album is entitled "I Dreamed I Saw St. Augustine." In it, Dylan makes a direct allusion to "Joe Hill" with the line "I dreamed I saw St. Augustine alive as you and me." *Rolling Stone* magazine writer Alan Rinzler pointed out the similarities between "St. Augustine" and "Joe Hill" in both melodies and lyrics. *Rolling Stone* writer Greil Marcus sensed the same connection, claiming that "St. Augustine" finds its way back to "I Dreamed I Saw Joe Hill."[8] These and other commentators suggest that the song might indicate Dylan's repentance for leaving the Joe Hill and Woody Guthrie acoustic tradition during his recent heavily electrified phase. An uncredited writer on the Website *thefatangelsings* simply refers to the song as a surreal riff on the labor standard "Joe Hill."

Be that as it may, *John Wesley Harding* stands firmly as a link in the chain from Joe Hill through Woody Guthrie to Bob Dylan. Music historian and archivist Lori Elaine Taylor has pointed out that, in emulating Woody Guthrie, Bob Dylan was, by extension, emulating Joe Hill.

ONE YEAR LATER folk singer Phil Ochs recorded his own Joe Hill song on his *Tape from California* album. The twenty-two-verse ballad retells the Hill legend to the tune of the Carter Family's "John Henry," and features guitar accompaniment and harmony singing by Ramblin' Jack Elliott.

American master, American tragedy: this was Phil Ochs. Born in 1940 in El Paso, Texas, Ochs became enamored of the music of Woody Guthrie and Pete Seeger while studying journalism at Ohio State University. Moving to New York the same year that Bob Dylan arrived, Ochs quickly became recognized as a powerful songwriter and performer, best remembered for his protest songs—though he liked to refer to himself as a "singing journalist." His work earned him a file at the FBI, which frequently misspelled his name as "Oakes."

But while Dylan enjoyed ever-increasing stardom, Ochs, despite the wide acceptance of his songs, such as "There but for Fortune" and "Changes," could not quite achieve comparable success. He apparently was also suffering from either undiagnosed bipolar disorder or manic depression. Phil Ochs had become one the most celebrated folk singers in America, but his career and life unraveled. In 1976 he committed suicide.

Woodstock

WHEN ALFRED HAYES and Earl Robinson collaborated on "Joe Hill," in 1936, America was deep in the grip of the Great Depression and the

Dust Bowl, and to many people the Communist Party USA appeared to offer viable alternatives to a failing capitalist system. When Joan Baez sang "Joe Hill" at Woodstock in August 1969, America was deep into the quagmire of the Vietnam War, where we were supposedly fighting to prevent the spread of communism.

American contact with Vietnam dates back to the 1919 Paris Peace Conference at the conclusion of World War I. It was during this meeting that Vietnamese leader Ho Chi Minh petitioned President Woodrow Wilson for help in creating a Vietnam independent of French colonialists. Wilson ignored him. The United States' direct involvement in that country stretches back at least as far as the fall of 1950, when President Harry Truman deployed the Military Assistance Advisory Group to Vietnam, purportedly to supervise the use of $10 million in military equipment authorized for the French. Truman's successor, Dwight Eisenhower, sent the same group to train the Army of the Republic of Vietnam.

In 1961, newly elected President John F. Kennedy faced three crises: the failed Bay of Pigs invasion of Cuba, the construction of the Berlin Wall, and a settlement between the pro–Western government of Laos and the Pathet Lao communist movement. Wary of enduring another setback, Kennedy remained committed to the bipartisan, anti-communist policies in Vietnam that he inherited from Truman and Eisenhower. No less an authority on the matter than Charles de Gaulle warned Kennedy that in Vietnam he would sink step by step into a bottomless military quagmire, however much America spent in men and money.

In 1965, two years after Kennedy was assassinated, President Lyndon Johnson sent 3,500 Marines into Vietnam, the first American ground troops to be so deployed.

It would known forever as Woodstock, while in fact the three-day music festival of that name actually took place on a farm in nearby Bethel, New York. Formally billed by the Woodstock Music & Arts Fair as "An Aquarian Exposition," three days of peace and music that, as it turned out, coincided with a combination of heat, humidity, rain, and mud. By the time of the festival, more than 500,000 American troops were actively engaged in Vietnam, and anti-war protests were a major component uniting the counterculture of the time, as was that counterculture's music.

In one sense Joan Baez seemed out of place at Woodstock, given the overwhelming rock-and-roll content of the program. But as a highly regarded artist and a well-known political activist, her every gesture

Joan Baez at Woodstock in August 1969, where her *a cappella* rendition of "Joe Hill" introduced it to a new generation, the most important milestone in the evolution of the song since its adoption by Paul Robeson.

could be examined for its message. Six months pregnant at the time, she was the closing act of the festival's first day, August 15, but was finally able to take to the stage hours after midnight on the morning of August 16. "Good morning," she said to the hundreds of thousands in the audience out in the dark. After performing the traditional gospel song "Oh Happy Day," Tom Paxton's "The Last Thing on My Mind," and Bob Dylan's "I Shall Be Released," she paused to tell the audience that federal marshals had recently arrested her husband, David Harris, for resisting the draft.

Then she sang "Joe Hill" *a cappella*.

FIRST, THE CREATION: A song was born when Alfred Hayes handed Earl Robinson his poem. Then Paul Robeson, one of the world's most recognizable concert artists, made the song his own. Now came Joan Baez.

It was dark in the wee hours of the morning, but fireworks may as well have gone off when Baez sang "Joe Hill." The significance of her performance of the song at Woodstock cannot be overemphasized. It was the third major milestone in the "Joe Hill" story and a monumental turning point in its evolution. With the insertion of "Joe Hill" into the context of current events Baez not only reinvented the song for a new generation, she broadened its application into yet another anti-war movement, as Robeson and others had done with the song during the Spanish Civil War.

As Josh Dunson has written, for a topical song to survive beyond the original context in which it was written, "it must be able to reach out and touch people who have not lived through the experience or emotion described in the song."[9] Joan Baez accomplished this. She would become as identified with the song as Robeson was and would record it several times, as he did. One of her albums on which she included "Joe Hill" is entitled *Carry It On* (1971). That is what Joan Baez and all others who sing it to this day continue to do for "Joe Hill."

Years later, writing in his autobiography, Joe Glazer said that Earl Robinson once facetiously told him that the Robinson family gives a prayer of thanks to Joan Baez every night.

In 1970 Swedish film director Bo Widerberg produced a film entitled *Joe Hill*, and John McDermott wrote a novelization of the screenplay, released concurrently with the movie. Earl Robinson and Joan Baez met during recording sessions for the film project. The song is one of Joanie's most requested numbers, Robinson later wrote, "so I expect she'll be singing it for many years to come."

Baez

JOAN BAEZ was born on Staten Island, New York, in 1941. Her father was from Puebla, Mexico, and her mother from Edinburgh, Scotland. Her paternal grandfather had left the Catholic Church to become a Methodist minister, and her maternal grandfather was an English Anglican priest. The family converted to Quakerism when Joan was quite young, which contributed to her lifelong pacifism.

Being half Mexican, Baez was no stranger to the kind of racism that plagued Paul Robeson and other people of color. As a high school girl she felt isolated from her peers. She had a Mexican name, skin and hair: the Anglos wouldn't accept her because of all three, and the Mexicans wouldn't accept her because she didn't speak Spanish. Her experience contributed to her identification with outsiders, whether they were minorities, laborers, or prisoners, and to her lifelong political activism and anti-war pacifism. "One of the saddest, stupidest things in our world is the segregation and discrimination of different races," she wrote as a high school senior, which is included in her memoir. She singled out Robeson, among others, as demonstrating what people of color are capable of.

Like Robeson before her, when she discovered she had been gifted with a voice to sing she chose not to have it professionally trained. And like Pete Seeger, whom her parents took her to hear when she was thirteen, and whose music deeply influenced her, she first tried the ukulele. It wasn't long after she learned to accompany her clear soprano voice with the guitar that she began singing in coffee houses around Harvard Square in Boston. She first came to wide public notice at the 1959 Newport Folk Festival, when she was invited on stage by Bob Gibson, the same Bob Gibson who had told Seeger about the Ku Klux Klan involvement in the Peekskill riots. On the strength of that appearance, Vanguard Records signed her to a recording contract.

In the summer of 1960, at the age of nineteen, she released her first album, and by Christmas *Joan Baez* was number three on the top 100 best-selling albums in the country, Soon enough the former coffee house singer was performing before 20,000 people in the Hollywood Bowl, and to her repertoire of traditional folk ballads she added songs that spoke out about civil rights and social issues.

David Bowie called Joan Baez the moral center of the anti-war and social justice issues that rose up in the Sixties. Her expanding repertoire would include such songs as the civil rights anthem "We Shall Overcome," Malvina Reynolds's anti-nuclear song "What Have They Done to the Rain," and Phil Ochs's "There but for Fortune." "Joe Hill" became a favorite, as it had with Paul Robeson before her.

His Truth

THE WOODSTOCK FESTIVAL took place almost twenty years to the day after the first, aborted Peekskill concert. While that earlier event descended into what Seeger biographer David Dunaway called the first full-scale riot of America's cold war, Woodstock fulfilled what it promised—peace and music with no violence. The two events forever linked together Paul Robeson and Joan Baez as champions of the song "Joe Hill."

Robeson was seventy-one at the time of Woodstock. Four years earlier, on the occasion of his sixty-seventh birthday, he had been honored at a gathering sponsored by *Freedomways* magazine that drew two thousand people to New York's midtown Americana Hotel. Among the participants in the event were writers James Baldwin and Paule Marshall; actors Roscoe Lee Brown, Ossie Davis and Ruby Dee; and musicians Dizzy Gillespie, John Coltrane, Earl Robinson, and Pete Seeger. Robeson embraced Seeger, who later in the program sang "We Shall Overcome."

Late in the evening Robeson rose to thank those assembled, and directed special attention to Lawrence Brown, whom he identified as an authority on Negro and classical music and his friend and partner in concerts for forty years. He then said that in all his time out of the country he never lost touch with the progress of civil rights in America, adding that achieving those rights for black people would not endanger them for whites, but would strengthen democracy for all Americans.

A significant component of that event was the participation of such young civil rights activists as Bob Moses and John Lewis. Fresh from facing the dangers of 1964's Freedom Summer voter registration drive in Mississippi and 1965's marches in Selma, Alabama, respectively, Moses and Lewis indicated by their presence that the new generation of movement leaders recognized Paul Robeson as a vital forerunner in the struggle for civil rights, and that they would be continuing the political activism for human rights that Robeson had been practicing for years. Lewis, who admittedly knew little about Robeson at the time, read remarks drafted for him by a fellow SNCC member that caught the flavor of the occasion: We are Paul Robeson's spiritual children; we, too, reject gradualism and moderation. Lewis quoted from Robeson's autobiography *Here I Stand* to the effect that the goal of equal rights could be achieved, adding that we hope to best honor you by performing that task.

The presence of those young, new activists and leaders solidified once and for all the knowledge that Paul Robeson was a pioneer of the civil rights movement. Lewis later said that meeting Robeson was a highlight of his life.

Paul Robeson's truth would go marching on.

☰ 10 ☰

Which Side Are You On?

"If a song is good, it keeps on ringing down through the years."—Pete Seeger

THE BOATS EMBARKED from Canada and Mexico, carrying members of the Venceremos Brigade who were bound for Cuba and a rendezvous with Fidel Castro's revolution. Founded in 1969 by members of the Students for a Democratic Society (SDS) and officials of the Republic of Cuba, the Venceremos Brigade was an organization of international volunteers who traveled to that island to work side by side with Cubans and to protest American embargo policies against that country. On board one of those boats in the winter of 1969–70 was a young man named David Beckwith, and en route he heard someone singing a song he was not familiar with.

"I learned 'Joe Hill' from an old commie on the Brigade," Beckwith said. "*Venceremos:* 'We will win! We shall overcome!'"

Beckwith, a former principal of the Great Lakes Institute in Toledo, Ohio, was a consultant who focused on strategic planning, organizational development, and organizing for social justice nonprofits and philanthropic organizations, similar to the work of Josh Dunson. He had been a community organizer, trainer, and consultant since 1971, and it was during training sessions and organizational rallies that he would turn to "Joe Hill." "The last line of that song will live forever," Beckwith once said. "The unfair execution of activists continues. That story moves us forward."[1]

Beckwith called Joe Hill the master of what he termed the zipper song, referring to how he could take on the Salvation Army street ministry bands and their songs and zip in new words. One memory Beckwith held of a time involving the song "Joe Hill" was a fundraising concert for the Farm Labor Organizing Committee (FLOC), the organization that had been founded by the renowned union organizer Baldemar

Velasquez and his father in 1967. Born in Texas in 1947 into a family of migrant workers, Velasquez would volunteer with CORE—the Congress of Racial Equality—before founding FLOC. For his lifelong activism he would receive a MacArthur "Genius" Award in 1989 and, in 1994, Mexico's Order of the Aztec Eagle, the highest honor that country awards to a non-citizen.

For the FLOC concert Beckwith arranged an event in a building in East Toledo that had been the union hall for the Toledo IWW. A "One Big Union" logo was still visible on the wall above the stage. Everyone sang "Joe Hill," led by a Canadian musician who had a leather pouch that contained some of Joe Hill's ashes that were sent to Wobblies after the execution. It was, Beckwith recalled, a powerful moment.

THE MUSICIAN'S NAME was Len Wallace. The "Squeezebox from Hell" is a phrase that has been used to describe Wallace's fiery accordion playing. A classically trained musician, Wallace has nevertheless claimed the accordion for folk music. He once commented that no other instrument has been so established in the homes of working people for so many years, and while the accordion has been the butt of endless jokes and disparaging remarks it remains an instrument that is central to folk traditions from Celtic and Quebecois music to Cajun, Zydeco, Tex-Mex, Klezmer and traditional American folk music. Believe me, he once said, you've never heard "Union Maid" until you've heard it on the accordion.

Wallace performs in many traditions, including Celtic, Irish and Scottish music, but singing for working people has always been at the forefront of his career. He has performed on picket lines, at rallies and demonstrations, in marches—for workers wherever the cause is just.

Sometime before participating in the FLOC fundraiser Wallace had received a gift from the Toronto members of the IWW, a red leather locket containing a pinch of the remaining ashes of Joe Hill. The union was honoring Wallace for his devotion to keeping the rebel tradition of Hill alive. He wears it every time he performs, and it was this pouch that David Beckwith saw at the Ohio event. The ashes came to Wallace after Mimi Conway, a Labor Heritage Foundation board member, conducted research in the National Archives in 1989. She checked a list of items the Archives was about to dispose of and saw that one item was an envelope containing ashes of Joe Hill. A reporter for the United Auto Worker magazine *Solidarity* got wind of the story and published it. The story caught the eye of someone in the Chicago office of the IWW and the ashes were turned over to the IWW. A pinch of them eventually wound up in Len Wallace's pouch.

Walter Reuther

1970: THE SONG "JOE HILL" reached yet another international audience when the Irish band The Dubliners, featuring the voice of Luke Kelly, included the song on its album entitled *Revolution*. The year also witnessed two significant deaths in the world of American labor: Walter Reuther, president of the United Auto Workers, was killed in a plane crash, and Ammon Hennacy, a legendary pacifist, activist, and Wobbly union organizer, died on a picket line.

In 1970 Alfred Hayes and Earl Robinson's "Joe Hill" turned thirty-four. From its beginnings it had been picked up and disseminated by and through labor unions and similar organizations and, in its most important leap forward, had been learned and taken into the repertoires of Paul Robeson and Joan Baez. But the death of Reuther and Hennacy demonstrated the song's further outreach. It had become a favorite not only of workers at home and abroad but also by leaders of those workers. Walter Reuther and Ammon Hennacy were two of those.

WALTER REUTHER WAS BORN in 1907 in West Virginia to German-American parents. From his father, who operated a horse-drawn beer wagon and was a Socialist and union organizer, Walter absorbed the lessons of unionism and the struggles and aspirations of working people. His mother would stage home debates so that her sons learned to think on their own about women's suffrage, child labor, and civil rights. Reuther's parents also practiced frugality, a habit Walter, neither a smoker nor a drinker, carried throughout his life.

At 19, Reuther left home for Detroit, talked himself into a job at Ford Motor Company, finished high school, enrolled at Detroit City College (now Wayne State University), organized rallies for Socialist Party political candidates, then went off on a three-year adventure with his brother, Victor. They worked in the Soviet Union, helping workers there decipher the production methods that Henry Ford had sold to that country. Later they traveled all over Europe, where they saw people of every race, religion, and nationality working for the same things—jobs with some degree of security and dignity, opportunities for their children, and essential freedoms. These lessons led Walter Reuther into the American labor movement.

By 1946, when he was elected president of the United Automobile Workers (UAW), Reuther had led successful union efforts against several of the major automobile companies, most notably the 1932 walk-out at the giant Ford River Rouge Complex in Dearborn, Michigan, a suburb of Detroit. This resulted in vicious beatings of union workers and organizers, including Reuther himself, by thugs enlisted by Henry Ford. During World War II, his ideas to transform the auto industry's capacity for the purpose of producing fighter planes for the Allies, subsequently called the "Reuther Plan," received the support of both union members and President Franklin Roosevelt.

In addition to his union advocacy, Reuther was a staunch supporter of the Civil Rights Movement and Cesar Chavez and the United Farm Workers. As a boy he had witnessed other boys throwing rocks at black people, and his father told him to never treat another human being like that. He marched with Martin Luther King, Jr., in Birmingham, Jackson, Montgomery, and Selma. He arranged funds for King's release from the Birmingham jail. He helped organize and fund the 1963 March on Washington, where he spoke before Dr. King's famous "I Have a Dream" speech. He served on the board of the NAACP. On the 25th anniversary of the UAW King wrote him a letter stating that more than anyone in America, Reuther stood out as the shining symbol of democratic trade unionism, and that one day all of America would be proud of him.

Reuther became president of the Congress of Industrial Organizations (CIO) in 1952, until it merged with the American Federation of Labor three years later, and continued as president of the UAW until his death. He survived two assassination attempts only to die in a plane crash on May 9, 1970. The National Transportation Safety Board later determined that various parts of the plane had either been incorrectly installed or were missing, fueling speculation that Reuther had been murdered. Coretta Scott King spoke at his funeral, saying that Reuther was to black people the most widely known and respected white labor leader in the nation. He was fighting the whole world's fight, she said.

"Joe Hill" was Walter Reuther's favorite song. At his funeral Earl Robinson sang it. Joe Glazer, who had sung the song with Reuther at the merger of the AFL-CIO, also performed at the ceremony. Years later Reuther was posthumously awarded the Presidential Medal of Freedom by President Bill Clinton, who remarked that although Reuther died a quarter of a century ago the nation had still not caught up to his dreams.

Ammon Hennacy

BORN IN 1893 and raised on an Ohio farm by Quaker parents, Ammon Hennacy seemed destined to activism, passive resistance to authority, and self-styled Christian anarchy. He grew up a Baptist, resisted conscription during World War I, joined the Socialist Party and the Industrial Workers of the World in the early 1910s, and took part in defense activity for Joe Hill in 1915. He was a non-smoking, non-drinking veg-etarian who espoused simple living and activism in opposition to war and nuclear proliferation.

In the 1930s he met activist Dorothy Day, a former Chicago social-ist and IWW activist who had converted to Catholicism in 1927. On May Day 1933 she appeared in New York's Union Square selling (for a penny) a new newspaper, the *Catholic Worker*. This marked the begin-ning of a new kind of radical movement. Day believed in socialist ideas that were rooted in Christian gospel, not in the works of Karl Marx. She founded the Catholic Worker Movement and began offering meals and shelter to destitute people in the first "hospitality house." Hennacy remained an associate of Day's for years, but in 1961 he moved to Salt Lake City where he established Joe Hill House.

Joe Hill House was designed to be a welcoming place for transients and migrants who might otherwise be scorned by society. The *Salt Lake City Tribune* reported that the city was minding its own business when Ammon Hennacy blew into town. "Don't say you weren't warned." It is no small irony that Hennacy named his hospitality house for Joe Hill, in the city where Hill was executed. The hierarchy of the Catholic Church, not to mention the FBI and many other organizations and individu-als on both the political right and left, distrusted the Catholic Worker movement. But Ammon Hennacy was a firebrand who started the Joe Hill House largely as a one-man operation. He would eventually leave the Catholic Church altogether, denouncing it and any organized reli-gion for supporting exploitation and war. He never paid federal taxes because they helped fund war.

ONE PROMINENT ASSOCIATE of Hennacy's was Utah Phillips. Bruce Duncan Phillips was born in Cleveland, Ohio, in 1935. His father was a labor organizer, and his parents' activism would prove critical to Phil-lips's later development. After his parents divorced and his mother remarried, Phillips grew up in Salt Lake City. He served in the United States Army for three years in the 1950s, and the devastation and suf-fering he witnessed during the Korean War traumatized him. Follow-ing his discharge, he took to hoboing, riding the rails, and writing songs as a way to clear his head and straighten out his political think-ing. When he returned to Salt Lake City, Phillips joined Hennacy at Joe Hill House.

Phillips worked at Joe Hill House for eight years, during which time he helped Hennacy publish *If I Were Free: A Collection of Songs Sung Every Friday Night at the Joe Hill House* under the imprint of the Utah Wobbly Press. The typewritten booklet included two introductions by

Hennacy—one a sketch of Joe Hill's life and another on Hill House—as well as four Hill songs and the Hayes/Robinson ballad.

In 1965, the fiftieth anniversary of Joe Hill's execution, the Friends of the Salt Lake Library sponsored a lecture and concert entitled "If I Were Free." Hennacy delivered the introduction to the event, and when the *Deseret News* reported on it, the article concluded with the verses of "Joe Hill."

Five years later Ammon Hennacy died of a heart attack while on a picket line. His ashes were scattered around the Haymarket monument, now Forest Home Cemetery, in Chicago, where fifty-four years earlier some of Joe Hill's ashes had been scattered and where several of the Haymarket martyrs are buried, as are Helen Gurley Flynn, Lucy Parsons, Emma Goldman, and Franklin Rosemont, among others. In the future Utah Phillips would often mention Hennacy during a concert, calling him a regular one-man revolution in America.

Honoring Paul

ON APRIL 8, 1968 London's Royal Festival Hall was the site of a celebration of Paul Robeson's life. Among those who participated were actresses Peggy Ashcroft and Mary Ure, the two British Desdemonas to Robeson's Othello, as well as actors Peter O'Toole and Michael Redgrave. Tributes poured in from the likes of actor John Gielgud and violinist Yehudi Menuhin. That same year twenty-seven countries held celebrations of Robeson's seventieth birthday.

In 1971 an entire issue of *Freedomways*, the quarterly journal of the Freedom Movement, was devoted to Robeson. The publication referred to Robeson as "The Great Forerunner." In that same year *Ebony* magazine named him one of the "10 Greats of Black History."

The Song Keeps on Ringing

As JOAN BAEZ was bringing "Joe Hill" to a new generation, Alfred Hayes was enjoying success as a writer for such television programs as *Alfred Hitchcock Presents, Twilight Zone, Nero Wolfe* and *Mannix*. In 1972 labor historian Archie Green began a series of letters to Hayes, hoping to discuss "Joe Hill." The letters went unanswered.

That same year Barrie Stavis published a new edition of *The Man Who Never Died*, with an introduction by Pete Seeger. "A song is an insubstantial thing," Seeger wrote. "When the echo dies, it's gone.

But if it is a good song, the echoes will be sent ringing again and again through the years.... The song about Joe Hill, written in the late 1930s by Earl Robinson and Alfred Hayes, carried the name of Joe Hill around the world."[2] The song, then thirty-six years into its journey, had kept on ringing, and would continue to ring around the world due to the efforts of people like Earl Robinson, Paul Robeson, Pete Seeger, Utah Phillips, and Joan Baez. There would be many more.

Another important publication in 1972 was Pete Seeger's *The Incompleat Folksinger.* Commenting on the book's title, editor Jo Metcalf Schwartz explains that it is a takeoff on *The Compleat Angler,* published in 1653 by Izaak Walton. That book, says Schwartz, was a tutor of fishing skills, but it lives on because it brings to life an enthusiastic, honest human being who wishes to be of service to his fellow men—a sentence that well describes Pete Seeger. In *The Compleat Folksinger* Seeger refers to the Industrial Workers of the World as the singingest union America ever had and Joe Hill as one of the union's best songwriters. Hill, Seeger writes, was brave, generous, lighthearted, single-mindedly dedicated to his cause, thoughtful toward others, and always militant.

ON CHRISTMAS DAY 1972 Lawrence Brown died. The accomplished pianist, researcher, and sometime vocalist had accompanied Paul Robeson for forty years. He had been a pioneer in the introduction of Negro spirituals to the public, as early as his publication *Spirituals: Five Negro Songs* in 1923, and Robeson credited with awakening him to much of his own people's music. Brown had retired in the early 1960s. He last saw Robeson when the singer's health was beginning to decline, and his own health was failing. He lived in his home on West 135th Street for four decades until he passed away at Harlem Hospital. Lawrence Brown was 79.

Harlan County USA

IN 1973 MINERS at the Brookside Mine in Harlan County, Kentucky, went on strike against the Eastover Coal Company, owned by Duke Power Company, seeking better wages, fair labor practices, and safer working conditions. For Harlan County, it was *déjà vu* to a similar situation forty years earlier.

In 1931 miners in the county had gone on strike against company owners, seeking the same kind of concessions that miners were now demanding in 1973. But in the midst of the Great Depression, the 1930s strike stretched out into a near-decade long confrontation, with miners and union organizers on one side and owners and law enforcement—and

hired thugs—on the other side. The situation was marked by violence
and deaths on both sides, and the county came to be known as "Bloody
Harlan." At long last the miners won the right of union representation.

Two notable side results of that 1931 strike were the emergence of
the folk singer known as Aunt Molly Jackson and the creation of the
famous labor song "Which Side Are You On?" written by Florence
Reece. A native of Kentucky, Mary Magdalene Garland Stewart Jackson Stamos—forever known as Aunt Molly Jackson—was no stranger to
mining and its dangers. She had lost one husband to a mining disaster;
her father was temporarily blinded in another. She joined United Mine
Workers and began writing and performing protest songs.

In the midst of the Harlan strike a group of writers, including Theodore Dreiser and John Dos Passos, came to Kentucky on a fact-finding
mission. Jackson sang them her song "Hungry Ragged Blues," on
the basis of which they encouraged her to go to New York. There she
became active in the folk and radical communities and performed with
Woody Guthrie and Pete Seeger. At the time of her death, on September
1, 1960, she had recorded a few original songs, some of which were later
included on an anthology issued by Rounder Records.

Reece, whose husband Sam was a union organizer, wrote her song
after the local sheriff came looking for him. In *The Incompleat Folksinger*, Pete Seeger describes the incident this way: Mrs. Reece was home
one day when Sheriff J.H. Blair and his "deputies" came to her house.
They poked their rifles into closets, under beds, even into piles of dirty
clothes before leaving. She tore a calendar off the wall and wrote her
song on the back. Fitted to an old hymn tune, "Which Side Are You
On" remains one of the most widely beloved of all union songs. Years
later, when he shared the stage with then elderly Reece at a Washington,
D.C., rally, Joe Glazer asked if she was nervous before the audience of
300,000. Why should I be? she retorted. I wasn't scared when those gun
thugs were trying to break up the union in Kentucky!

Kahn and McCutcheon

IN LATE SUMMER 1973 a young but seasoned community and civil rights
organizer stopped off to visit his cousin in Pittsburgh, where the United
Mine Workers of America was holding its annual convention. He discovered his cousin, a union employee, flat on his back on his hotel bed,
a wet washcloth over his eyes, moaning. He was groaning over the state
of the miners' strike in Harlan County. He asked his organizer cousin
for help.

The young organizer was Si Kahn. He was born in 1944, the son of a Pennsylvania rabbi, who was a cantor and violinist, and a mother who was an accomplished classical pianist and who liked to recite poetry. Kahn grew up surrounded by music in synagogue and at home, where he also gained a firm grounding in family values and social justice. After studying at Harvard, he began his career as an organizer in 1965 when for several months he worked with the Student Nonviolent Coordinating Committee (SNCC), the militant student wing of the Southern Civil Rights Movement. Kahn was stationed in Forrest City, Arkansas, named for the slave trader Nathan Bedford Forrest, a former Confederate general who in 1867 had been elected the first "Grand Wizard of the Invisible Empire" (the Ku Klux Klan) at the Maxwell House Hotel in Nashville, Tennessee.

At Harvard, Kahn had majored in medieval history and literature, not because he saw it as preparatory to becoming an organizer—"At that time in my life, I didn't even know there was such a thing as an organizer"[3]—but because he liked it. As it turned out, his knowledge of feudalism proved useful in trying to do community and civil rights organizing in the rigid, caste-conscious South. One particular aspect of his medieval studies that fascinated Kahn were the troubadours of the twelfth and thirteenth centuries. "At some subliminal level, I must have known even then that I was going to become not only a community organizer but a folksinger."

Kahn has said that he first became a songwriter after falling in love with the old songs he heard in the 1950s on old Library of Congress recordings, among them music by Texas Anna Gladden, known for her Appalachian ballad singing; John "Sin-Killer" Griffin, a hymn-singing evangelist from Louisiana, bluesman McKinley Morganfield (later known as Muddy Waters), and Aunt Molly Jackson. In the 1960s and 1970s he discovered that many of the musicians he admired were still alive and well, and heard them not on record but on front porches and in churches. He heard Sarah Ogan Gunning, a singer from the eastern Kentucky coal fields, like her half-sister Aunt Molly Jackson; Florence Reece; the Appalachian banjo and guitar player Roscoe Holcomb; the "high, lonesome" sound of bassist and guitarist Hazel Dickens from West Virginia; and the SNCC Freedom Singers, led by Bernice Reagon, who later founded the *a cappella* group Sweet Honey in the Rock.

"I put Si in the same category as Woody Guthrie and Pete Seeger," said writer and musician Rosanne Cash, "and, in a strange way, as my dad, who shared his righteous sense of humanity and his love of the 'meek,' who he truly believed who inherit the earth."[4]

His experience with SNCC inaugurated Si Kahn's career as a

community organizer, a path that has continued uninterrupted for six decades. In Harlan in 1973 the strike was not as violent as its predecessor, although at one point both sides began to openly brandish weapons. It wasn't until the fatal shooting of miner Lawrence Jones by a company guard that the two sides finally sat down at the bargaining table to settle the thirteen-month confrontation. The on-location presence of filmmaker Barbara Kopple and her team also likely contributed to the reduced violence. Kopple's resulting work, *Harlan County USA*, would win the 1976 Academy Award for best documentary film.

During the strike, Si Kahn met another musician who had come to Harlan to support the miners. This was John McCutcheon.

AUGUST 28, 1963. The television was on in the afternoon in the McCutcheon house in Wisconsin—a most unusual occurrence. McCutcheon's mother was watching the March on Washington for Jobs and Freedom. It was the centennial year of the Emancipation Proclamation. Young John joined her to watch as 250,000 people gathered along the reflecting pools before the Lincoln Memorial. The day's program began with the National Anthem sung by Marian Anderson, the world-renowned contralto who during her long career performed everything from opera to spirituals around the world. In 1939 the Daughters of the American Revolution had denied Anderson, because of her race, the opportunity to sing at Constitution Hall. First Lady Eleanor Roosevelt responded by helping Anderson perform at an open-air concert that same year on the steps of the Lincoln Memorial. Twenty-four years later she stood on those steps again.

McCutcheon and his mother listened to speeches by John Lewis and Walter Reuther and, of course, Martin Luther King, Jr. Beyond the speeches, something else caught John McCutcheon's attention—the music. In addition to Marian Anderson and Mahalia Jackson there were folk singers, the like of which John had not heard before. Here were Peter, Paul, and Mary; Joan Baez; and Bob Dylan. It was McCutcheon's introduction to folk music and spirituals. He was riveted, and sought out more. He also listened to Paul Robeson recordings. At that time he didn't even know that Joe Hill was a real person. By the time he arrived in Harlan County, McCutcheon knew about Joe Hill and was playing the guitar—and would go on to master many stringed instruments.

"John McCutcheon is not only one of the best musicians in the U.S., but a great singer, songwriter, and song leader," said Pete Seeger. "And not just incidentally he is committed to helping hard working people everywhere to organize and push this world in a better direction."[5]

The significance of the Kahn and McCutcheon meeting to

American folk music cannot be overstated. It would prove invaluable not only to their individual careers but also to the ongoing folk song movement in America and to the endurance of the song "Joe Hill." Si Kahn would, in the future, name his own company Joe Hill Music, and he and McCutcheon formed a friendship that continues to this day. Both men have developed into prolific songwriters, they frequently collaborate on projects, and have each gone on to create substantial bodies of original work.

Joe at Joe's

IN 1974, UNDER the auspices of the United States Information Agency, Joe Glazer made one of his many tours of Scandinavia. In Sweden his hosts escorted him to the Hägglund family home at 28 Nedra Bergsgatan in Gävle, which is now a Swedish national historical landmark. Once there, Glazer was greeted by labor leaders and members of the print and radio press. Soon he found himself giving a mini-concert of Joe Hill songs and telling the story of Hill's short life and tragic death in the United States. Glazer, of course, had sung Joe Hill's songs at a hundred meetings in the United States and other countries, but he was thrilled to sing them in the very home where Hill had been born almost a century earlier. The audience could not get enough of the adventures of their hometown celebrity. Glazer closed his impromptu concert with the Hayes/Robinson ballad. Echoing what he and Edith Fowke had written in *Songs of Work and Protest*, Glazer told those assembled that the song is the most important factor perpetuating the memory of Joe Hill.

    The song "Joe Hill" had now come full circle, sung in the very house in which Hill had been born.

ONE YEAR AFTER Joe Glazer's visit to Sweden, Pete Seeger and Arlo Guthrie released a double album called simply *Together in Concert*. They had sung together before and would continue to do so, but this selection of performances from different American cities represented one of their earliest recorded collaborations. It was like a reunion of the Seeger and Guthrie clans, a friendship that dated back to the 1940s when Pete and Woody traveled together across the country. Seeger had included "Joe Hill" on his 1964 album *Songs of Struggle and Protest 1930–1950*. Now "Joe Hill" became a prominent feature of the Pete and Arlo set list.

    Pete Seeger never failed to show which side he was on during his solo performances, as he did at a 1977 fund-raiser in Homestead, Pennsylvania, for Ed Sadlowski, who was running for president of the

Steelworkers Union. As Joe Klein described it in *Rolling Stone*, Seeger "was almost stunned by the explosion from the audience when he hopped onto the stage."[6] Homestead was the site of an infamous 1892 strike when some 300 armed Pinkerton agents were sent to break the strike at Carnegie Steel Works. They were met there by 10,000 strikers who were armed and ready to fight. The Pinkertons were routed and sent running.

In 1975 FINLAND'S Turku Student Theatre, founded in 1946, released an album of Joe Hill's original songs, along with the Hayes/Robinson ballad.

One of the most unusual performances of "Joe Hill" took place in March 1975. In New York for some concerts, Earl Robinson called Cathy Douglas, wife of Supreme Court Justice William O. Douglas. Robinson had met the justice and his wife before and had visited them at their summer home in Goose Prairie, Washington. There he had sung to Douglas his cantata entitled "Ride the Wind," inspired by the justice's work. Now, in New York, Justice Douglas, who graduated from Columbia Law School in the same class as Paul Robeson, was recovering from a stroke. Robinson took his guitar and, Mrs. Douglas at his side, sat at the foot of the justice's bed and sang. He repeated "Ride the Wind" and performed "Joe Hill" as well as some of Joe Hill's original songs. The event turned into a mini-concert when hospital staff crowded around the door of Douglas's room to listen.

THAT SAME YEAR Josh Dunson launched Real People's Music, an organization that specialized in diversity and multicultural programming. Over the years his artists and activists have included Peggy Seeger, Laura Fuentes, Joe Heaney, Ola Belle Reed, and Si Kahn, who has remained a close friend. Dunson himself learned "Joe Hill" from Paul Robeson recordings. "My parents were happy that I learned it," he says. "We all loved Paul's singing."[7]

Heaney, a native of County Galway, Ireland, grew up accustomed to evenings when families would gather together to sing and tell stories. He believed that traditional music should be presented as it was taught to him but also injected with creativity, the non-purist kind of approach singers have used regarding "Joe Hill." Reed, a native of North Carolina, very early learned the claw hammer banjo style and regularly sang old-time mountain songs with her family. She was named a recipient of a National Heritage Fellowship in 1986 in recognition of her contributions to American folk music.

Dunson says that it is personal connections and the love of the music that got him started in this business. When people ask him what he does for a living he answers, "make trouble." He is adamant when he says that he doesn't connect with anyone who doesn't connect with him. The kind of folk music he represents must reach out to people.

The Tallest Tree

ON JANUARY 23, 1976 Paul Robeson died at the age of seventy-seven. The towering figure who had been the leading ambassador of "Joe Hill" for almost four decades had been in declining health and lived his final years in relative seclusion, most frequently at his sister's house in Philadelphia. Marian Robeson Forsythe, a retired schoolteacher, was a seventy-two-year-old widow when Paul came to live with her in 1966. Some days Marian would invite Charlotte Bell, a piano teacher who lived close by, to visit and play for Paul, who would softly sing his favorites.

He had been celebrated with a "Salute to Paul Robeson," a seventy-fifth birthday gala at Carnegie Hall in 1973, which he could not attend but to which he sent a taped message. Speaking at the event Coretta Scott King proclaimed that Robeson has been buried alive because he championed human dignity and civil rights long before her husband had. A symposium on his life was staged at his alma mater, Rutgers.

In 1974 an article in the *Philadelphia Evening Bulletin* suggested that perhaps Paul Robeson had been born thirty years too soon. The writer, Hans Knight, further commented that the Robeson who was vilified as a communist in the past would be welcomed on talk shows now as a goodwill ambassador. Times have changed, Knight wrote, not least because of the courage of Paul Robeson.

Robeson's funeral service was held at Mother A.M.E. Zion Church in Harlem, where his late brother Ben had presided for many years. Despite the cold and rain some five thousand mourners came—black and white, liberal and conservative, famous and not famous, friends and complete strangers whose lives he had touched. Speaking again, as she had at the earlier gala, Mrs. King publicly deplored America's inexcusable treatment of a man who had the courage to point out her injustices. Other speakers included Robeson's friend Dr. Sam Rosen, who had shared the Peekskill riots with him; Lloyd Brown, who had attended those riots and helped Robeson write his autobiography; and Paul Jr. who said that while his father's last years contained disappointment because illness had forced him to retire, he did so undefeated and unrepentant.

Robeson's mistreatment at the hands of his own country's government was—and remains—a national disgrace. Since the early 1940s he had endured continued official harassment from the FBI—his mail opened, his phones tapped, agents trailing him, with the result that many people were afraid to be seen with him. What they have done to Paul has been the cruelest thing I have ever seen, said W.E.B. Du Bois. The persecution of Paul Robeson by the government has been one of the most contemptible happenings in modern history, said Bishop J. Clinton Hoggard, a boyhood friend. This was a man who bore on his body the marks of Jesus, marks of vengeance. Bishop Hoggard delivered the eulogy at Robeson's funeral, ending with a phrase that echoed Joe Hill—"Don't mourn for me, but live for freedom's cause."

When he was called before the HUAC in 1956, Robeson was asked why, if he liked the Soviet Union so much, he didn't stay there. He answered, "Because my father was a slave, and my people died to build this country, and I am going to stay here and have a part of it just like you. And no fascist-minded people will drive me from it. Is that clear?"[8] The reason you are here, a committee member said, is because you are promoting the communist cause in this country. To which Robeson shot back that he was there because he opposed the neo–Fascist cause that he saw arising in this committee. You are the real un–Americans, he told the committee members, and you should be ashamed of yourselves. Finally, in 1974, after more than three decades of persecuting Paul Robeson, the FBI declared that no further investigation of him was warranted. It was a concession that was far too little and far too late.

Purdue University had planned a celebration of Robeson's life and work. When word came of his death, the event was turned into a memorial. Earl Robinson composed a special tribute, which was performed on piano by Jenny Vincent, the New Mexico musician and political activist who had sung with Seeger and Robeson at the 1948 Progressive Party convention for Henry Wallace.

In 1977 television reporter and interviewer Gil Noble created the first documentary film about Paul Robeson. For a title to the documentary he referred back to a comment that educator Mary McLeod Bethune had made years earlier on the occasion of Robeson's forty-sixth birthday: Paul Robeson was "The Tallest Tree in Our Forest."

ONE YEAR after Robeson died, James Baldwin referred to him in an open letter that he wrote on behalf of a group of blacks that was protesting a play that they felt trivialized Robeson's life and misrepresented his character. Baldwin's letter stated that while Robeson is not yet a historical figure, he lives in the hearts and minds of the people whom he touched, the people for whom he was an example, and the people who gained from him the courage to resist.

Twenty years later a journalist named Lerone Bennett, Jr., celebrated Robeson, commenting:

> Before King dreamed, before Thurgood Marshall petitioned and Sidney Poitier emoted, before the big breakthroughs in Hollywood and Washington, before the Jim Crow signs came down and before the Civil Rights banners went up, before Spike Lee, before Denzel, before Sam Jackson and Jesse Jackson, there was Paul Robeson.[9]

What had formed the lifelong core of Robeson's ethic were convictions passed on to him from his father and from his study of the Fourteenth Amendment. William Robeson had taught his son that we are all brothers and sisters, and that we should remain true to our conviction without succumbing to bitterness or unkindliness. And from the amendment, that he had written his thesis about at Rutgers, no state should deprive any person of life, liberty, or property without due process of law. Considering the unjustifiable treatment that Robeson endured at the hands of his own government and many fellow Americans, it is a remarkable achievement that he retained his own sense of dignity, kindliness, and optimism. *New York Times* writer Arnold Lubasch later underscored Robeson's continued aspirations for human dignity regardless of race or nationality when he wrote:

> He traveled through much of the world but remained forever a man of America, with deep roots in his native land. We are left with the recordings of his wonderful voice singing songs of America—the many spirituals, the labor anthem "Joe Hill," the historic "Ballad for Americans," and his signature "Ol' Man River." His life should be remembered by our people, restored to it rightful place in our history, secured in the soul of our nation—it is a ballad of America.[10]

There were his two major ballads—"Ol' Man River" and "Joe Hill." In his adaptation of the song from *Show Boat* Paul Robeson had sung that he must keep fightin' until he was dyin.' That is exactly what he did. And in the very conduct of his life he echoed "Joe Hill": Where people stand up for their rights that's where you'll find Big Paul.

Unbending. Despite everything.

⇒ 11 ⇐

Telling It Like It Is

"This is one of the most important songs ever written."
—Gov. Tom Kean

NEARLY 10 YEARS after her performance at Woodstock Joan Baez again found herself at a rock concert, this time in Ulm, Germany. Backstage the promoters were betting that an audience that was there to hear rock and roll music might boo her off the stage. Baez was welcomed with polite applause, but her opening song flopped. She cut it short and talked about the Sixties and Woodstock. Then she sang "Joe Hill," and the crowd cheered.

Labor Heritage Foundation

IN 1978 JOE GLAZER and Archie Green, an expert on labor music and folklore, had a conversation about the future of labor union music— Glazer, the seasoned union operative as well as "Labor's Troubadour," and Green, the Canadian-born, Southern California-raised veteran of the Civilian Conservation Corps and the U.S. Navy. After earning a B.A. in political science from the University of California at Berkeley, Green spent twenty years at the San Francisco shipyards as a member of the United Brotherhood of Carpenters and Joiners. He later returned to academia for an M.L.S. degree from the University of Illinois and a Ph.D. in folklore, specializing in labor lore (the special folklore of workers), from the University of Pennsylvania. That love of folklore had been partially sparked in 1942, when Green bought Lead Belly's recording *Work Songs of the U.S.A.*

In his conversation with Glazer, Archie laid it on the line: Joe, he said, it's great that you and your music are in demand, but you can't do this alone and you can't do this forever. We must find young people and

135

nurture them so that in a few years we will have a whole stable of union singers across the country.

One result of that conversation was the creation of the Labor Heritage Foundation. Working with Glazer to establish that organization were Joe Uehlein, a musician and AFL-CIO staffer, and Saul Schniderman, a federal employee union member and labor history activist. As outlined in its mission statement, the Foundation serves to strengthen the labor movement through its participation in all the arts, to preserve and promote knowledge of the cultural heritage of the American worker, and to conduct research through written and oral histories. In other words, give the people the artistic tools and they will use them.

AT THE TIME the foundation was launched, Schniderman was a local officer of the American Federation of State, County, and Municipal Workers Employees. He had started his own musical sideline in 1975 with a trio called Folkworks, in support of a strike by *Washington Post* pressmen. The group remained active at union rallies, festivals, and on picket lines through the 1980s.

Schniderman is now chair of the Labor Heritage Foundation. He is the founder of the Inventory of American Labor Landmarks, a Foundation project that maintains a catalog of sites that commemorate the history and heritage of American workers. From 1982 to 1988 he edited *Talkin' Union*, a magazine of music, labor lore, and history. In 2000 he led the efforts to place a historical marker at the site of Mother Jones's death in Adelphi, Maryland. He has also served as the president of the Library of Congress Professional Guild, AFSCME Local 2910, and remains a board member of the Metro Washington Community Services Agency, AFL-CIO and of the Battle of Homestead Foundation that celebrates that 1892 strike and promotes relevant labor history.

Schniderman now writes an online newsletter entitled *Friday's Labor Folklore: Con Carbon, the Minstrel of the Mine Patch*, a weekly shout-out of critical information regarding both historical and contemporary milestones in American labor history. Con Carbon is a reference to Cornelius "Con" Carbon. Born into a mining family in Hazleton, Pennsylvania, in 1871, with his tenor voice and Irish brogue and wit Con Carbon became a singer and storyteller beloved to the labor community. He died in 1907. Schniderman's newsletter consistently highlights such heroic men and women as well as important moments in labor history.

Joe Hill was the subject of one such newsletter. In that edition of *Friday's Labor Folklore* Schniderman recounted the major events of Hill's life, stating unequivocally that he was convicted in an unfair trial in an atmosphere of anti-union hysteria. In that entry Schniderman includes five musical selections, "The Preacher and the Slave" by Mac McClintock, "The Rebel Girl" by Hazel Dickens, "Casey Jones the Union Scab" by Pete Seeger, "Joe Hill's Last Will" by John McCutcheon, and the Paul Robeson version of "Joe Hill."

JOE UEHLEIN learned "Joe Hill" at home. He grew up in a union family on the banks of Lake Erie, where his father was a founder of the CIO in Lorain, Ohio, and worked in the steel mills. The elder Uehlein served with the United Steel Workers and as president of the Pennsylvania AFL-CIO. Uehlein's mother worked for the Amalgamated Clothing Workers Union (ACWU) and was editor of the CIO *Sun* in Cincinnati. Both were musical as well, Uehlein's father playing guitar and his mother the piano, and sing-a-longs were routine family fare.

"A lot of what we played were labor songs," Uehlein says. "My parents had a lot of recordings by Joe Glazer, Pete Seeger, and Woody Guthrie. I learned 'Joe Hill' from them. They sang it all the time."[1]

Uehlein played electric guitar in high school bands and then, at Penn State, turned back to the music of Glazer, Seeger, and Guthrie, as well as Paul Robeson. His experience reads like a working person's model resume: work in Pennsylvania mills, organizing in Mississippi, and, after settling in the Washington, D.C., area, founding the Labor Network for Sustainability and Voices for a Sustainable Future; a member of the National Advisory Board of the Union of Concerned Scientists, and serving in various capacities with the United States Climate Action Network (USCAN) and the AFL-CIO.

Uehlein plays roots-rock and Americana music with his band The U–Liners, and "Joe Hill" is a staple of the group's repertoire. He says:

> We should sing the song and talk about Joe Hill and the IWW and its theory of trade unionism. In recent years there have been strikes regarding the lack of covid-19 protective equipment, many by workers who don't have a union. We have seen workers strike in support of students demanding action on climate change, again without a union. We could be witnessing the birth of a new labor movement. It's important that people know about the IWW and Joe Hill, the man and the song.[2]

THE LABOR HERITAGE Foundation began with a three-day event called the Great Labor Song Exchange, held in 1979 in the George Meany Center for Labor Studies in Silver Spring, Maryland. The gathering attracted a dozen or so singers and musicians to share their music and writing and to discuss the effective use of music in labor activism. From that humble beginning the event, now renamed the Great Labor Arts

Exchange, has expanded to include all the arts and annually attracts hundreds of participants.

Interviewing Alfred

IN 1982 WRITER Gwen Gunderson interviewed Alfred Hayes in California. According to Archie Green, Gunderson found Hayes ambivalent about his original poem, claiming to have simply dashed it off one morning when he may have been as young as nineteen, while living with his parents on East Fremont Avenue in the Bronx. He recalled a little room overlooking an airshaft, where he got up one morning and wrote it in about a half-hour. He did not name any specific political or union event that had inspired the poem, nor did he tell her how or when he became aware of Joe Hill. And while he thought Earl Robinson's tune catchy, he did not think it was a song that would last.

That same year an interview conducted by Judith Spiegelman for the volume *Contemporary Authors* yielded a similar result: Hayes made no reference to "Joe Hill." What was clear at this point was that Alfred Hayes wanted his legacy to be based on what he considered his more mature and complex work, his novels and poetry, and not on "Joe Hill" or the political context in which it was written.

IN DECEMBER 1982 Earl Robinson's mother, Hazel, lay dying of cancer in a Seattle hospital. On his last visit with her, Robinson sat by her bed and, just as he had done for Justice William O. Douglas seven years before, played the guitar and sang to her. Hazel Robinson had been proud to know Paul Robeson, so her son sang the entire "Ballad for Americans" to her, as well as another song she held dear, "Joe Hill."

"I Get Chills"

IN 1983 FLYING FISH Records received an unsolicited cassette of original songs from an at-the-time-unknown folksinger. On the basis of the strength of those songs, the company offered the singer a recording contract, something almost unheard of in the music business. The resulting album announced the arrival of singer-songwriter John O'Connor.

O'Connor began working in factories in Waterloo, Iowa, when he was fresh out of high school. Those experiences and an interest in folk music in general and Woody Guthrie in particular led him to launch his career as a folk musician with a strong affiliation with the labor movement. He has issued several CDs of traditional as well as original songs, and he continues to perform and speak about labor and social movements.

"I don't remember when I learned 'Joe Hill' or who I first heard sing it," O'Connor said, but it must have been from someone in the labor movement in Iowa. It is part of a repertoire of labor songs I have been singing since 1971.

> The song's strength is that it can be sung without introduction. The audience doesn't even have to know who Joe Hill was. Paul Robeson and Pete Seeger popularized the song in the 40s and 50s, and millions learned the song when Joan Baez sang it at Woodstock with no context whatsoever. That is the genius of the song. It can be sung in almost any political context. It is difficult to think of another song in the canon of labor that is as moving as Joe Hill. There are great rallying songs like "Roll the Union On" or utopian songs like "Solidarity Forever," but I still get chills when I am singing "Joe Hill" properly.[3]

Carry It On

IN 1984, TWELVE years after his letters to Alfred Hayes had gone unanswered, Archie Green made one last attempt to contact the author of "Joe Hill." As he later wrote, "Caught between my respect for his privacy and my feeling that we needed his recollection of the ballad, I telephoned him at his San Fernando Valley home in Encino on February 12. Ascertaining my purpose, he terminated the conversation."[4]

ALFRED HAYES DIED on August 14, 1985, at the age of 74. With his passing the exact time and place of the origin of the poem "Joe Hill" was lost. Fortunately, the creation of the song had a specific time and place: Camp Unity, June 1936. Since World War II and launching his career as a scriptwriter for film and television Hayes had deflected attempts to associate him with the song. After his younger and more political days, during which he wrote "Joe Hill," he entered a period of political disillusionment. His first two novels, *All Thy Conquests* and *Shadow of Heaven*, had identified him as a writer of serious fiction, while his third, *The Girl on the Via Flaminia* (1949), brought him his first commercial success. Hayes, like many a writer before him with a novel or two to his credit, then moved to Hollywood, lured in part by the prospect of lucrative work. After a flurry of success, particularly in the 1950s, his film assignments tapered off and he turned to writing for television.

At the same time he continued to produce what he considered his serious writing—the novels *Love* (1953), *My Face for the World to See* (1958), *The End of Me* (1968), *The Temptation of Don Volpi* (1960), and *The Stockbroker, the Bitter Young Man, and the Beautiful Girl* (1973), as well as the poetry collections *Welcome to the Castle* (1950) and *Just Before the Divorce* (1968). In one poem from *Welcome to the Castle,* "As a Young Man," the narrator recalls his young self and wonders who remembers the volunteers in Spain or the miners in Lawrenceville? Time, he writes, has had the ultimate laugh.

While the first three of those novels from the 1950s have been reissued by the *New York Review of Books*, forming a kind of trilogy, and there have been recent essays devoted to Hayes, his work remains too often overlooked. As Alex Harvey claims, in his aforementioned documentary *The Lasting Worth of Alfred Hayes*, one reason for Hayes's invisibility in the United States may be that his refined sensibility and acute gaze is more European in its quality. The great irony is that his novels perfectly capture the texture of midcentury American life.

Herbert Mitgang opened the second paragraph of his *New York Times* obituary of Hayes with reference to "Joe Hill." In a similar fashion, the heading of the Hayes obituary in the *Chicago Tribune* read: "Alfred Hayes, screenwriter, 'Joe Hill' poet." As Earl Robinson later wrote in his autobiography, Hayes may have wanted to distance himself from "Joe Hill," but times came, years later, when "Joe Hill" saved both Hayes and himself from going broke.

Alfred Hayes deserves to be remembered for the substantial poetry and fiction he produced, and he deserves to be—and will forever be—remembered for "Joe Hill," which, to what might have been his surprise, has become one of the world's most long-lasting songs.

The year Alfred Hayes died, Pete Seeger and Bob Reiser published *Carry It On: A History in Song and Picture of the Working Men and Women of America*. The book contains eighty-four songs, dating from 1770 to the time of publication. Among those they thank in the Acknowledgments are Joe Glazer, for collecting and singing labor songs for more than forty years; Saul Schniderman, for keeping union history alive through his magazine *Talking Union*; and historians Philip Foner and Joyce Kornbluh.

Foner is the author of dozens of books on labor history, black history, and women in the labor force, including *The Case of Joe Hill*. He also served as editor of *The Letters of Joe Hill* and *Paul Robeson Speaks: Writings, Speeches, Interviews 1918–1974*. Kornbluh, a former executive secretary of the AFL-CIO Joint Minimum Wage Committee, edited and wrote introductions for the influential volume *Rebel Voices: An*

I.W.W. Anthology. Seeger and Reiser also thank John Uehlein, who transcribed and edited all of the songs in the book while finishing his thesis at Columbia University. Uehlein, who is Joe Uehlein's brother, also transcribed the music and language in the Labor Heritage Foundation Songbook.

In the Foreword to the book Seeger and Reiser write:

> With songs and pictures we try to tell how the working people of this country—women and men; old and young; people of various skin shades, various religions, languages, and national backgrounds—have tried to better their own lives and work toward a world of peace, freedom, jobs, and justice for all.[5]

The songs include several by Joe Hill as well as the Hayes/Robinson ballad, and Alfred Hayes is credited as the lyricist. The following year Seeger, Si Kahn, and musician and activist Jane Sapp collaborated on an album entitled *Carry It On*. Like Joan Baez's earlier album of the same name, the Kahn, Sapp, and Seeger collaboration contains "Joe Hill," and credits both Hayes and Robinson.

Pete Seeger, seen here in Newburgh, NY, in August 1987 doing what he did best—getting people to sing along—was a lifelong proponent of "Joe Hill," a song, he said, that rings on down through the years.

ABEL MEEROPOL, the prolific writer of "Strange Fruit," "The House I Live In," and many other songs, had continued his association over the years with Camp Unity, where he served as a counselor and counted among his charges the future jazz saxophone virtuoso Sonny Rollins. But since the early 1970s he had been suffering from Alzheimer's disease. Meeropol's oldest son would play "Strange Fruit" for him in the nursing home, and while Meeropol was beyond recognizing anyone, he seemed to know the song and perked up when he heard it. The man who had sung "Joe Hill" to his sons was now having his own song played back to him. Finally, in October 1986, fifty years after he heard "Joe Hill" debuted around a campfire at Camp Unity, Abel Meeropol passed away in a Jewish nursing home in Longmeadow, Massachusetts. He was eighty-three.

In 1999, sixty years after it had denounced "Strange Fruit" as NAACP propaganda, *Time* magazine named it the Song of the Century.

Rise Up

IN 1988, SING OUT PUBLISHERS released a songbook entitled *Rise Up Singing*. The book contains "Joe Hill" in its Work section, credited to both Hayes and Robinson. The lyrics, as they appeared, had undergone slight changes: In the fifth stanza the line

> "Where working men are out on strike"

was included as

> "Where workers strike and organize."

And in the following stanza

> "Where workers strike and organize"
> Says he, "You'll find Joe Hill"

was now rendered as

> "Where workers stand up for their rights/
> It's there you'll find Joe Hill."

In the introduction to the book, Pete Seeger writes, "If a song seems too complicated, skip it. Come back later. When a song seems inappropriate to you, note that in the margin. No one would want to sing all the songs in this book. I don't. Change a word. Add a verse. This is known as 'the folk process.'"[6] In those few words Seeger concisely describes the process by which songs are renewed time and time again to update them and make them fresh, precisely what Paul Robeson memorably did and many others continue to do with "Joe Hill."

No less stellar a folk and blues musician than Josh White once weighed in on the folk process, saying that if the story of a song doesn't run true to form you can write into it, add and subtract from it. That's one thing about folk songs, he said. You're at liberty to do this kind of thing.[7]

IN AUGUST of that same year Earl Robinson received phone calls from friends who told him that Governor Thomas Kean of New Jersey, the keynote speaker at that year's Republican National Convention, was reciting "The House I Live in," announcing to the nation that he had grown up with the song. Reading a transcript of Kean's speech, Robinson realized that the governor had recited a verse including the name of Frederick Douglass, the one-time slave who escaped his bondage to become a renowned author and abolitionist. This was a version of "The House I Live In" that only Paul Robeson had used.

Robinson wrote a letter to *The New York Times* to say that while he thanked Gov. Kean for quoting from the song, neither he nor the late lyricist Lewis Allan (Abel Meeropol) intended the song to be for the Republican Party or the Democratic Party or, for that matter, any "ism," but rather for people of all stripes and colors. "It is living proof," he wrote, "that a song may transcend politics and give a message to all Americans and people everywhere as to what our country is all about."[8]

On the strength of that letter Robinson received an invitation from the governor's office to meet with Kean in Trenton. When they met Governor Kean thanked Robinson for coming. "I've been looking forward to this. I'm a fan of Paul Robeson—he's a Jersey man, you know. I have every one of his records." Kean then declared that "Joe Hill" is one of the most important songs ever written. "It tells it like it is."[9]

ON THE FOLLOWING Christmas Eve Robinson received the news that Jessie Lloyd O'Connor had died. O'Connor was the granddaughter of Henry Demarest Lloyd, a nineteenth-century social reformer and author of *Wealth Against Commonwealth,* a denunciation of the oil industry. Her father, William Bross Lloyd, a prominent lawyer and active member of the Socialist Party and the Communist Propaganda League, had once been indicted for sedition. His defense lawyers included Clarence Darrow, the lawyer known for his involvement in the American Civil Liberties Union and for his defense of John Scopes during the so-called Scopes "monkey" trial. Jessie's mother, Lola Maverick Lloyd, was a pacifist and founder of the United States section of the Women's International League for Peace and Freedom.

Jessie had married Harvey O'Connor, a devoted socialist and

member of the Industrial Workers of the World. Harvey worked with Federated Press, a labor news service, and Jessie established herself as a labor journalist in her own right. She also had long been a benefactor of Earl Robinson. A gift from O'Connor had helped Robinson complete his 1986 recording *Earl Robinson Alive and Well*, an album that contained some of his best-known songs, including "Black and White," "Same Boat, Brother," "The House I Live In," and "Joe Hill." At O'Connor's memorial in Rhode Island Robinson made sure to include "Joe Hill," knowing how much she liked the song.

Don't Mourn—Organize!

AT THE GREAT LABOR Arts Exchange in 1989 the Labor Heritage Foundation inaugurated the Joe Hill Award to honor leaders and artists who have contributed to the successful integration of arts and culture in the labor movement. The foundation gives the award to individuals based on their dedication, participation, and promotion of labor, labor arts, culture, organizing, and/or history. Among the recipients of the award are Cesar Chavez, Hazel Dickens, Anne Feeney, Joe Glazer, Archie Green, John Handcox, Si Kahn, John McCutcheon, Utah Phillips, Saul Schniderman, Pete Seeger, and Joe Uehlein.

In January 1990 Earl Robinson discoursed on Joe Hill at a Labor Heritage Festival in San Francisco that was organized by California members of the AFL-CIO. Pete Seeger sang during the event. That same year Seeger collaborated again with Bob Reiser to publish *Everybody Says Freedom: A History of the Civil Rights Movement in Songs and Pictures.*

THE YEAR 1990 also witnessed an important development in the perpetuation of the life and legacy of Joe Hill himself—the creation of the Joe Hill Organizing Committee. Salt Lake City attorney Brian Barnard helped found the committee to arrange a 75th anniversary commemoration of Hill's death. Members of the committee were teacher and activist Robert "Archie" Archuleta, educator and artist Christine Leaming, musician Kate MacLeod, pipefitter Hyram Matthews, musician Duncan Phillips (son of Utah Phillips), historian John Sillito, Joe Hill biographer Gibbs Smith, screenwriter Bryan Stubbles, and historian Lori Elaine Taylor.

On Labor Day 1990 the committee sponsored a free concert in Sugar House Park, the site of the former prison where Hill was executed seventy-five years earlier. The Utah State Prison was closed in 1951 and its buildings razed to make room for the park. Performers included Joe Glazer, Utah Phillips, Earl Robinson, and Pete Seeger. Robinson sang

"Joe Hill," while Glazer, Phillips, and Seeger each performed one of Hill's own compositions. It was, Glazer said, a beautiful day under blue skies and warm sunshine and Joe Hill.

Another Joe Hill tribute appeared in 1990 in the form of a recording entitled *Don't Mourn—Organize! Songs of Labor Songwriter Joe Hill.* Released by Smithsonian Folkways, the record was compiled by Lori Elaine Taylor, then assistant archivist in the Smithsonian's Office of Folklife Programs. Taylor provided comprehensive liner notes on each song, adding:

> It is precisely through the rituals of mourning and commemoration that singers, speakers, and artists have organized their audiences. Performers participate in a dynamic musical and political tradition by perpetuating Joe Hill's ideals and following his example. The songs, the images, the legends and memories of Joe Hill—and of other songwriters within this tradition— are used to forge a sense of community.... The songwriters who followed Joe Hill are links in a chain of political music.[10]

She names as examples of those links Woody Guthrie, Bob Dylan, and Phil Ochs, as well as Pete Seeger, Si Kahn, Hazel Dickens, Utah Phillips, and others.

The disc includes two versions of "Joe Hill": the Paul Robeson version with Alan Booth on piano and one by Earl Robinson, accompanying himself on guitar. Alfred Hayes is credited in both versions. Because of this song in particular, Taylor writes, the story of Joe Hill has continued to touch a large audience. Other artists appearing on the recording include English-born singer Billy Bragg, Hazel Dickens, Joe Glazer, Cisco Houston, Harry "Haywire Mac" McClintock, Utah Phillips, and Pete Seeger, as well as Elizabeth Gurley Flynn with a short-spoken narrative.

The same year that *Don't Mourn—Organize!* was released Bragg issued a recording entitled *The Internationale Live & Dubious.* The EP contains his own song "I Dreamed I Saw Phil Ochs Last Night," using Earl Robinson's "Joe Hill" music. Bragg has said that hearing the rock band The Clash in concert in London in 1977 marked his initiation into the use of music in support of political activism. *The Internationale* is a political album, and a later reissue of the recording included additional tracks not on the original release, among them a version of "Joe Hill."

Change of Address

ON JULY 20, 1991, Earl Robinson was killed in Seattle when the car he was driving was hit head-on by a drunk driver. He was identified in the first sentence of his *New York Times* obituary as the man who composed the music for the song "Joe Hill." His hometown *Seattle Post Intelligencer* headed his obit: "'Joe Hill' Composer Robinson." *Los Angeles Times* writer Burt Folkart referred to the song as an unofficial anthem for the Flower Children of the '60s and '70s, as it had been for their working class mothers and fathers.

At the conclusion of his autobiography *Ballad of an American*, written with Eric Gordon, Robinson drew attention to his late-in-life interest in yoga and spirituality. "Having come to the end of this book, you can appreciate the continuity of themes in my life," he wrote. "There is in fact no separation between the Old Left and the New Age Robinson. I point again to the song 'Joe Hill': That line 'I never died' forms the natural bridge between the old and new Earls. I don't need to give up one for the other." After all, he once quipped, death is just a change of address. He concluded the book, writing, "I thank whatever powers are responsible for leading me to the words of 'Joe Hill.' For that song brought me to this clarity."[11] Earl Robinson was eighty-one.

In the liner notes to Robinson's 1963 album *Earl Robinson Sings*, Irwin Silber, then the editor of *Sing Out!* magazine, recalled a time when People's Songs had been asked by striking maritime workers to send some singers to entertain a large meeting at St. Nicholas Arena in New York. The singers were struggling to hold the seamen's attention when someone at the back of the hall shouted, "How about 'Joe Hill'?" That did it. Suddenly five thousand tough, striking seamen began singing. The packed hall, wrote Silber, became unified in a way that is hard to describe. He recalled that when the singers were finished, there were no other songs to sing, and no others were necessary.

Silber remembered little else about that strike, but that one incident remained clear in his mind because he recognized that he had participated in one of those moments of history which are rarely recorded in a book but which have a significant impact on men's lives—the creation of a spirit of solidarity among men with common problems and a common task. It is no small thing, he said, for a composer to have created a work that lives in men's hearts the way "Joe Hill" has. If Earl Robinson had done no more than write the music for "Joe Hill" he would have the right to feel that his "walk in the sun" had meaning.

EARL ROBINSON will forever be remembered as the composer of "Ballad for Americans," "Lonesome Train," "Black and White," "The House I Live In" and many other songs, as well as "Joe Hill." But whereas Alfred Hayes later distanced himself from the song, Robinson never deflected his connection with it. He promoted it and performed it openly and gladly for the rest of his life. As he wrote in his autobiography:

I suppose that for fifty-five years my close identification with this song has served to almost pass Joe Hill's mantle to me, though this could be said of others, too, like Woody Guthrie or Pete Seeger, or later Bob Dylan or Phil Ochs.... But in truth there is no mantle. Each of us is unique. The important thing is that our song lasted and lasted, encouraging each new generation to study Joe Hill's life, and find in it the strength to keep up the struggle.[12]

While both men went on to create other substantial work, it is not at all farfetched to say that their most lasting creation is this one song about a martyred labor icon. Perhaps "Joe Hill" was, in the beginning, a statement born out of youthful idealism and exuberance. With Robinson's music, it became a song of mature and defiant optimism.

It became, in other words, a song of ongoing international relevance.

≈ 12 ≈

Fellow Workers

"There is no room for wimps in this business."
—Maxine Waters

PAUL ROBESON, Alfred Hayes, and Earl Robinson were gone. Woody Guthrie, John Steinbeck and Abel Meeropol were gone. With their passing a chapter closed on "Joe Hill." But spearheaded by Pete Seeger, Joe Glazer, Joan Baez, Utah Phillips and others, "Joe Hill" was in good hands as it approached the twenty-first century and its own sixth decade.

No Root, No Fruit!

AFTER HIS EXPERIENCE at Joe Hill House, Utah Phillips launched his own career as a folksinger and storyteller. His 1983 live recording *We Have Fed You All a Thousand Years* is a collection of songs from the IWW *Little Red Song Book* and includes the Hayes-Robinson ballad. Like Joe Hill before him, Utah Phillips and the Industrial Workers of the World were made for each other. In addition to becoming a consummate performer of folk and labor songs and a walking archive of labor lore and hobo history, he was a member of the IWW, proudly carrying Card #X318003. A self-proclaimed Christian anarchist pacifist, no one spread the Wobbly gospel more effectively than did Utah Phillips.

In the liner notes to *We Have Fed You All for a Thousand Years*, Phillips wrote that he sing these songs for a damn good reason, because they gave him a history he never got in school. His high school books gave him a history of the ruling class, he complained, a history of the industrialists, the bankers and the presidents that didn't get caught. And all the military leaders. So, he felt that when he went out into the working world to barter his labor for a paycheck he was armed with the tools that were somebody else's class background.

We need a whole new history of our people, because the one we've got doesn't serve us very well, he concluded. "That's why I sing these songs. That's why I tell these stories, dammit. No root, no fruit!"[1]

As *New York Times* reporter Nikole Hannah-Jones has written, "We all suffer for the poor history we've been taught."[2]

Utah Phillips now stood as one of the most prominent agents for folk and labor music in general and "Joe Hill" in particular. He and Pete Seeger, Joe Glazer, and Joan Baez would be joined by a number of like-minded performers and songwriters who have sung and recorded "Joe Hill" and songs by Joe Hill. These are the singers and songwriters—the witnesses and fellow workers—who testify to the ongoing relevance of the song.

Springsteen

WITH THE RELEASE of his 1975 album *Born to Run* Bruce Springsteen firmly established himself as a leading rock-and-roll star and, at the same time, a powerful voice for working people.

In 1981 a chance meeting with Vietnam veteran Ron Kovic, author of *Born on the Fourth of July*, led Springsteen to front a benefit concert for the Vietnam Veterans of America. That experience, and his subsequent reading of Henry Steele Commager's *A Pocket History of the United States* and Howard Zinn's *A People's History of the United States*, further engaged his thinking about what it means to be an American; and Joe Klein's *Woody Guthrie: A Life* led him to a deeper exploration of Guthrie's America.

That exploration showed in Springsteen's next release, the 1982 album *Nebraska*. On this recording Springsteen sounded unlike any of his previous records. The album is like nothing so much as a small movie about people stuck between the proverbial rock and a hard place. Instead of the high-energy rock and roll that had been his trademark, Springsteen presented a series of bleak acoustic songs dealing with blue-collar people who were facing difficult challenges and critical turning points in their lives. The album solidified Springsteen as standing squarely in the musical and political traditions of not only Woody Guthrie and Bob Dylan but of Joe Hill himself. *Nebraska* also showed that he had inherited the mantle of John Steinbeck as a voice for the people. In the ensuing years he would alternate between his rock and roll statements and this other side of himself.

THE YEAR 1981 also saw the release of a double album entitled *An English Folk Music Anthology*, a compilation of folk songs recorded in the 1970s and 1980s by Sam Richards and Tish Stubbs. "Joe Hill" leads off Side 4 under the heading "Recent Songs of Known Authorship."

In his liner notes to the anthology Richards, a London-born writer, composer, jazz pianist, and folk singer and song collector, writes:

> Conceivably the best known industrial or political song in the British trade union and labour movement is the American composition "Joe Hill" by Alfred Hayes and Earl Robinson. There is hardly a union activist who has not heard it, many can sing along with it, and all who in any way concern themselves with singing informally at weekend schools and conferences seem to know it.[3]

The version of "Joe Hill" on the anthology is sung by the English folk musician George Strattan, who was known in his country for many years as a folk singer, trade unionist, and peace campaigner who included the song in his regular repertoire. (Strattan died in 2009).

As Richards wrote elsewhere, some idea of the popularity of "Joe Hill" can be gained from a trade union colleague of Strattan's named Ian Parr. He claims that when he sings there is the automatic assumption: "You must know 'Joe Hill,' Sing us 'Joe Hill.'" When Richards asked Parr who requested the song at his weekend and conference appearances, whether it was solely agitators and politicos, Parr replied, "No. Anybody really. Anybody."[4]

Why Was He Shot?

IN 1984 historian William Adelman, vice president of the Illinois Labor History Society (ILHS), took stacks of petitions requesting an official pardon for Joe Hill to Utah's Governor Scott Matheson. The effort had been directed for several years by ILHS president Leslie Orear from his tiny East Harrison Street office in Chicago. Orear was optimistic about the campaign drive, but Gov. Matheson refused to receive Adelman. The governor said in a television appearance that exoneration was not possible because the Hill case was still unclear, to which IWW historian Fred Thompson retorted, "If the case in unclear why was Joe Hill shot?"[5]

A Legend of the Sea

IN FEBRUARY 1986 nearly 1,000 people crowded into the Los Angeles Hilton Hotel to cheer Harry Bridges, founder of the International Longshoremen and Warehousemen's Union (ILWU), as he approached his eighty-fifth birthday. A dozen speakers praised the man as "a legend of the sea" who had become one of the most powerful labor leaders in American history, the man who led workers through the bloody strike in 1934 that shut down San Francisco, the man who defied government attempts to deport him due to alleged subversive activities.

"Harry Bridges symbolizes and epitomizes what the labor movement is all about," said Assemblywoman Maxine Waters (D–Los Angeles). "You've got to be prepared to shut them down, to go to the streets and I mean everything. There is no room for wimps in this business."[6]

Harry Bridges was no wimp. He had outlived all opposition. At the ceremony singer Ronnie Gilbert, a former member of The Weavers who, as a child, had attended Camp Wo-Chi-Ca, led the assembled in several songs that praised working people, concluding with "Joe Hill."

The Ghost of Tom Joad

FOLLOWING HIS READINGS in American history and the life of Woody Guthrie, Bruce Springsteen drew further inspiration from John Steinbeck's *The Grapes of Wrath* and John Ford's film version of that book. The result was the 1995 album *The Ghost of Tom Joad*. This album was Springsteen's comment on the economic divisions of the eighties and nineties, on the hard times facing many of the people whose work and sacrifice had created America. It features a title track that directly references Steinbeck's protagonist. Springsteen has his own protagonist sitting down in the campfire light, declaring that wherever there is hatred in the air, he'll be there.

That same year filmmaker B.J. Bullert produced a documentary on Earl Robinson entitled *Ballad of an American*. In the film Robinson discusses the creation of "Joe Hill," adding that the song has been traveling ever since.

IN 1997 UTAH PHILLIPS teamed up with folk musician Mark Ross to release a recording entitled *Loafer's Glory*. The two are pictured on the cover of the disc sitting around—what else—a campfire. In the liner notes for the album Ramblin' Jack Elliott wrote that Utah Phillips made him wish that he hopped a few more freights, an experience that has given him a wealth of songs and stories about a disappearing America. In his own notes to the recording, Phillips writes that the album is a collection of songs and stories about the traveling life, most from three decades on western freight trains. Loafer's Glory, he says, is the name of a hobo jungle under the old Western Pacific water tower by Keddie, California, at the top of Feather River Canyon.

Mark Ross grew up in a liberal Democratic household in New York, where his parents, who were not themselves musicians, nevertheless listened to a lot of music. Among the music he remembers hearing was Paul Robeson's version of Earl Robinson's "Ballad for Americans." Then, at the age of eight, he heard Pete Seeger and The Weavers. Ross has played the banjo ever since, and has added guitar, mandolin, and harmonica.

Ross dates his own political activism to the 1960s, when, at the age of seventeen, he joined the folk music boom that was happening in New York. There he met Utah Phillips, and the first song he heard Utah sing was Joe Hill's "Preacher and the Slave." During the 1970s Ross did a residency at the Folklore Center, where his repertoire included "Joe Hill" and other labor songs. He has lived in Oregon for the last twenty years, as this is written.

Also in 1997 Phillips launched *The Loafer's Glory: A Hobo Jungle of the Mind,* an eclectic radio program broadcast from Nevada City, California, where he lived. Referring to himself in a typically self-deprecating manner as "the Golden Voice of the Great Southwest," he offered up what he called music known and unknown and years of sheer recollection hammered together, proving once again, he said, that no matter how long he vacuumed the bag was never full. Among the subjects of his earliest programs were Woody Guthrie, Ammon Hennacy, Joe Hill, Billie Holiday, Aunt Molly Jackson, and Earl Robinson.

IN 1999 UTAH PHILLIPS recorded "Joe Hill" again, this time on a song and spoken word collaboration with Ani DiFranco entitled *Fellow Workers.* In the liner notes to that compact disc historian Howard Zinn wrote that listening to "Joe Hill" by Phillips and DiFranco reminded him of the Industrial Workers of the World—the IWW or Wobblies—that magnificent bunch of people who in the early years of the twentieth century formed One Big Union and brought everyone in, including people who had been shut out of the old conservative unions—among them black workers, women, and immigrants.

WITH THE BANDS Rage Against the Machine and Audioslave, guitarist and songwriter Tom Morello became known as much for his strong political views as for his music. Born in New York's Harlem and raised in Illinois, Morello came by his political convictions early. His African father participated in the Mau-Mau uprising from 1952 to 1960 that ended British rule in Kenya, and later served as Kenya's first ambassador to the United Nations. His mother, of Irish/Italian heritage, started Parents for Rock and Rap, an organization that protested censorship in music. His paternal great-uncle, Jomo Kenyatta, was the first elected president of Kenya and a friend of Paul Robeson.

In addition to his band affiliations Morello performs a solo acoustic act known as The Nightwatchman. In this guise he recorded a version of "Joe Hill" for his 2011 EP *Union Town,* using Alfred Hayes's lyrics but with original music. Morello calls Joe Hill the poet laureate of the working class—hero, martyr, and uncompromising rebel—whose life and music laid the groundwork for Woody Guthrie, Dylan, Springsteen, The Clash, and Rage Against the Machine.

In an interview with C.J. Gronner of *No Depression* magazine, Morello claimed Joe Hill as his favorite musician even though there are no known recordings of him. Hill, said Morello, was on the front lines risking life and limb to try to create a better, more just world. That's why they killed him. But as the song says, Joe Hill ain't dead. Wherever, whenever you raise your fist, Morello added, your voice, or your guitar in the name of justice and freedom, Joe Hill is right there by your side.

The interview took place on November 19, 2015, two days after a Joe Hill Centenary Concert at The Troubadour club in Los Angeles, an event that featured Morello, Joan Baez, and others, and concluded with everyone singing "I Dreamed I Saw Joe Hill Last Night."

JOAN BAEZ could have been in this song, said Steve Earle of "Christmas in Washington," from his 1997 album *El Corazon.* Written by Earle, the song calls on Woody Guthrie, Martin Luther King, Emma Goldman, Joe Hill and Malcolm X—all of whom were involved in the struggles of their times and all of whom remain iconic and inspiring figures long after their deaths—to rise again and address our turbulent contemporary times. Earle explained that Baez is a hero to him because she sang "Joe Hill" at Woodstock and continues to sing it.

Earle launched his music career in 1974 as a songwriter in Nashville. Soon enough he began recording his own songs, later forming a group called The Dukes as his music became harder-edged and more influenced by rock. At the same time he became more outspoken in his political views. He has on numerous occasions invoked the spirit of Joe Hill, as when he read Hill's last will and testament during a Voice of the People's History of the United States event in November 2006 and sang "Joe Hill" at an Amnesty International meeting in Madison, Wisconsin.

Robeson at 100

IN APRIL 1998 former Wo-Chi-Ca campers held a reunion, the first since 1976 when they had gathered to mourn the death of their friend and hero, Paul Robeson. Now, twenty-two years later, they came together to mark the centennial of Robeson's birth. They joined in on old camp songs and sang along to Robeson's recordings of the "Ballad for Americans" and "Joe Hill."

In *The Guardian* of April 8, 1998, Martin Kettle wrote that along with Louis Armstrong and Joe Louis, Paul Robeson was one of the most famous black Americans of his times. But whereas Armstrong and Louis each honed one skill superbly, Robeson was an athlete, linguist, actor, singer, and political activist—a role model for all people, whatever their color.

In the Robeson centennial year the operatic bass Kevin Maynor released an album entitled *Paul Robeson Remembered.* Four years later another operatic singer, Willard White, followed suit with this recording *The Paul Robeson Legacy.* And in 2006 the father-son duo of Leon and Eric Bibb released *Praising Peace: A Tribute to Paul Robeson.* All three recordings include "Joe Hill."

Extraordinary Jobs

ON SEPTEMBER 29, 2006, Joe Glazer died at his home in Silver Spring, Maryland. Four years earlier he had released his autobiography, *Labor's Troubadour,* the story of his half-century of writing, singing, and organizing on behalf of union and labor movements in this country and around the world. And as Glazer's daughters can testify, their father's activism was a family affair. Patti Glazer recalls:

> My sister, Emily, and I grew up marching on picket lines, stuffing envelopes for various causes while sitting around the dining room table, and standing on street corners handing out pamphlets at election time while my father sang political jingles. Although Joan Baez helped make the song "I Dreamed I Saw Joe Hill Last Night" famous at Woodstock, I grew up singing that song. I thought labor-organizing songs like "Joe Hill," "We Shall Overcome," and "Solidarity Forever" were typical folk songs that all kids grew up singing![7]

Pete Seeger, who knew Glazer for fifty years, said that he had done an extraordinary job in his life, not letting people forget the great union songs. Labor folklorist Archie Green credited Glazer with leaving a legacy of lasting value to the labor movement through his own songs and his recordings of union classics. Singer/songwriter Bucky Halker has written, "Although there are plenty of musicians who are performing labor songs, Joe Glazer is the only person around who worked within the mainstream union structure and kept music at the forefront of his work. The story of his life as a labor songsmith is absorbing and important."[8]

That same year the World Folk Music Association had awarded Glazer its Lifetime Achievement Award, in recognition of a life of unwavering passion and purpose.

"Protest songs use humor, they tell about terrible conditions, but you still have to be able to laugh and sing and tell a joke," Glazer once told *The New York Times*. "You know, that is an important thing—life goes on." Glazer's best known original song was "The Mill Was Made of Marble," wherein a mill worker dreams of a heaven where nobody ever gets tired and nobody ever grows old. Joe Glazer's good works will never grow old. He was eighty-eight.

THE FOLKSONG and labor music world lost another towering figure who had done an extraordinary job when Utah Phillips died in Nevada City, California, on May 23, 2008. Phillips once described his mentor, Ammon Hennacy, as a one-man revolution in America. The same might be said of him. Labor organizer, storyteller, folksinger, songwriter, radio broadcaster—Utah Phillips was all of these, as well as a vital inspiration to a younger generation of like-minded musicians and activists.

In his *New York Times* obituary of Phillips, music writer Jon Pareles quoted Phillips's comment from a podcast to the extent that after his traumatic experience in the Korean War, his lost period of drifting, and his experience at Joe Hill House, he finally found his calling as a singer and songwriter. "I discovered a dignified, ancient, elegant trade, one where I could own what I do and never have to have a boss again."[9]

He plied that trade like few others before or after him. What Utah Phillips did over the years was to present concerts that were as much history lessons as songfests, during which he would expound on labor lore, the Wobblies, and the value of direct political action, and he could deliver his messages with what Pareles referred to as a trove of "one-liners," memorable comments that never failed to bring laughter from his audiences and underscore Joe Glazer's emphasis on the importance of humor. His songs were recorded by many other artists, among them Ani DiFranco, Emmylou Harris, Rosalie Sorrels, Ian Tyson, and Tom Waits. By the time health issues in his last years curtailed his public appearances he had become an elder statesman of the folk community and a keeper of the flame of labor songs. Utah Phillips was seventy-three.

IN 2009 SOME FORTY ARTISTS, including Joan Baez, Ani DiFranco, Arlo Guthrie, Richie Havens, Kris Kristofferson, Taj Mahal, Dave Matthews, Roger McGuinn (whose group The Byrds had turned many rockers on to such Seeger songs as "Turn, Turn, Turn"), John Mellencamp, Bruce

Springsteen, and others joined to mark Pete Seeger's 90th birthday at a celebration in Madison Square Garden, New York. Springsteen had been drawn into the Seeger orbit in 1997, when he had been invited to contribute a song to a planned tribute album to Pete. Knowing little about Seeger at the time, Springsteen immersed himself in Pete's music and was overwhelmed by what he found. The result was his 2006 album *We Shall Overcome: The Seeger Sessions*.

That same year the Veterans of the Abraham Lincoln Brigade published a special issue of its magazine, *The Volunteer*. Entitled "Robeson in Spain," the twenty-seven-page issue commemorates, in graphic art, the trip to Spain that Paul and Eslanda Robeson made from January 23 to 31, 1938.

A Sydney Story

ANOTHER JOE HILL STORY is featured on John McCutcheon's 2009 album *Untold*, a double CD half of which was recorded live at the National Storytelling Festival in Jonesborough, Tennessee. In the track entitled "Sydney/Joe Hill" McCutcheon relates a story about winding up his first tour of Australia twenty years earlier. Playing three nights in Melbourne, McCutcheon noticed the same man in the same seat in the front row each night. It was not his geography that caused McCutcheon to recognize him—it was his clothes. The man was dressed in pink short shorts and a sleeveless shirt, and was covered in tattoos—not the kind of appearance you necessarily expect of a 70-something-year-old guy. During an intermission McCutcheon spoke with him, and the man asked if McCutcheon would take a request. McCutcheon said, "You've earned it." The man named the song and why he wanted to hear it.

Twenty years earlier, the man had worked as an electrician on the construction of the Sydney Opera House. One day a limousine pulled up to the site and out stepped a towering black man wearing a beret. He was an American, very friendly, and introduced himself around to the workers, not the bosses. He had been on tour in Australia and heard about the building of the opera house, and before he returned home to the United States he wanted to be the first to sing at the site. The former electrician told McCutcheon that the man sang for almost two hours. And when he finished he told the workers that their work was not done—that they now had to go home and tell their children who it was that really built that opera house—that it was them, the workers, not the architects and the financiers, but the day-to-day construction workers, because if they didn't tell their children, nobody else would. They all had tears in their eyes—a construction site packed with hundreds of workers with tears in their eyes!

That day he ended up with a song that all of the workers knew—and that they joined in singing. The singer, of course, was Paul Robeson; the song, of course, was Robeson's special favorite.

In 2011 Si Kahn's one-man musical play *Joe Hill's Last Will* was produced in California, featuring John McCutcheon in the title role. The scene is Hill's cell in the Utah State Prison in Salt Lake City, ninety minutes before dawn on November 19, 1915, the day Hill is scheduled to die. A reporter from a local paper arrives to record Hill's last words, but before that happens Hill reprises the story of his life as well as his thinking on a number of topics. Based on Joe Hill's own words as well as from newspaper reports and court documents, the play addresses not only the story of Hill's life but that of labor, immigration, and workers' resistance in the early years of the twentieth century, and features many of Hill's original songs.

That same year the American band Anti-Flag released an album entitled *The General Strike*. The band included on this recording an original song, "1915," about the execution of Joe Hill, saying that every word he wrote, he spoke, he sang, we are still singing today.

The Almanac Trail

Sesame Street: This television show is where an aspiring musician in East Brunswick, New Jersey, first saw Pete Seeger. The young musician's name is Rik Palieri. He grew up in a household with parents who were not musicians but who had an extensive record collection of everything from show tunes and Italian opera to Elvis, Ray Charles, and Harry Belafonte. It was after he watched Pete Seeger that he became fascinated with the longneck banjo, just like Seeger back in 1936. When he finally obtained a banjo he bought Seeger's book *How to Play the Five-String Banjo* and practiced it obsessively.

One day Palieri played hooky from school to attend a Seeger concert at Douglass College, not far from where he lived. After the program he ventured backstage where Pete and his wife Toshi were having people sign a petition opposing the war in Vietnam. Palieri mustered up his courage and spoke with Seeger. As he later walked away Palieri felt his life changing. That day was the beginning of a friendship that would last the rest of Seeger's life. Palieri became a frequent visitor to the Seeger home in Beacon and soon was involved in Seeger's campaign to clean up the Hudson River.

At one point Palieri read Seeger's *The Incompleat Folksinger* and learned about the 1941 cross-country tour that the Almanac Singers had undertaken singing for unions. Palieri became fixated on the idea of recreating that trip, an idea that remained just that until 2012, when he met a fellow folksinger named George Mann.

George Mann was nine years old when he heard Joan Baez's version of "Joe Hill" on the Woodstock soundtrack recording. Growing up as a teenager on Long Island in the 1970s, Mann was into rock and roll, but later turned to folk music. Mann's parents were union members, and he came into his own as a political activist when he went to work for the musicians union in New York City and met a man named Julius Margolin.

The multi-faceted Margolin was a World War II veteran, a former merchant seaman, a union electrician, and a longstanding member of the CIO and the International Alliance of Theatrical Stage Employees (IATSE). Mann and Margolin met at the 1996 Great Labor Arts Exchange. That meeting inaugurated ten years of playing and recording together, during which they released three CDs, among them a series entitled *Hail to the Thief* during the presidency of George W. Bush. When he died, in August 2009 at the age of 93, scores of tributes and memories poured in, commemorating him for his lifelong activism on behalf of working people. One contributor wrote that like Joe Hill, Julius would always be standing right beside us in the struggle for social justice.

With his own work background and his collaborations with Margolin, Mann, a member of the IWW, launched his own career as a singer and songwriter devoted to the labor movement, and has released a number of recordings of his original songs.

When Rik Palieri contacted Seeger about recreating the Almanac Singers' trip, Pete responded with memories about the original journey. Before they embarked on the tour, Rik and George recorded an album entitled *The Almanac Trail*, covering songs of the original Almanacs Singers, as well as a version of "Joe Hill" that they did not include on the CD but kept for their road repertoire. When Rik mailed the finished CD to Seeger, just before he and George took to the road in July 2013, Pete's daughter drove him to the post office to pick it up. Seeger insisted on hearing the recording in its entirety in the car in the parking lot. "He was very happy," says George. "We had brought him full circle, in a sense."[10]

Rik and George launched their tour in Pittsburgh, as the Almanac

Singers had done seventy-two years earlier. It was their first stop on a thirty-two day tour playing for unions at twenty-three concerts in fifteen states. Joining them for several early concerts was activist and singer-songwriter Anne Feeney, whose most widely known song is "Have You Been to Jail for Justice?".

At several of their tour stops Palieri and Mann invited local artists to join them, including Larry Penn in Milwaukee, Bob and Diana Suckiel in Kansas City, and Joe Hickerson in Portland, Oregon. In San Francisco they visited 98-year-old Faith Petric, the longtime head of the San Francisco Folk Music Club who was known as the "Fort Knox of Folk Music" for her ability to remember the lyrics of thousands of songs. And across the bay in Berkeley they performed at a senior living facility where they met June Gordon, who presented Rik with a copy of her memoir of Camp Wo-Chi-Ca.

"The trail that Rik and I are on started with our mutual love for songs that tell stories and especially for these songs [of the Almanacs]," said George. "By carrying forward the work of people like The Almanacs, Utah Phillips, Joe Hill, and others, we are also paying back what we owe to them."[11]

There Will Never Be Another

ON JANUARY 17, 2014, Pete Seeger died in New York City. He had devoted his entire adult life to the causes of political freedom, civil liberties, the abolition of racism, the elimination of war, respect for the environment, and more, and in his last years he had not slowed down.

In October 2011, at the age of 92, Seeger participated in a march to express solidarity with the Occupy Wall Street movement. Dubbed "Occupy the Circle," the march culminated in Columbus Circle in upper Manhattan. There he performed with his grandson Tao Rodríguez-Seeger, Arlo Guthrie, David Amram, and other musicians. Rodríguez-Seeger feared the worst when a policeman approached, but the cop just reached out and shook his hand, saying, "Thank you. This is beautiful."

The following month, on Veterans Day, November 11, Joan Baez sang "Joe Hill" yet again during the Occupy Wall Street protest. In 2012 Seeger participated, along with Harry Belafonte and others, in a concert to bring awareness to the almost four-decade incarceration of Native American activist Leonard Peltier.

As much as any individual, Pete Seeger had demonstrated the power of song to stir the hearts and minds of people and inspire them to do what is right. Through his unceasing encouragement for people to sing together, he further demonstrated the magic of music to capture a single moment or energize a full movement. At his death the tributes poured in.

"Pete spent his life scattering seeds," said Rik Palieri. "Everywhere he went he would plant some seeds. He would say that some might fall on stone, but some might grow into tall oak trees. He lives on in our daily lives. Every time we gather together with friends to sing a song, walk in a picket line or go to recycling a bit of Pete is with us. I am just one of thousands that he touched and whose lives he changed."[12] In honor of his friend and mentor Palieri wrote a tribute song he called "I Dreamed I Saw Pete Seeger," using Earl Robinson's music from "Joe Hill."

Seeger's friend John Cronin, who taught a course entitled "Citizen Advocacy in the Evolution of American Democracy" at Pace University, tells a story that captures the Seeger charisma. In 2001 Cronin invited Seeger to meet his class because he could talk from first-hand experience about the movements the class was discussing—labor, civil rights, peace, environment. Seeger showed up with his banjo, and the classroom full of young people, who didn't know Seeger from Adam, looked at each other, whispering, "What? Who is this?" These were street-smart students steeped in rap and hip-hop—a hard group to impress. Within five minutes, Pete had them singing the union song "Joe Hill." At the next class they talked about him for forty-five minutes.[13]

At Seeger's 90th birthday celebration, Bruce Springsteen had paid tribute to the honoree, saying that "[a]t some point, Pete decided he'd be a walking, singing reminder of America's history, a living archive of America's music and conscience, a testament of the power of song." Springsteen added, "At 90, he remains a stealth dagger through the heart of our country's illusions about itself ... remind[ing] us of our immense failures as well as shining a light toward our better angels and the horizon where the country we've imagined and hold dear we hope awaits us."

"The key to the future of the world," Seeger once said, "is finding the optimistic stories and letting them be known." "My own biggest thing in life," he added, "is simply being a link in a chain." Pete Seeger was ninety-four.

⇒ 13 ⇐

Freedom Is a Constant Song

"And Woody Guthrie and Dylan and Pete Seeger and
Johnny Cash and Paul Robeson singing 'Joe Hill'—the
true popular poets of America"
                                        —Lawrence Ferlinghetti

FOUR MONTHS AFTER Pete Seeger died, Bruce Springsteen opened
a May Day concert in Tampa, Florida, by singing "Joe Hill." He chose
it to honor International Workers Day. In her online article "Joe Hill
Returns," Felicia Miyakawa wrote: "Backed by an impressive brass and
saxophone section ... backup singers join Springsteen's vocals and more
band members add their instruments to the growing sound. The effect
is metaphorical: when we come together we are powerful. When we sing
together our voices are stronger and our message is louder."[1]

WHEN WE SING together our voices are stronger. When we sing together
our message is louder. Pete Seeger had been hammering this message
home all of his adult life: "The revival of audience singing is an integral
part of the whole revival of interest in folk songs.... If we really love folk
music, we will get people singing with us."[2]

There are people all over the country who are carrying on the
folk traditions, says musician Ellen Harper, owner of the long-running
Folk Music Center in Claremont, California. "They are teaching and
playing and singing the folk songs that keep alive the voices of people past and present. When people come together to sing, be it in a
band, church, temple, picket line, protest march, ukulele club, or living room, wherever voices are raised together in song, that is a folk
music revival."[3]

ONE OF SI KAHN's recent songs is entitled "Freedom is a Constant Song."
From his fifth-floor window Kahn heard Black Lives Matter marchers

"singing back the fear, against the chill of a dream gone wrong," and wrote:

> They bring us courage, hope, and love
> For freedom is a constant song[4]

That is precisely what today's folksingers and songwriters are doing: they are singing back against the fear of things gone wrong, of things that may go wrong. They stand as witnesses whose art and activism testify to the continued relevance of songs like "Joe Hill," and in so doing they give us the strength to carry on fighting for freedom, to go to jail for justice. As Joe Hill wrote to ten-year-old Katie Phar, before his execution, "as long as we can keep singing and keep the spirit up, we are bound to win."[5]

Nothing More Thrilling

SHE HAD JUST FINISHED performing a multimedia program entitled "Troublemaker Working Albertans, 1900–1950" for the Pacific Northwest Labor History Association. When applause invited an encore, she started to sing "I dreamed I saw Joe Hill last night." For Maria Dunn, it was a magical moment. "Once I started the song the whole theatre audience sang it with me. There is nothing more thrilling than hearing all those voices sing it with you!"[6]

Born in Scotland, Dunn immigrated as a child with her family to Ontario, Canada, and now lives in Alberta. She trained in classical piano from a young age, later immersing herself in folk music as a volunteer disk jockey while enrolled at the University of Alberta. She soon began writing her own songs, and to date has released seven albums of original material.

Her most recent recording, *Joyful Banner Blazing*, continues her ongoing support of workers through such songs as "Heart in Hand," that commemorates the 1986 strike in northeast Edmonton's meatpacking district, and "Waltzing with the Angels," that celebrates the ironworkers who helped built Edmonton's CN Tower, that city's first high-rise. The song title refers to how those workers described called their dangerous jobs.

Dunn learned "Joe Hill" from *Sing Out!* magazine. Like many who sing "Joe Hill" Dunn has tweaked the song, specifically the line "Where workingmen are out on strike," the single line that most singers change in order to make the song more gender inclusive. Dunn sings, "Where workers fight and organize." Dunn says that while she has not recorded a version of "Joe Hill," she keeps "Joe Hill" in her back pocket because it is such a classic and because it has such a beautiful melody.

The workingmen line that Dunn changes is the same line that New Jersey lawyer Bennet Zurofsky similarly changes. A longtime subscriber to *Sing Out!*, Zurofsky dedicates his practice to the causes of labor, peace, and social justice. He heard versions of "Joe Hill" by Paul Robeson and Joan Baez and others, and says, "I pretty much picked it up from the oral tradition with the help of written and recorded sources."[7]

When not in court Zurofsky can be found supporting unions and responsible government, often as director of the Solidarity Singers of the New Jersey Industrial Union Council. Zurofsky says the preferred venue of the Singers is a picket line, where they try to lift people's spirits and help them carry on. We don't all know how to read music, he says, but we know which side we're on.

Get Folks Singing

Elena Klaver, a court certified interpreter (Spanish/English) based in Colorado, says she sings "Joe Hill" all the time. She learned the song from Robeson and Baez albums and, like many others, changes "working men," in her case to "working folks."

"When I introduce the song I say who it was written by, that Joe Hill was a real person—some people don't know that, sadly—and that it continues to inspire," she says.[8] She once sang it at a book presentation and signing of the book *When We Fight, We Win*, edited by Greg Jobin-Leeds, at a big bookstore in Denver. *When We Fight We Win* is a compilation of front-line stories by leaders of some of the successful civil and human rights movements of recent years. Its cumulative message dovetails precisely with that of Pete Seeger and the IWW: when we are together we are stronger.

Klaver feels that the IWW struggle, tactics, and perspective are very pertinent today. While the actual IWW, or what remains of it, might not be viable, she believes the values represented by the union can and should be revived in any struggle against a system that continues to operate for the benefit of a tiny minority.

Lift Every Voice

One of the programs affiliated with the Labor Heritage Foundation is the DC Labor Chorus. According to former foundation Executive

Director Elise Bryant, the chorus sings for workers rallies, demonstrations, and picket lines. "We sing for solidarity," she says. "We sing for peace. We sing for jobs. We sing for justice. We sing for joy. And we sing 'Joe Hill.' I learned it from some labor singers in Detroit at a workers' culture school that I organized. I also heard Earl Robinson sing it at the Western Workers Labor Arts Exchange."[9]

Before moving to Washington, D.C., in the 1990s and forming the chorus, Bryant was the artistic director of the University of Michigan's labor theater project "Workers' Lives/Workers' Stories." A former professor at the now-defunct National Labor College, she has since been elected president of the Coalition of Labor Union Women.

In May of 1994 Bryant joined a group of unionists, labor educators, and artists from the United States—among them Saul Schniderman and Anne Feeney—that undertook an eleven-day tour of Sweden, led by Stanley Rosen of the University of Illinois Labor Education Program and Lars-Göran Pettersson of Sweden's ABF/LO Kulturforum (ABF is the Workers Education Association of that country and LO is Sweden's largest trade union confederation). The group visited Sweden's cultural institutions and held exchanges with Swedish cultural workers and trade union leaders. The tour included a stop at the Joe Hill Museum in Gävle, the former Hägglund family home where Hill was born.

Regarding the strategic use of "Joe Hill" today, Bryant thinks that someone could add a verse about essential workers. It would also be cool, she said, to work in the words of the late Rich Trumka, former president of the AFL-CIO, who said that the labor movement is not a building, it is a living collection of working people who will never stop fighting for economic, social, and racial justice. We will clean up the glass, he said, sweep away the ashes, and keep doing our part to bring a better day out of this hour of darkness and despair.

INTO THE 1990s and 2000s composers and performers continued to create versions and adaptations of the song and the story about the man celebrated in the song.

In 1995, at the inaugural Raise Your Banners festival of political song in Sheffield, England the Sheffield Socialist Choir performed "Joe Hill" in an arrangement by English record producer Nigel Wright. In 2005 the British anarcho-rock band Chumbawamba included a song entitled "By and By" on its album *A Singsong and a Scrap* that incorporates the first stanza of Alfred Hayes's lyric, and in 2007 multi-instrumentalist Ry Cooder included a song entitled "Three Chords and the Truth," written with his son Joachim, on his album *My Name is Buddy*. The song invokes Joe Hill, Paul Robeson, and Pete

Seeger, saying the only "crime" they ever committed was three chords and the truth.

In 2008 Seattle composer and bandleader Wayne Horvitz created a musical tribute to Joe Hill entitled "Joe Hill: 16 Actions for Orchestra, Voice and Soloist." One year later the American band Among the Oak & Ash released an eponymously titled album of traditional folk songs, plus two originals, one of which, penned by singer and songwriter Josh Joplin, was "Joseph Hillstrom 1879–1915." The state couldn't kill you, the song says, it never ever could and it never ever will. "Struggle on, struggle on," rings a recurring chorus.

In 2010 folksinger Otis Gibbs released an album entitled *Joe Hill's Ashes.* The title song, a Gibbs original, carries the same title as an earlier song by Mark Levy that appeared on the 1990 Smithsonian compilation *Don't Mourn—Organize.* Every time I dream about better times, Gibbs sings, I can feel Joe's ashes stirring deep inside. Born and raised in Indiana, where he once worked as a tree planter, Gibbs writes and sings songs about everyday life, songs that tell stories. One of Gibbs's YouTube posts is entitled "Joe Hill: The Grandfather of All Folksingers."

Further tributes to Joe Hill include the 2012 album *The General Strike* by the band Anti-Flag, a recording that features the song "1915," which tells Hill's story. In 2013 trombonist Roswell Rudd and the New York City Labor Chorus recorded a four-movement tribute to Joe Hill on his *Trombone for Lovers* album.

2015: The Centennial

THE YEAR 2015 marked the centennial of Joe Hill's execution, and workers, singers, and songwriters commemorated the occasion on many fronts. Chicago-based singer/songwriter Bucky Halker released a CD entitled *Anywhere but Utah: The Songs of Joe Hill*, echoing Hill's last request to Big Bill Haywood. The recording features eighteen of Joe Hill's songs as well as a clip of Elizabeth Gurley Flynn speaking about Hill and a reading of Joe Hill's last will in Swedish and English.

Clark "Bucky" Halker, a scholar of labor history as well as a professional folksinger and songwriter, grew up in Ashland, Wisconsin, a small industrial town on Lake Superior. As a youth he experimented back and forth between acoustic and electric instruments. But while he logged in time playing rock and roll, there were some die-hard folkies in town that eventually hooked Halker on the music of Woody Guthrie, Lead Belly, and other giants of folk music and the blues. His introduction to Joe Hill came in 1970 when, as a high school student, he was invited to perform at a folk festival at Northland College near Ashland. There he met Utah Phillips and listened intently as Phillips told stories about labor history, music, and the Wobblies.

Halker met Woody Guthrie's second wife, Marjorie, when he was invited to perform at the opening of the Huntington's Disease Clinic in Minneapolis. He did graduate work at the University of Minnesota, and in 1991 published *For Democracy, Workers, and God: Labor Song-Poems and Labor Protest, 1865–95*, an examination of song-poems written by workers during the Gilded Age.

Halker has since embarked on his own career as a folksinger and songwriter, releasing a number of recordings, among them *The Ghost of Woody Guthrie*, a song cycle of original Guthrie-inspired tunes as well as a cover or two of Woody's songs. As he recounts in the liner notes to that CD Halker first encountered the music of Woody Guthrie in the second grade, when his teacher distributed to the class a music book that included "This Land Is Your Land." With *Anywhere but Here: The Songs of Joe Hill*, Halker affirmed his place as a link in the direct chain from Joe Hill and Woody Guthrie and beyond.

2015 SAW THE RELEASE of another important recording. This was *Joe Hill's Last Will* by John McCutcheon, whose many previous albums include the aforementioned *Untold*. McCutcheon dedicated the album to the late Utah Phillips, who, he said, did more to introduce folks to Joe Hill, his music, life and ideas than anyone else. *Joe Hill's Last Will* contains McCutcheon's takes on thirteen Hill songs, as well as Hill's last will and testament. In the liner notes McCutcheon wrote:

> What we have left today, 100 years after his death, is far more than ashes. We have not only his music but, more importantly, the example of writing songs designed to be sung, to be useful. Joe Hill was not writing songs for the ages. He was writing songs to do a job. And, like any good worker, to pull their shift, and then go home.
>
> Hill's work inspired Woody Guthrie, who inspired the likes of Pete Seeger, of Bob Dylan, of Huddie Ledbetter, of so many more throughout the years. The music of the Civil Rights Movement was almost entirely comprised of updated hymns. Songs that were sung to educate, to humor, to create solidarity. And here we are, a century later, in the throes of yet another anti-immigrant surge. Workers rights have eroded. Wages have stagnated. The gap between the wealthy and the rest yawns ever more widely.

In this landscape, Joe Hill's music is more than historical curiosity. He taught us to tackle the hard stuff with both courage and humor. Be clear. Be brave. Be loyal. And, above all, be useful.[10]

The Joe Hill 100 Road Show

TWO MAJOR COMMEMORATIONS during the Hill centennial year were the Joe Hill Road Show and the concert conceived and staged by the Joe Hill Organizing Committee.

The idea for the road show was hatched a year earlier by two railroad men, Ron Kaminkow and John Paul (JP) Wright. Raised in Baltimore by pro-union parents who opposed the Vietnam War, Kaminkow first became aware of Joe Hill and the Hayes/Robinson song in his late teens. He studied forestry at Virginia Tech, and became a self-taught political radical, reading Ralph Chaplin's autobiography *Wobbly*, studying about America's involvement in the overthrow of Salvador Allende in Chile, as well as living briefly in Margaret Thatcher's England. For a time he alternated periods of hopping freight trains with involvement in union activities in Chicago and Wisconsin, later going to work for the railroad and joining the IWW.

In Madison, Wisconsin, Kaminkow helped organize weekly labor sing-a-longs in Mickey's Tavern as well as events in recognition of International Workers Day. He has been a brakeman, conductor, and engineer and an outspoken and tireless advocate on issues of railroad safety and working conditions. Fix the hazards, he says, don't blame the engineers. "Let's face it," he said in a recent interview. "It's large corporations, big business, that are largely running this country, and the rest of us are all too often fighting each other. In a sane economy, one that's based on human needs rather than private profit, we would be able to have both a safe and healthy environment and good-paying union jobs for all."[11]

Kaminkow saw the Joe Hill Road Show concept not only as a series of commemorative concerts but also, as with his railroad activism, an opportunity to build a labor community alliance.

Through the Railroad Workers United he met John Paul Wright. Wright grew up in Louisville, Kentucky, in a family of German Catholic railroad people, political activists, and musicians—a very union family. He credits part of his own activism to his mother, who went back to college at the University of Louisville late in her life and joined the Progressive Student League, a group that held meetings to pressure the university to divest funds that supported South African Apartheid. Wright's father was an electrical contractor with the International Brotherhood of Electrical Workers 369 in Louisville.

Singing was part of everyday family life. JP bought his first guitar with money earned on his paper route and has played it ever since, writing songs and releasing CDs. He also became involved in local union activities, first as a member of the United Transportation Union after going to work on the railroad.

When once asked about some of his favorite labor stories he immediately said Joe Hill. "What I like about his story is how important he really was to the process of culture and the IWW."[12]

Wright didn't know that much about Joe Hill until he met Ron Kaminkow, who gave him a copy of *The Little Red Songbook.* "Then I began to recognize that the more we are pushed out of community realms the more we lose the interlocking way of speaking with one another."[13] Kaminkow also introduced Wright to the music of Utah Phillips, and approached him with the idea of the Joe Hill Road Show. Kaminkow and Wright began contacting people, and among the first they reached out to was George Mann.

With his Almanac Trail experience fresh in his recent past, Mann was a natural for the Joe Hill Road Show. He has said that the song "Joe Hill" has always been one of the most requested songs at his concerts.

Kaminkow and Wright were thinking in terms of a single concert tour that would travel the country, and Mann countered with the concept of different concerts in different parts of the country. Mann himself would end up performing around the West Coast and as far afield as Australia. For his programs he provided a biographical background on Joe Hill, performed songs and discussed their contexts, even read Hill's last will.

THE JOE HILL Road Show formally premiered in May at The Hideout in Chicago. It would be the first of some forty road show concerts held around the country. Wright opened with a Joe Hill–like parody of Stephen Foster's "My Old Kentucky Home," followed by Hill's "Casey Jones the Union Scab" and Florence Reece's "Which Side Are You On?".

Among those who followed Wright were Alexis Buss, a union organizer and six-term general secretary-treasurer of the Industrial Workers of the World, who discussed Joe Hill and the IWW; Anne Feeney, who sang her favorite Joe Hill song, "The Preacher and the Slave" ("Pie in the Sky") and an original song about mining disasters; Swedish songster Jan Hammarlund singing Malvina Reynolds's "Jailhouse Door," then "Joe Hill" with the first verse in Swedish; and Bucky Halker, who sang

Hill's "Rebel Girl" and "My Dreamland Girl of Mine," as well as Harry "Haywire Mac" McClintock's "Hallelujah I'm a Bum," and Lead Belly's "Bourgeois Blues." The show concluded with everyone singing "Solidarity Forever."

If ever there was a singer/songwriter made to order for the Joe Hill Road Show it was Anne Feeney, who two years earlier had joined Rik Palieri and George Mann for several of their Almanac Trail tour shows. Utah Phillips once referred to her as the best labor singer in America. Feeney reportedly quipped, "Not a bad compliment, coming from the best labor singer in America." Born in 1951 in Charleroi, Pennsylvania, Feeney was early influenced by her grandfather, William Feeney, who was a first-generation Irish immigrant and a mineworkers' organizer. He also played the violin in support of labor causes. Anne graduated from the University of Pittsburgh School of Law and practiced as a trial lawyer for twelve years, representing refugees, among others. She also joined the IWW.

Leaving the law behind, Feeney launched her career as a folksinger and songwriter in 1969 at a Vietnam War protest. She soon established herself as a major figure in folk circles, performing shows in the United States and Europe for workers on strike, in union halls, and at protests. She released twelve record albums, and appeared with Pete Seeger, Loretta Lynn, Billy Bragg, and John Prine, among others. Her song "Have You Been to Jail for Justice?" was covered by many artists, most notably Peter, Paul, and Mary.

Regarding her work, Feeney once said that "music is a fantastic way of empowering people and giving them strength and energy. I've spent a good part of my life trying to find and write music that will empower people to resist and stand up for what's right."[14]

AMONG THE OTHER artists who took part in the Joe Hill Road Show were two husband-and-wife teams, the Shelby Bottom Duo and Magpie. Michael J. August and Nell Levin formed the Shelby Bottom String Band in 2008, and continue today as the Duo. With a repertoire that ranges from original songs to obscure traditional tunes, they play festivals, house concerts, benefits for social and environmental causes, and such major auditoriums as Nashville's Ryman. They have also developed their own road show, "A Musical History of Joe Hill and the Early Labor Movement," and have released a companion CD entitled the *Joe Hill Road Show*.

Multi-instrumentalists Greg Artzner and Terry Leonino formed Magpie in Ohio in 1973. The following year they moved to Washington, D.C., where they were regulars on the local folk music scene for over thirty years before relocating to upstate New York. Artzner and Leonino both hail from working class families, and there is a strong working class dimension to their performances. Pete Seeger referred to Magpie as links in the chain.

"So many people are interested in unions and Joe Hill now," Artzner and Leonino have said. "We can make a connection today."[15] Among the recordings they have released to make that connection is the 2017 CD *When We Stand Together: Songs of Joe Hill, the IWW, and Fellow Workers*. The recording is dedicated to "our friend and mentor" Joe Glazer. On the Joe Hill Road Show they consistently played with George Mann and singer/songwriter Charlie King.

Born and raised in Brockton, Massachusetts, Charlie King has enjoyed a long career as a folksinger and a political activist. He has said that his major musical influences were the folk revival of the 1960s, the Civil Rights Movement, and the Vietnam War. He is active in Local 1000, the traveling musicians union of the American Federation of Musicians, as well as the Peoples Music Network for Songs of Freedom and Struggle, an organization that promotes artists in all media who work for a just and peaceful world.

King has released numerous albums under his own name as well as several with the group Bright Morning Star and compilations with other artists. He frequently tours for Journey for Hope, a group working to end the death penalty. His songs have been recorded and sung by Pete Seeger, Holly Near, Ronnie Gilbert, Arlo Guthrie, John McCutcheon, and others. His art and activism have received frequent recognition, including the War Resisters League Peacemaker Award, the Sacco-Vanzetti Social Justice Award, and the Joe Hill Award from the Labor Heritage Foundation. Seeger once remarked, "If we had more Charlie Kings in the world I'd be less worried," to which singer-songwriter Tom Paxton added, "Luckily, we have him!"

BUCKY HALKER followed up his participation in the opening program of the Joe Hill Road Show with a number of appearances in Wisconsin. There he was joined on several dates by multi-instrumentalist Mark Revenson, who tours professionally as Lil' Rev. He plays guitar, mandolin, and harmonica, but it was while growing up in Milwaukee that he received a banjo ukulele as a gift. That instrument led him to a career as a nationally recognized ukulele virtuoso, whose performances include not only music but also workshops and storytelling. He has released more than twenty recordings and instrument instruction books.

Speaking at a radio interview during the Road Show tours, Lil' Rev said that Joe Hill fought for a lot of things that people still believe in, adding that so many of the causes that the IWW stood up for are just as apropos today as they were more than 100 years ago.

Halker said that we could all use a reminder of Hill's legacy. "It's part of our history, and I think it often gets neglected in the schools or shuffled under the carpet," he said. "It's important to remember these stories. And Joe Hill is a way to bring that story of small people and their fight for bigger issues."[16]

ANOTHER MUSICIAN who participated in Joe Hill centennial activities was David Rovics. Growing up in Connecticut, Rovics absorbed the political and musical passions of his parents, both of whom were left-leaning Democrats and classical pianists. At home they played recordings by Guthrie, Robeson, and Seeger.

First dabbling with the cello and, later, psychedelic rock, Rovics turned to folk music. He dropped out of college, traveled back and forth across the country playing in various bands and busking in subways before settling in Seattle in the 1990s. He has since established a career as a solo singer-songwriter. While he performs almost exclusively original music, he keeps certain established songs in his repertoire. "Joe Hill" is one of those songs. Says Rovics:

> There are so many reasons, in my life as a singer and political activist who is interested in history, to keep coming back to Joe Hill and the song about him. The song is part of the lifeblood of the English-speaking left around the world—and the Swedish speaking left, of course. It is a placeholder for history. There are certain songs that can introduce people to whole periods of history, and "Joe Hill" is one of those. It opens people up to what was an impactful moment in history, the whole world of the labor movement of the time. It is a brilliantly written and composed song, a highly emotional song that has been reinforced for our own times by Paul Robeson, Joan Baez, and many others.[17]

Before joining the Joe Hill Road Show in America, where he toured the West Coast with George Mann and others, Rovics did a tour in Sweden in the company of Swedish musician and composer Kristian Svensson. Growing up in Halmstad, in southern Sweden, Svensson first heard Joe Hill's own songs, as well as the Hayes-Robinson ballad, after he joined the *Unga omar*, the Young Eagles, a Social Democratic children's labor movement. At first Svensson didn't realize that the songwriter identified as Joe Hill was Swedish, and that he was hearing Swedish translations of English lyrics.

By the age of eleven Svensson was playing the guitar, and the mid–1980s, inspired partially by the songs of Bruce Springsteen, Svensson began writing his own material. He says:

The very "Americaness" of Joe Hill is one of the reasons I got into contact with his story and songs. When his lyrics were translated into Swedish in the 1960s it was all part of the folk music revival of that age, and anything tying the Big Hip Country in The West to little Sweden seems to have been welcomed with open arms. It's also obvious that Hill was part of the extremely eclectic cultural mix that was special in the United States in his day and age, long before it sparked youth culture worldwide.[18]

Svensson and Rovics performed throughout Scandinavia, winding up with a concert in the garden of the house in Gävle where young Joel Hägglund grew up. Svensson has written a musical entitled *The Man Who Never Died*, a work for eight-piece orchestra, and he also holds combined concerts and lectures for branches of the Swedish labor movement that feature Hill's songs and contemporary works. In addition, he has initiated an interactive, political folk festival for trade union members, where every artist teams up with members of the audience to write what he calls "new Joe Hill songs" for our day and age ("When we sing together…").

Salt Lake Commemoration

THE ACTIVITIES of the Joe Hill Organizing Committee culminated on September 5, 2015, with a daylong commemoration and concert in Salt Lake City's Sugar House Park. Chairing the committee was Lori Elaine Taylor, the former Smithsonian archivist who spearheaded the *Don't Mourn—Organize* CD and who was a member of the committee that staged the 75th anniversary of Joe Hill's execution.

A native of Salt Lake City who still lives there, Taylor did graduate work at George Washington University, where she wrote her master's thesis on "The Politicized Legend of the Singing Hero: Joe Hill, Woody Guthrie, Pete Seeger, Bob Dylan, and Bruce Springsteen." While there she produced and wrote the liner notes for the recording *Don't Mourn—Organize!* The lives of charismatic leaders often get stretched after they die, she said. They become important symbols. All of her academic work has been about how people shape and create such symbols.

Among the performers at the concert were Judy Collins (whose set included "Joe Hill"), Conjuntos Familia Castillos, Guy Davis, Anne Feeney, Joe Jencks, Lab Dogs, Timothy Mason, Mischief Brew, Rio Bravo, Mark Ross, David Rovics, Lovisa Samuelsson, Triggers and Slips, and many others.

The centennial event also included a meeting between descendants of John Morrison, the man whom Joe Hill was accused of killing, and members of the Hägglund family, including performer Samuelsson, who is Joe Hill's great-great-niece; her mother, Pia Samuelsson; and her uncle, Rolf Hägglund, all descendants of Joe Hill's brother Efraim. "The Morrison and Hill families meeting was the most important thing I did that year," said Lori Taylor. "It was rewarding just to have members of the two families together."[19]

"An interesting part of the Joe Hill story is that his family over in Sweden didn't know about his life as a union man and hero until the 1950s, long after the birth of the song," said his great-nephew Rolf Hägglund. "He got lost in the new big country." He sent a couple of postcards the first decade to his family, but that stopped when he got busy with the IWW and, of course, was later executed. And they only knew him as 'Julie,' his nickname. They wouldn't have understood that the Joe Hill in the song was their brother.

"But the U.S. authorities knew who he was," Hägglund continued, "and mailed all his belongings, mostly papers, to his uncle in Gävle. Since he had been executed for murder, all of those papers were put in an attic and forgotten until the uncle died. Then his widow burned the papers!"[20]

THE FEELINGS of many of those present at the centennial were summed up by Jencks, a veteran of many decades on the international folk circuit and an award-winning songwriter who has performed in every venue from coffee houses and folk festivals to New York's Carnegie Hall and Lincoln Center. His many albums include *Links in a Chain*, which features a version of "Joe Hill." In a videotaped interview, Jencks said that Joe Hill means a lot to him because he himself comes from a family of immigrants from Sweden, Ireland, and France by way of Quebec—a working family that believes in the idea of people banding together, of coming together for the purpose of improving their situation collectively. We live in a culture steeped in the ideal of the rugged individual, said Jencks, but the fact is none of us do it alone. We are all in community with each other, and the question is do we work together in solidarity or do we take advantage of those relationships in a predatory manner? For Jencks, the labor movement has always been about coming together and uplifting each other in solidarity.

100 Years to the Day

DAWN: WEDNESDAY, November 19, 2015. Si Kahn and John McCutcheon are standing in Sugar House Park in Salt Lake City, the former site of the Utah State Prison where the Joe Hill Centennial Concert had been held two months earlier. As Kahn recalls, as the early morning sun began climbing up the Wasatch Mountains they stood in a silent shivering circle with two dozen others, surrounding the spot where Joe Hill was tied to a chair and blindfolded, exactly one hundred years ago to the day.

In June 2015 McCutcheon performed Kahn's play *Joe Hill's Last Will* in cities and towns throughout California, as well as in Richmond, Virginia. He would present the play four more times after November 19, in Denver, Colorado, Cedar Rapids, Iowa, Madison, Wisconsin, and, finally, in Washington, D.C. But on that night of November 19, 2015, John brought Joe Hill back to life on stage in Salt Lake City. Here are Joe Hill's last words as imagined by Si Kahn:[21]

> The deputy is the one who has to give the order: "Ready, aim, fire." I'm going to let him say those first two words. But I will not allow him to say the last one. That one's for me alone.
>
> Because every fellow worker has got to take control of his death, just like he's got to take control of his work and his life. I refuse to hand that over to them. I refuse to give them that power.
>
> It's going to get real quiet, real still, in the yard, and all around the world. The deputy is going to say, "Ready." I'll hear the sound of those boys cocking their rifles. Then he's going to say, "Aim."
>
> That's when I'm going to say my true last word, the one I've been holding back all this time. I'm going to shout, as loud as I can, so they will hear it for a thousand years.
>
> "Fire! Go on and fire!"

> I dreamed I saw Joe Hill last night
> alive as you and me,
> Says I, "But Joe, you're ten years dead."
> "I never died," says he.
> "I never died," says he.
>
> "In Salt Lake, Joe," I says to him,
> him standing by my bed.
> "They framed you on a murder charge."
> Says Joe, "But I ain't dead."
> Says Joe, "But I ain't dead."
>
> "The copper bosses killed you, Joe,
> they shot you, Joe," says I.
> "Takes more than guns to kill a man."
> Says Joe, "I didn't die."
> Says Joe, "I didn't die."

And standing there as big as life
and smiling with his eyes.
Says Joe, "What they could never kill"
went on to organize,
went on to organize.

"Joe Hill ain't dead," he says to me,
"Joe Hill ain't never died."
Where workers stand up for their rights
Joe Hill is at their side.
Joe Hill is at their side.

"From San Diego up to Maine
in every mine and mill.
Where workers strike and organize,"
Says he, "you'll find Joe Hill."
Says he, "You'll find Joe Hill."

I dreamed I saw Joe Hill last night
alive as you and me.
Says I, "But Joe, you're ten years dead."
"I never died," says he.
"I never died." Says he.

Epilogue

"As long as we keep singing and keep the spirit up we are bound to win."—Joe Hill

ON JUNE 16, 2016 British Member of Parliament Jo Cox was shot and stabbed to death outside of a library in the town of Birstall, near Leeds in northern England, where she was scheduled to hold a meeting of her constituents. The attacker was a 52-year old man named Thomas Mair, a white supremacist with links to neo–Nazi groups. This was during the time when Britain was on the eve of a referendum to either leave the European Union or stay in it. Cox, a forty-one-year-old wife and mother of two young children, favored remaining in the EU. Mair also stabbed Bernard Kenney, a 77-year-old local man who tried to stop the attack. (Kenney survived.) Eyewitnesses to Cox's murder later testified at Mair's trial that he had shouted, "This is for Britain" or "Britain will always come first."

Searching his home, police found a library full of materials about the Nazis, German military history and white supremacy, kept in a bedroom bookshelf topped with a gold Third Reich eagle with swastika. Mair also subscribed to a rightwing magazine, the *SA Patriot*, which had begun publication in South Africa but later moved to England under the new name *SA Patriot in Exile.* In 1991 Mair wrote a letter to the magazine expressing his fear that the white race was in for a long and bloody struggle.

Jo Cox was a first-term Member of Parliament whose advocacy for people's rights had made her a respected figure in England. Her death sent shock waves throughout the nation, both in and beyond the political arena.

In response to this tragedy Malcolm Hawksworth of the nonprofit group Peace Through Folk, an organization that sponsors concerts and performances that celebrate peace and reconciliation, used Earl

Robinson's music "and borrowed the spirit of Joe Hill" to create a tribute song, "I Dreamed I Saw Jo Cox Last Night."[1] Guitarist Pete Morton and violinist Phoebe Rees performed an early rendering of the tribute, which can be viewed on YouTube.

In the wake of Cox's murder and the adaptation of the song "Joe Hill" in her honor, Phoebe Rees's father, John Ridgman, himself a political and anti-war folk song activist, wrote to the present author saying that his introduction to Joe Hill came through Hawksworth's adaptation of the song. Following are excerpts from Ridgman's comments:

> When the world is heading down a path that seems all wrong to me, leaving me feeling helpless and worried, there is some solace to be found in voicing those concerns to people through a song. One of the ways of galvanizing workers is to educate them about the struggle and sacrifices of the past. Real events, such as the murder of Joe Hill and the stories behind them, can be learnt about by way of songs being sung and passed on down the generations. When downright lies are fed to the populous as truth and accepted by too many as such, it is vital that history has a way by which it can be handed on to the future generations in pure unadulterated form.
>
> Joe Hill stands as an inspirational figure. His story needs to be out there. The song "Joe Hill" tells it as it was. Someone was killed for standing up for people's rights, for encouraging the notion of solidarity and for trying to make people aware that their labour was theirs to use, amongst other things, as a bargaining tool to fight for fair pay and working conditions and a better life.[2]

ON NOVEMBER 11–12, 2016 a conference was held in Galway, Ireland entitled "Ireland and the Wobbly World: Irish Labor Radicals and the IWW in the Early 20th Century," hosted by the Irish Centre for Histories of Labour and Class. Retired Irish Transport & General Workers Union official Francis (Francy) Devine opened the proceedings by singing "Joe Hill."

ON JANUARY 29, 2017, a memorial plaque to Joe Hill was dedicated in San Pedro, California. The location was Liberty Hill Plaza near the waterfront, the site of a 1923 IWW strike and the arrest of muckraking journalist Upton Sinclair (*The Jungle*). Following an introduction by longshoreman Jerry Brady, the eight-foot-wide, three-and-a-half foot high bronze plaque was unveiled.

The plaque is based on an original drawing by Suzanne Matusmiya, the graphic designer for San Pedro's alt-weekly newspaper *Random Lengths*. The front of the memorial features Joe Hill holding a guitar, with the logo of the Wobblies over his head as if a halo. Hill gazes on a sea of workers being confronted by policemen, their clubs raised. The

In January 2017 this memorial to Joe Hill and fellow workers was dedicated in San Pedro, California, near the docks where Hill worked.

local *OC Weekly* newspaper reported that the other side displays an image of incarcerated workers along with couplets from Joe Hill's song "Workers of the World, Awaken."

Among those participating in the ceremony were IWW member Arthur Almeida, harbor historian, former longshoreman, and author of *Wobblies of San Pedro*, who proudly waved a copy of the *Little Red Songbook*; Dr. Vivian Price, the labor studies chair holder at California State University Dominguez Hills; James Preston Allen, editor of *Random Lengths*, who sang "Joe Hill," substituting San Pedro for San Diego; and David Arian, past president of International Longshore and Warehouse Union Local 13.

Price offered a capsule history of the labor movement in California, adding, "We have to know the past. We have to celebrate our heroes, and then find the heroes among us who are courageous and willing to speak up today." Arian concluded the dedication ceremony, saying, "This plaque now becomes part of that progressive history that we can remind America of over and over again. This is who we are; this is the real America."

ON NOVEMBER 18, 2023, a memorial to Joe Hill was unveiled in Sugar House Park, the former site in Salt Lake City of the Utah State Penitentiary where Hill was executed. The inscription on the front of the memorial reads:

> Songwriter, Itinerant Laborer,
> Union Organizer.

Hill was born October 7, 1879 in Gävle, Sweden
and executed at the Utah State Penitentiary
on November 19, 1915.

In hobo jungles, on picket lines and at workers'
rallies, Hill was well-known as the author
of popular labor songs and as a member
of the Industrial Workers of the World (IWW).
Thanks in large part to his songs
"The Preacher and the Slave" and
"There is Power in a Union" in addition to
his stirring, well-publicized call to his fellow
workers on the eve of his execution—
"Don't waste time mourning, organize!"

Hill became, and has remained, the best-
known IWW member and a labor folk hero.

The other side of the memorial features lyrics from Joe Hill's song
"There is Power in a Union," the logo of the Central Utah Federation
of Labor AFL-CIO, and the inscription "Dedicated in 2023 to workers
past, present, and future of the Union Labor Movement."

The memorial project was the result of years of negotiations among
representatives of local labor unions, city officials, community organizations, and the Sugar House Park Authority. The Authority agreed to
the formation of a subgroup to pursue the issue of a Joe Hill memorial.
Subsequent discussions revealed that the controversy over Hill's guilt
or innocence had not been resolved in the 108 years since his execution.

"That was a significant hurdle to overcome," said Brandon Dew,
president of the Central Utah Federation of Labor, who participated
throughout the campaign to have the memorial installed. "We were able
to convince everyone that what we wanted was not simply a memorial to
Joe Hill, but a historical marker that celebrated Hill as a representative
of the labor movement. That perspective—commemorating labor in the
larger sense—was an important element of our proposal."[3]

With funding by donations, ninety percent of which came from
labor unions, the plan was finally approved for a six-foot by six-foot by
one-foot marker that resembled another already in the park, one that
celebrates sons and daughters of Utah pioneers.

Among those who spoke at the unveiling, in addition to Dew, were
Erin Mendenhall, mayor of Salt Lake City; Holly Nichols, president
of the Sugar House Park Authority; Landon Clark of the Sugar House
Community Council; Brad Asay, vice president of the Utah AFL-CIO,
and historian Lori Taylor. For Taylor, the former archivist at the Smithsonian who had produced the 1990 *Don't Mourn—Organize!* CD, and

whose efforts were instrumental to the 75th and 100th anniversary celebrations of Joe Hill, it was the realization of something she had championed for decades. She also read a welcoming note from the Hägglund family in Sweden.

Dew commented that the project had started in 2021, when he and Will Kocher, secretary-treasurer for The American Federation of State, County and Municipal Employees Local Union No. 1004 and vice president of the Central Utah Federation of Labor, decided they wanted to do something to give back to their union brothers and sisters. He added:

> This historical marker was, in our minds, less about Joe Hill and more about the working men and women who have fought and continue to fight daily for their rights in the workplace. We hope that those who come to see this historical marker, whether it be for Joe Hill or for the union labor movement in general, will take a moment while they are here to ponder what they can do and have done to make this a better world for those who come after them.[4]

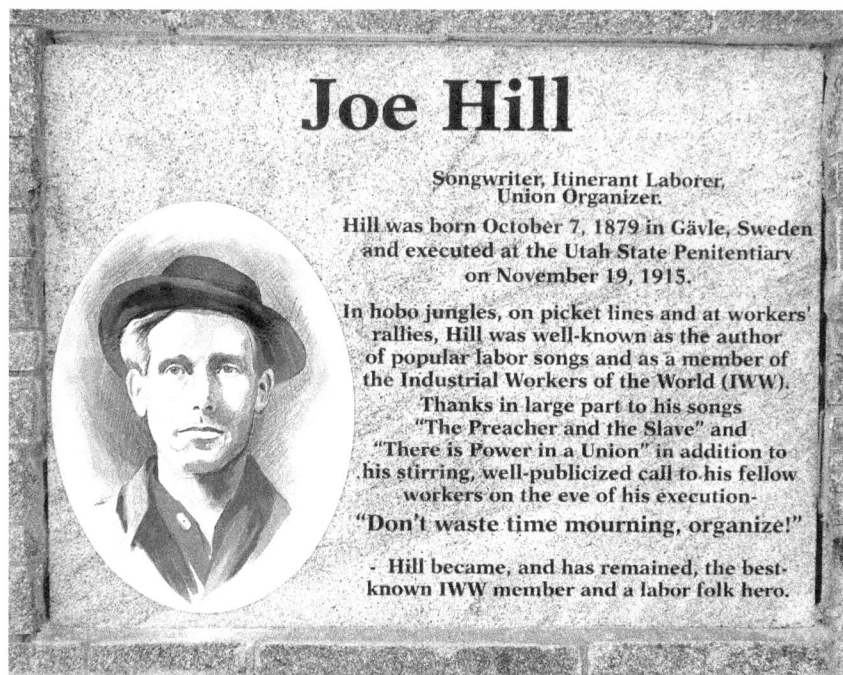

Joe Hill

Songwriter, Itinerant Laborer, Union Organizer.

Hill was born October 7, 1879 in Gävle, Sweden and executed at the Utah State Penitentiary on November 19, 1915.

In hobo jungles, on picket lines and at workers' rallies, Hill was well-known as the author of popular labor songs and as a member of the Industrial Workers of the World (IWW). Thanks in large part to his songs "The Preacher and the Slave" and "There is Power in a Union" in addition to his stirring, well-publicized call to his fellow workers on the eve of his execution-

"Don't waste time mourning, organize!"

- Hill became, and has remained, the best-known IWW member and a labor folk hero.

Joe Hill and the larger labor movement of which he was a representative were remembered by this memorial, unveiled in November 2023 in Salt Lake City's Sugar House Park, site of the former Utah State Prison where Hill was executed in 1915.

Make this a better world: That is what the immigrant Joel Hägg-lund tried to do. When he encountered repression of working men and women instead of the land of unlimited opportunity he had been led to expect, he turned to a labor organization that was committed to help-ing create a better world. Hill paid for his idealism with his life. With his death Joe Hill became a martyr, based largely on the song by Alfred Hayes and Earl Robinson, two very different people who were neverthe-less united in their efforts to make a better world.

Is "Joe Hill" a classic song? To be considered a classic implies a memorable melody with meaningful lyrics and an emotional impact on a wide audience and on culture itself. As labor lore historian Archie Green puts it:

> Songs and stories lead individuals to conceptual questions about them-selves and their institutions. "I Dreamed I Saw Joe Hill Again," the original poem, and "Joe Hill," the Camp Unity contribution, help all who toil sense the conjunction of truth and myth, manifesto and tale, chain maker and chain breaker.[5]

Born as a brief poem, "Joe Hill" grew into a song that outleaped its original context as an ode to a fallen fellow worker. The song became a wakeup call for workingmen and women to stand up for their rights. It became a rallying cry for downtrodden peoples everywhere to overturn their oppressors. It became an anti-war anthem. From one generation to another it has been adapted to the temper of changing times.

"Joe Hill" brings its history with it. Every time it is sung a new dimension is added to that history. It rings on down through the years, and when it does it brings us together to lift us up in solidarity toward freedom—and freedom is a constant song.

Acknowledgments

EARLY MORNING: a Sunday in June. There are no final ceremonies being conducted; no interment is in progress. There is no one else in sight. My wife, Lynda, and I are standing in a corner of Ferncliff Cemetery in the Westchester County hamlet of Hartsdale, some twenty miles north of New York City. At our feet is the grave marker that is inscribed,

PAUL ROBESON

APRIL 9, 1898   JAN. 23, 1976

"THE ARTIST MUST ELECT TO FIGHT
FOR FREEDOM OR SLAVERY. I
HAVE MADE MY CHOICE. I HAD
NO ALTERNATIVE."

Adjacent to Robeson's grave are those of his wife, Eslanda Goode Robeson, his longtime piano accompanist Lawrence Brown, and the author James Baldwin who once said of Robeson, "At a time when there seemed to be no hope at all, Paul Robeson spoke out for all of us."

Robeson is one of those principal players in the story of the song "Joe Hill" who were long gone before I came to this project. They include the song's lyricist and composer, Alfred Hayes and Earl Robinson, as well as John Steinbeck, Pete Seeger, Woody Guthrie, Utah Phillips, Joe Glazer, and, more recently, Anne Feeney. The folk song and labor movements lost one of their most effective voices when Feeney passed away in February 2021 of covid-19, before I could reach out to her.

It is the stories and legacies of people like these and the ongoing stories of those who are still active that compose the substance of this book, just as it is the lives of the people one meets on the journey from cradle to grave that provide the wealth of one's own story.

I have many to thank for their time and important insights: James Preston Allen, Arthur Almeida, David Beckwith, Greg Artzner, Elise Bryant, Brandon Dew, Maria Dunn, Josh Dunson, Patti and Emily

Glazer, Bucky Halker, Ron Kaminkow, Elena Klaver, Terry Leonino, Lil' Rev, George Mann, John McCutcheon, Robert Meeropol, John O'Connor, Rik Palieri, David Rovics, Saul Schniderman, the staff at the Tamiment Library and Robert F. Wagner Archives at New York University, Lori Elaine Taylor, Joe Uehlein, John Paul Wright, and Bennett Zurofsky. Their wisdom and perspectives were indispensable to this book.

My friend and music buddy, the late author John Nichols, was a source of unfailing encouragement. "John Nichols ain't never died."

Thanks as well to those I reached out to outside of the United States, and who responded with enthusiasm and valuable information: Malcolm Hawksworth and John Ridgman in England, and Rolf Hägglund and Kristian Svensson in Sweden.

I am also indebted to Alfred Hayes's daughter, Josephine Hayes Dean, for reviewing sections of the book relating to her father, making several critical corrections, and offering photographs of him, Her help is greatly appreciated.

It was our friend Jenny Vincent who planted the seed that ultimately led me to this journey. In 2002 Lynda and I attended the wedding of our son in Taos, New Mexico. Jenny and her trio were playing for the event. Jenny was born into well-to-do circumstances in Chicago, where she enjoyed early piano studies both classical and by ear, as well as exposure to international folk music. Jenny eventually embraced a more down-to-earth existence in northern New Mexico, whose peoples and cultures had captured her interest and her heart. By then she had picked up the accordion, which became her primary instrument. She became a regular volunteer performer for farmers' organizations, for the International Union of Mine, Mill and Smelter Workers (known as Mine Mill), and public schools, where she championed the use of Spanish in classrooms at a time when it was outlawed—despite the fact that ninety percent of New Mexico children at the time were native Spanish speakers.

Jenny joined Pete Seeger and others to sing for Henry Wallace at the 1948 Progressive Party presidential convention, provided piano accompaniment for Paul Robeson at a Wallace rally in Denver, and later performed with Earl Robinson at the Purdue University memorial for Robeson. She also sang with the women on the picket line during the Salt of the Earth strike in southern New Mexico. She did not, as she told us with a sly smile, sing for the Senate equivalent of the HUAC, which subpoenaed her after the notorious FBI informant Harvey Matusow falsely accused her of subversive activities.

Jenny was eighty-nine when Lynda and I met her. I thought she could be the subject of an interesting article, one that would likely require only a single interview. How wrong I was! After a year of weekly interviews, I published her biography with the University of New Mexico Press.

During our conversations Jenny would mention the names of the many people who visited her New Mexico guest ranch. Among them was Earl Robinson. At the time I was not familiar with Robinson. "He composed the music for 'Joe Hill,'" she said. That rang a bell: didn't Joan Baez sing something called "Joe Hill" at Woodstock? In 2016 Jenny died at the age of 103. Several years later I thought of her and Earl Robinson and "Joe Hill." It was time to find out more.

SI KAHN: I owe incalculable thanks to Si. When I first reached out to him to speak with him about all things Joe Hill, Si responded with great enthusiasm. After several telephone conversations and emails, he personally contacted on my behalf a dozen or more key players in the folk music field, people who responded with invaluable emails and interviews. Si read over an entire draft of the manuscript and gifted me with several hours of interview time, during which he offered many helpful suggestions. The book owes much, including its title, to him and his encyclopedic knowledge and experience, not to mention his terrific sense of humor.

LYNDA: I dedicate this book to my wife, Lynda, with love. There are no words that can adequately thank her for the unwavering patience and steadfast support she gave me during the progress of this project over several years. She walked the site of Camp Unity and the site of the Peekskill riots with me. She talked me through moments of doubt with unfailing encouragement. There would be no book—or anything else worth doing—without her.

Errors? Inaccuracies? Misinterpretations? All are my responsibility.

Discography

Any listing that presumes to call itself a discography cataloging all of the recordings of the song "Joe Hill" should instead call itself "selective." Such an attempted list will inevitably commit the sin of omission. What follows, then, inevitably leaves out deserving artists and recordings that should appear here. I regret any oversights, for they are unintentional. I have not attempted to catalog recordings outside of the United States.

Baez, Joan: *One Day at a Time*, Vanguard, 1970. *Woodstock Soundtrack,* Atlantic, 1970. *From Every Stage*, A&M Records, 1993. *The Best of Joan Baez*, Vanguard 1995. *Bowery Songs*, Vanguard 2004. *Carry It On*, Vanguard, 2007.

Bibb, Eric, and Leon Bibb: *Praising Peace: A Tribute to Paul Robeson*, Stony Plain Music, 2006.

Bragg, Billy: *The Internationale, 1990.*

The Dubliners: The: *Revolution*, CHYME Music, 2014.

Feeney, Anne: *Have You Been to Jail for Justice?* CD Baby, 2003.

Glazer, Joe: *The Songs of Joe Hill*, Folkways Records, 1954. *We've Only Just Begun: A Century of Labor Songs*, Collector Records, 1981. *Joe Glazer Sings Labor Songs*, Collector Records, 2009.

Jencks, Joe: *Links in a Chain*, Turtle Bear Music, 2022.

Kahn, Si: *Carry It On*, Flying Fish Records, 1987. *Joe Hill's Last Will* (DVD), Charlotte: Joe Hill Music LLC, 2015.

Maynor, Kevin: *Paul Robeson Remembered*, Fleur de Son, 1998.

McCutcheon, John: *Live at Wolf Trap*. Rounder, 1991. *Untold*, Appalseed Productions, 2009. *Joe Hill's Last Will* (DVD), Charlotte: Joe Hill Music LLC, 2015.

Morello, Tom (as The Nightwatchman): *Union Town*, New West Records, 2011.

Ochs, Phil: *Tape from California*, 1968. A&M Records. *Live in Montreal*, Rockbeat, 2017.

Phillips, Utah: *We Have Fed You All a Thousand Years*, Philo/Rounder Records, 1983. *Fellow Workers*, Righteous Babe Records, 1999.

Robeson, Paul: *Live at Carnegie Hall*, Vanguard Records, 1965. *Songs of Struggle*, Regis Records, 2005. "Joe Hill" is included in several other Robeson collections, among them *On My Journey, The Odyssey of Paul Robeson*, and *The Peace Arch Concerts*.

Robinson, Earl: *Strange Unusual Evening*, UAW Records, 1970. *Alive & Well*, Aspen, 2010. *Walk in the Sun,* Folkways Records, 1957.

Rovics, David: *The Other Side.*

Samuelsson, Lovisa: *Main Magma Chamber,* 2014

Seeger. Pete: *The Complete Bowdoin College Concert*, Smithsonian Folkways, 1960. *Carry It On*, Flying Fish Records, 1987. *Together in Concert* (with Arlo Guthrie). *If I Had a Hammer: Songs of Hope & Struggle*, Smithsonian Folkways, 1998.

Shelby Bottom Duo: *Joe Hill Road Show*, 2015.

Various Artists: *Don't Mourn—Organize! Songs of Labor Songwriter Joe Hill*, Smithsonian Folkways Records, 1990.

White, Willard: *The Paul Robeson Legacy*, Linn Records, 2002.

Many other artists and groups who have produced recordings of Joe Hill's original songs, Wobbly songs, or songs inspired by Joe Hill have been mentioned in the text of this book, and I encourage the reader's attention to them. Examples of these recordings include:

Gibbs, Otis: *Joe Hill's Ashes*, otisgibbs.com.

Halker, Bucky: *Anywhere but Utah: Songs of Joe Hill*, Revolting Records, 2015.

Magpie (Greg Artzner and Terry Leonino): *When We Stand Together: Songs of Joe Hill, the IWW, and Fellow Workers*, Long Tail Records, 2017.

McCutcheon, John: *Joe Hill's Last Will*, Appalsongs, 2015.

Various Artists: *Classic Labor Songs*, Smithsonian Folkways, 2006.

Various Artists: *Power to the People! Protest Songs*, Master Classics, 2009.

Various Artists: *Songs of Civil Rights and Protest*, Acrobat, 2022.

Image Credits

The author is grateful to the following individuals and institutions for supplying the images in this book:

Joe Hill: Public domain, courtesy of Judy Dencker and her colleagues at the Salt Lake Police Museum and Jeremy Harmon, *Salt Lake City Tribune*.

Alfred Hayes: Photo courtesy of Josephine Hayes Dean.

Earl Robinson and Paul Robeson: Archive PL / Licensed to Alamy Stock Photos

Paul Robeson in Oakland: Science History Images / Licensed to Alamy Stock Photos.

Joe Glazer and Walter Reuther: Unknown photographer. Photo courtesy of Patti and Emily Glazer.

Joan Baez: Collection Christophel / Licensed to Alamy Stock Photos.

Pete Seeger: Francis Specker / Licensed to Alamy Stock Photos.

San Pedro Memorial: Photo by Lynda Smith, reprinted by permission.

Salt Lake City memorial: Photo by Milan Q. Foley, reprinted by permission.

Chapter Notes

Preface

1. Earl Robinson, *Ballad of an American* (Lanham, MD: Scarecrow Press, 1998), 54.

Prologue

1. Joan Didion, "John Wayne: A Love Song," *We Tell Ourselves Stories in Order to Live* (New York: Alfred A. Knopf, 2006), 34.
2. Rachel Nuwer, "How Conversations Around Campfires Might Have Shaped Human Cognition and Culture," *Smithsonian.com*, September 2014.

Chapter 1

1. Carl N. Degler, *Out of Our Past* (New York: Harper Colophon, 1984), 412.
2. Will Rogers, willrogers.com/quotes.
3. Kathryn A. Flynn and Richard Polese, *The New Deal: A 75th Anniversary Celebration* (Salt Lake City: Gibbs Smith, 2008), 10.
4. John Maynard Keynes, Introduction, *The Economic Consequences of the Peace* (Online Library of Liberty).
5. Orrick Johns, *New Masses*, 1934.
6. Alan M. Wald, *Exiles from a Future Time: The Forging of the Mid-Twentieth-Century Literary Left* (Chapel Hill: University of North Carolina Press, 2002), 215.
7. Alex Harvey, "The Lasting Worth of Alfred Hayes," *The Los Angeles Review of Books*, July 2018.

8. Earl Robinson, *Ballad of an American*, 4.
9. Robinson, *Ballad of an American*, 52.

Chapter 2

1. Joyce L. Kornbluh, ed., *Rebel Voices: An I.W.W. Anthology* (Ann Arbor: University of Michigan Press, 1968), 1.
2. William M. Adler, *The Man Who Never Died* (New York: Bloomsbury, 2011), 91.
3. Josh Dunson, *Freedom in the Air* (New York: International, 1965), 14.
4. Philip S. Foner, ed., *The Letters of Joe Hill* (Chicago: Haymarket, 1965), 44.
5. Arthur Almeida, *Wobblies in San Pedro* (self-published, 2012), 110.
6. Foner, *The Letters of Joe Hill*, 60.
7. Foner, *The Letters of Joe Hill*, 67.
8. Chaplin, "Joe Hill's Funeral," *International Socialist Review*, December 1915. Quoted in Kornbluh, *Rebel Voices*, 155.

Chapter 3

1. Robinson, *Ballad of an American*, 53.
2. David Margolick, *Strange Fruit* (Philadelphia: Running Press, 2000), 29.
3. Ed Cray, *Ramblin' Man: The Life and Times of Woody Guthrie* (New York: W.W. Norton, 2004), 21.
4. Darryl Holter and William Deverell, *Woody Guthrie L.A. 1937 to*

1941 (Santa Monica: Angel City Press, 2015), 63.

5. John Steinbeck, *The Grapes of Wrath* (New York: Penguin, 1992), 477.

6. Robinson, *Ballad of an American*, 93.

Chapter 4

1. Paul Robeson, *Here I Stand* (Boston: Beacon Press, 1958), 10.

2. Robeson, *Here I Stand*, 27.

3. Robeson, *Here I Stand*, 9.

4. Foner, *Paul Robeson Speaks*, 12.

5. W.E.B. Du Bois, *The Autobiography of W.E.B. Du Bois* (Brooklyn: Diasporic Africa Press , 2013), 397.

6. Maurice Jackson, liner notes, *Steal Away: Spirituals, Hymns and Folk Songs*, recording by Charlie Haden, bass, and Hank Jones, piano (Polydor/PolyGram, 1995).

7. Robeson, *Here I Stand*, 15.

8. Martin Bauml Duberman, *Paul Robeson* (New York: Alfred A. Knopf, 1988), 159.

9. Foner, *Paul Robeson Speaks*, 124.

Chapter 5

1. Robinson, *Ballad of an American*, 53.

2. Louis Menand, *The Metaphysical Club* (New York: Farrar, Straus and Giroux, 2001), xii.

3. Robeson, *Here I Stand*, 31.

4. Robinson, *Ballad of an American*, 94.

5. John Steinbeck, *The Grapes of Wrath*, 572.

6. Robert Santelli, *This Land Is Your Land: Woody Guthrie and the Journey of an American Folksong* (Philadelphia: Running Press, 2012), 39.

7. Woody Guthrie, *Dust Bowl Ballads* (New York: Buddha Records, 2000).

8. Michael Loring and the TAC Singers, *Joe Hill*, Earl Robinson, piano (New York: TAC Records, Modern Record Co. Series A, No. 1, 1939).

9. Franklin Rosemont, *Joe Hill: The IWW and the Making of a Revolutionary Workingclass Counterculture* (Chicago: Charles H. Kerr, 2015), 201.

10. June Levine and Gene Gordon, *Tales of Wo-Chi-Ca: Blacks, Whites, and Reds at Camp* (San Rafael, CA: Avon Springs Press, 2001), 5.

11. Greg Vandy and Daniel Person, *26 Songs in 30 Days: Woody Guthrie's Columbia River Songs and the Planned Promised Land in the Pacific Northwest* (Seattle: Sasquatch, 2016), xiv.

12. Robinson, *Ballad of an American*, 128.

Chapter 6

1. Robinson, *Ballad of an American*, 220–221.

2. David King Dunaway, *How Can I Keep from Singing: The Ballad of Pete Seeger* (New York: Villard, 2008), 144.

3. Duberman, *Paul Robeson*, 342.

4. liquisearch.com/peekskill_riots/paul_robesons_remarks_in_paris.

5. Duberman, *Paul Robeson*, 342.

Chapter 7

1. Madeline Albright, *Fascism: A Warning* (New York: HarperCollins, 2018), p. 2.

2. Barrie Stavis, *The Man Who Never Died* (South Brunswick: A.S. Barnes, 1972), 65.

3. Foner, *Paul Robeson Speaks*, 234.

4. Foner, *Paul Robeson Speaks*, 239–240.

5. Unnamed authors, *Eyewitness: Peekskill U.S.A.* (self-published, 1949), unpaginated.

6. Kurt J., *Eyewitness: Peekskill U.S.A.*

7. Paul Robeson, *Negro Weekly, New York Age* of September 17, 1949, reprinted in *Eyewitness: Peekskill U.S.A.*

8. Dunaway, *How Can I Keep from Singing*, 14.

Chapter 8

1. Margaret Bradford Boni, *The Fireside Book of Folk Songs* (New York: Simon & Schuster, 1947), 5.

2. Rosemont, *Joe Hill*, 430.

3. Rosemont, *Joe Hill*, 431.

4. Jack Kerouac, *The Dharma Bums* (New York: Viking, 1976), 9.
5. Levine and Gordon, *Tales of Wo-Chi-Ca*, x.
6. Levine and Gordon, *Tales of Wo-Chi-Ca*, 109.
7. Stavis, *The Man Who Never Died*, 49.
8. Foner, *Paul Robeson Speaks* (New York: Citadel Press, 1968), 389.
9. Joe Glazer, *Labor's Troubadour* (Urbana: University of Illinois Press, 2001), 33.
10. Foner, *Paul Robeson Speaks*, 441.
11. Robeson, *Here I Stand*, 64.
12. Duberman, *Paul Robeson*, 463.

Chapter 9

1. Robert Meeropol, email to the author.
2. Joe Glazer and Edith Fowke, *Songs of Work and Protest* (Mineola: Dover, 1973), 5.
3. Glazer and Fowke, *Songs of Work and Protest*, 21.
4. Pete Seeger, introduction to Woody Guthrie, *Bound for Glory* (New York: Plume, 1983), vii.
5. Studs Terkel introduction to Cray, *Ramblin' Man*, xv.
6. Cray, *Ramblin' Man*, 188.
7. Ted Anthony, *Chasing the Rising Sun: The Journey of an American Song* (New York: Simon & Schuster, 2007), 151.
8. Greil Marcus, *Rolling Stone*, July 23, 1970.
9. Dunson, *Freedom in the Air*, 13.

Chapter 10

1. David Beckwith, interview with the author.
2. Stavis, *The Man Who Never Died*, 37.
3. Si Kahn interview with the author.
4. Si Kahn, *Creative Community Organizing* (Oakland: Barrett-Koehler, 2010).
5. Pete Seeger, liner notes, McCutcheon, *Live at Wolf Trap*,
6. Joe Klein, *Rolling Stone*, March 10, 1977, pp. 18–19.
7. Josh Dunson, interview with the author.

8. Foner, *Paul Robeson Speaks*, 427.
9. Lenore Bennett, Jr., *Let Paul Robeson Sing!* (Wales: Paul Robeson Trust/National Library of Wales, 2003), 7.
10. Arnold H Lubasch, *Robeson: An American Ballad* (Lanham, MD: Scarecrow Press, 2012), 211.

Chapter 11

1. Joe Uehlein, interview with the author.
2. Uehlein, interview with the author.
3. John O'Connor, interview with the author.
4. Archie Green, *Wobblies, Pile Butts, and Other Heroes* (Urbana: University of Illinois Press, 1993), 89.
5. Pete Seeger and Bob Reiser, *Carry It On! A History in Song and Picture of the Working Men and Women of America* (New York: Simon & Schuster, 1985), 9.
6. Peter Blood-Patterson, ed., *Rise Up Singing* (Bethlehem, PA: Sing Out Corporation, 1988), iii.
7. Anthony, *Chasing the Rising Sun*, 81.
8. Robinson, *Ballad of an American*, 414–15.
9. Robinson, *Ballad of an American*, 415.
10. Lori Elaine Taylor, *Don't Mourn—Organize! Songs of Labor Songwriter Joe Hill*, Smithsonian Folkways Records, 1990.
11. Robinson, *Ballad of an American*, 423.
12. Robinson, *Ballad of an American*, 55.

Chapter 12

1. Utah Phillips, liner notes, *We Have Fed You All a Thousand Years*.
2. Nikole Hannah-Jones, Preface, *The 1619 Project* (New York: The New York Times, 2019), xxii.
3. Sam Richards, liner notes, *An English Folk Music Anthology* (Washington: Smithsonian Folkways, 1981).
4. Sam Richards, "The Joe Hill Legend in England," Archie Green, ed., *Songs About Work: Essays in Occupational*

Culture (Bloomington: University of Indiana Press, 1993), 317–329.

5. Rosemont, *Joe Hill*, 150.

6. Maxine Waters, celebration for Harry Bridges.

7. Patti Glazer, email to the author.

8. Bucky Halker, book jacket blurb, Glazer, *Labor's Troubadour*.

9. Jon Pareles, *The New York Times*, May 27, 2008.

10. George Mann, interview with the author.

11. George Mann, liner notes to *The Almanac Trail* CD.

12. Rik Palieri, interview with the author.

13. Anecdote from Alex Wilkinson, *The Protest Singer: An Intimate Portrait of Pete Seeger* (New York: Alfred A. Knopf, 2009), 15–16.

Chapter 13

1. Felicia Miyakawa, *The Avid Listener*, July 24, 2020.

2. Seeger, *The Incompleat Folksinger,* 330.

3. Ellen Harper, *Always a Song: Singers, Songwriters, Sinners & Saints* (San Francisco: Chronicle Books, 2021), 239.

4. Si Kahn, email to the author and "Freedom Is a Constant Song" reprinted by permission.

5. Foner, *The Letters of Joe Hill*, 25.

6. Maria Dunn, interview with the author.

7. Bennet Zurofsky, email to the author.

8. Elena Klaver, e-mail to the author.

9. Elise Bryant, interview with the author.

10. McCutcheon, CD liner notes, *Joe Hill's Last Will.* Used by permission.

11. Ron Kaminkow, interview by Trish Kahle, *Jacobin.com*, February 4, 2015.

12. John Paul Wright, interview by Jae Carico, *The Fifth Column*, March 23, 2016.

13. John Paul Wright, interview with the author.

14. Anne Feeney in conversation as reported by Saul Schniderman.

15. Greg Artzner and Terry Leonino, interview with the author.

16. Bucky Halker, email to the author.

17. David Rovics, interview with the author.

18. Kristian Svensson, e-mail to the author.

19. Lori Elaine Taylor interview with the author.

20. Rolf Hägglund e-mail to the author.

21. Si Kahn, *Joe Hill's Last Will*, reprinted by permission.

Epilogue

1. Malcolm Hawksworth, email to the author.

2. John Ridgman, email to the author.

3. Brandon Dew, interview with the author.

4. Dew, Salt Lake City, November 18, 2023,

5. Green, *Wobblies, Pile Butts, and Other Heroes*, 94.

Bibliography

Adler, William M. *The Man Who Never Died: The Life, Times, and Legacy of Joe Hill, American Labor Icon.* New York: Bloomsbury USA, 2011.

Almeida, Arthur A. *Wobblies in San Pedro: Conversations with Paul Ware and Bob Bigelow.* Self-published, 2012.

Anthony, Ted. *Chasing the Rising Sun: The Journey of an American Song.* New York: Simon & Schuster, 2007.

Baez, Joan. *And a Voice to Sing With.* New York: Summit Books, 1987.

Boni, Margaret Bradford. *The Fireside Book of Folk Songs.* New York: Simon & Schuster, 1947.

Chandler, Russ. *Hold the Line: Echoes of the Peekskill Riots.* London: Redwords Pamphlet (The Socialist Bookshop), 2019.

Cohen, Phil. *Fighting Union Busters in a Carolina Carpet Mill: An Organizer's Memoir.* Jefferson, NC: McFarland, 2020.

Cray, Ed. *Ramblin' Man: The Life and Times of Woody Guthrie.* New York: W.W. Norton, 2004.

Duberman, Martin Bauml. *Paul Robeson.* New York: Alfred A. Knopf, 1988.

Dunaway, David King. *How Can I Keep from Singing: The Ballad of Pete Seeger.* New York: Villard Books, 2008.

Duncan, Dayton, and Ken Burns. *The Dust Bowl: An Illustrated History.* San Francisco: Chronicle Books, 2012.

Dunson, Josh. *Freedom in the Air: Song Movements of the 60's.* New York: International, 1965.

Fast, Howard. *Peekskill USA.* Mineola: Dover, 1951.

Flynn, Kathryn A., and Richard Polese. *The New Deal: A 75th Anniversary Celebration.* Salt Lake City: Gibbs Smith, 2008.

Foner, Philip S., ed. *Fellow Workers and Friends: IWW Free Speech Fights as Told by Participants.* Westport: Greenwood Press, 1981.

Foner, Philip S., ed. *The Letters of Joe Hill.* Chicago: Haymarket Books, 1965.

Foner, Philip S., ed. *Paul Robeson Speaks.* New York: Citadel Press, 1978.

Fowke, Edith, and Joe Glazer. *Songs of Work and Protest.* Mineola: Dover, 1973.

Geiser, Carl. *Prisoners of the Good Fight: Americans Against Franco Fascism.* Westport, CT: Lawrence Hill & Company, 1986.

Glazer, Joe. *Labor's Troubadour.* Urbana: University of Illinois Press, 2001.

Green, Archie. *Wobblies, Pile Butts, and Other Heroes.* Urbana: University of Illinois Press, 1993.

Green, Archie, ed. *Songs About Work: Essays in Occupational Culture.* Bloomington: Indiana University Press, 1993.

Guthrie, Woody. *Bound for Glory.* New York: Plume, 1983.

Harper, Ellen. *Always a Song: Singers, Songwriters, Sinners & Saints.* San Francisco: Chronicle Books, 2021.

Holter, Darryl, and William Deverell. *Woody Guthrie L.A. 1937–1941.* Santa Monica: Angel City Press, 2015.

Kahn, Si. *Creative Community Organizing.* Oakland: Berrett-Koehler, 2010.

Kornbluh, Joyce L., ed. *Rebel Voices: An I.W.W. Anthology.* Ann Arbor: University of Michigan Press, 1968.

Levine, June, and Gene Gordon. *Tales of Wo-Chi-Ca: Blacks, Whites and Reds at Camp.* San Rafael: Avon Springs Press, 2002.

Margolick, David. *Strange Fruit: Billie Holiday, Café Society, and an Early Cry for Civil Rights.* Philadelphia: Running Press, 2000.

Nuwer, Rachel. "How Conversations Around Campfires Might Have Shaped Human Cognition and Culture." *Smithsonian.com,* September 2014.

Palieri, Rik. *Banjo Man: Adventures of an American Folk Singer.* Self-published, 2020.

Rauchway, Eric. *The Great Depression & The New Deal: A Very Short Introduction.* New York: Oxford University Press, 2008.

Renshaw, Patrick. *The Wobblies: The Story of the IWW and Syndicalism in the United States.* Chicago: Ivan R. Dee, 1999.

Robeson, Marilyn, writer; Janet Hulstrand, ed. *Paul Robeson: Bearer of a Culture* exhibition catalog. New York: The Paul Robeson Foundation and the New-York Historical Society, 1998.

Robeson, Paul, with Lloyd Brown. *Here I Stand.* Boston: Beacon Press, 1988.

Robeson Wales Trust. *Let Paul Robeson Sing!* National Library of Wales, 2003.

Robinson, Earl, with Eric Gordon. *Ballad of an American: The Autobiography of Earl Robinson.* Lanham, MD: Scarecrow Press, 1998.

Rosemont, Franklin. *Joe Hill: The IWW & the Making of a Revolutionary Workingclass Counterculture.* Oakland: PM Press and Chicago: C.H. Kerr, 2015.

Ruehl, Kim. *A Singing Army: Zilphia Horton and the Highlander Folk School.* Austin: University of Texas Press, 2021.

Santelli, Robert. *This Land Is Your Land: Woody Guthrie and the Journey of an American Folksong.* Philadelphia: Running Press, 2012.

Seeger, Pete. *The Incompleat Folksinger.* Lincoln: University of Nebraska Press, 1972.

Seeger, Pete, and Bob Reiser. *Carry It On! A History in Song and Picture of the Working Men and Women of America.* New York: Simon & Schuster, 1985.

Smith, Gibbs M. *Joe Hill.* Salt Lake City: Peregrine Smith Books, 1984.

Stavis, Barrie. *The Man Who Never Died.* South Brunswick: A.S. Barnes, 1972.

Steinbeck, John. *The Grapes of Wrath.* New York: Penguin, 1992.

Steinbeck, John. *The Harvest Gypsies.* Berkeley: Heyday Books, 1988.

Vandy, Greg, and Daniel Person. *26 Songs in 30 Days: Woody Guthrie's Columbia River Songs and the Planned Promised Land in the Pacific Northwest.* Seattle: Sasquatch, 2016.

Wald, Alan M. *Exiles from a Future Time: The Forging of the Mid-Twentieth-Century Literary Left.* Chapel Hill: University of North Carolina Press, 2002.

Wilkinson, Alec. *The Protest Singer: An Intimate Portrait of Pete Seeger.* New York: Alfred A. Knopf, 2009.

Index

195